THE SHRINKING
OF AMERICA

Also by Bernie Zilbergeld, Ph.D.

MALE SEXUALITY   A Guide to Sexual Fulfillment

THE
SHRINKING
OF
AMERICA

MYTHS OF PSYCHOLOGICAL CHANGE

Bernie Zilbergeld, Ph.D.

LITTLE, BROWN AND COMPANY   BOSTON   TORONTO

FIRST EDITION

Library of Congress Cataloging in Publication Data

Zilbergeld, Bernie.
   The shrinking of America.

   Bibliography: p.
   Includes index.
   1. Psychotherapy—United States. 2. United States—
Social conditions. 3. Personality change. 4. Psycho-
therapy—Evaluation. I. Title.
RC480.5.Z54 1983   616.89'14   82-21712
ISBN 0-316-98794-8

BP

Designed by Dede Cummings

*Published simultaneously in Canada
by Little, Brown & Company (Canada) Limited*

PRINTED IN THE UNITED STATES OF AMERICA

To Carol, Claire, and Monica

For Bringing Love and Beauty Into My Life

Acknowledgments

The work of many people went into this book and I welcome the opportunity to publicly express my deep appreciation for their assistance.

- The one hundred and forty men and women who took the time to tell me and my assistants about their psychotherapy experiences, and the four people who helped me collect this information: Carol Craig, Libi Cape, Jacqueline Hackel, and Tom Hidus.
- The friends and colleagues who read all or part of earlier drafts and offered their comments, many of which have been incorporated into the text: Bernard and Connie Apfelbaum, Lonnie Barbach, Allen Bergin, Harvey Caplan, Phillip Cowan, Michael Evans, Peter Kilmann, Arnold Lazarus, Jay Mann, Gerald Mendelsohn, Harley Shands, Douglas Wallace, and Daniel Wile.
- The therapists, not already mentioned, who answered my questions about their work and about people-changing generally: Ben Ard, Hilde Burton, Stewart Emery, John Enright, Charles Garfield, Kenneth Pelletier, Lillian Rubin, Kurt Schlesinger Skanda, and Verneice Thompson.
- Two marvelously helpful editors at Little, Brown, Bill Phillips and Mike Mattil.
- The best collaborator, in-house editor, and friend I've ever had, Carol Rinkleib Ellison, and her daughter Monica, who efficiently handled copying and mailing tasks.

To all the above, a salute and my heartfelt gratitude.

Contents

THE SHRINKING
OF AMERICA

Perfectibility
and Psychotherapy

"We do have faith in our power to change human behavior."

— B. F. SKINNER

"One waits in vain for psychologists to make clear to the general public the actual limits of what is known."

— NOAM CHOMSKY

NOT LONG AGO I ATTENDED A PARTY where one of the topics of conversation was personal change. As soon as I voiced some skepticism about the extent of modifications made in psychotherapy and other change processes, a woman joined the discussion, insisting that therapy had changed her life. Not to be outdone, a man reported that reading *I'm OK — You're OK* had changed his life. After thinking for a moment, he added that five or six other books had had a similar effect on him. It wasn't just traditional psychotherapy and self-help books that made significant modifications in people's lives. I soon heard what I had heard so many times before: that new therapies, spiritual practices, physical exercise (especially jogging), certain diets, celibacy, and a host of other things all led to the same end. Life-altering experiences seem to have reached epidemic proportions, causing one writer to note that "the problem is not that so many are constantly looking for enlightenment these days, but that so many are constantly finding it."

Our culture is strongly committed to the proposition that people are highly malleable. Three key assumptions of the present age are that human beings should change because they are not as competent or as good or as happy as they could be; that there are few limits to the alterations they can make; and that change is relatively easy to effect. If only the right methods are used and the right attitudes are held, people can make significant changes and become almost whatever they want.

These ideas are not entirely new in America, a land always re-

ceptive to utopian notions. The settlers of this country believed in
the perfectibility of man or, as the perceptive Tocqueville put it,
"that man is endowed with an indefinite faculty for improvement."
Given the proper conditions — freedom, equality, adherence to
this or that interpretation of God's words, universal education, economic progress — people would improve themselves, find contentment, and fashion a society unlike any other on this earth. In this
sense America was a human potential society more than two hundred
years before the advent of the Human Potential Movement. It is
not surprising that the imminent coming of the millennium has
often been proclaimed here, with promises of an end to intemperance, extravagance, war, and other bad things, and a beginning of
"great enjoyment, happiness, and universal joy," and other good
things. Snake oils and sundry schemes to relieve aches and pains,
to achieve wealth and success, and to make other desirable changes
have usually enjoyed a brisk business. The first people to state in
a political document that they were endowed with an unalienable
right to the pursuit of happiness (which soon was construed as the
right to be happy) were not about to let opportunities for improvement go unused.

For better or worse, the millennium never did quite arrive, and
it is doubtful that Americans were or are any happier than other
people, but for a number of reasons the early dreams were kept
alive. The faith in human malleability and the idea that nothing
was impossible always had enough support at least to hold their
own and, more typically, to grow. For a long time, however, such
notions were to some extent held in check by the fact that most
people were too busy trying to secure adequate food and shelter to
have much time for perfecting themselves and also by countervail-
ing religious teachings about the necessity of restraint (rewards
would come in the hereafter, life on earth being inherently limited).

Then, eighty or so years ago, America entered the modern age, a
time characterized by a vastly improved standard of living, rapid
social change, secularization, and the belief that people could exert
considerable control over their lives. Modernity brought with it a
new understanding of what life is about, greatly expanded expecta-

tions, and a number of problems. Closely tied to the new worldview, and feeding off its increased expectations and discontents, was a sensibility that soon became the dominant cultural ideology. In the therapeutic sensibility the notions about human malleability that for so long constituted part of the American scene achieved their ultimate development. The malleability theses were broadened and harnessed to methods supposedly capable of fulfilling them. The era of psychological man and change without limit had arrived.

Psychology has become something of a substitute for old belief systems. Different schools of therapy offer visions of the good life and how to live it, and those whose ancestors took comfort from the words of God and worshiped at the altars of Christ and Yahweh now take solace from and worship at the altars of Freud, Jung, Carl Rogers, Albert Ellis, Werner Erhard, and a host of similar authorities. While in the past the common reference point was the Bible and its commentaries and commentators, the common reference today is a therapeutic language and the success stories of mostly secular people-changers. In the past, what we now call the media were filled with the words of Christ; while the religious messages are still there, they now must give equal time, and in many places far more than equal time, to the words of those that talk show host Phil Donahue calls Dr. Feelgoods.

Caution has been thrown to the winds. As one of the leading proponents of the psychological society puts it: "Well, what do you say to the design of personalities? Would that interest you? The control of temperament? Give me the specifications, and I'll give you the man!" He promises "a society in which there is no failure, no boredom, no duplication of effort!", while another expert says that among the blessings of behavioral technology "may be the elimination of mental illness, crime, and even war." Other equally impressive accomplishments are proclaimed. One project, the offspring of a popular therapeutic program, proposes to end starvation but not, as you might imagine, by feeding the hungry. Instead, it offers the simple expedient of getting individuals to sign cards saying they are "willing to be responsible for making the end of starvation an idea whose time has come." When an undisclosed number of people have in this way taken responsibility (one of the main slogans of the therapeutic sensibility), a "context" will have been created in which hunger will somehow end.

But what attracts most people are promises of personal change — radiant health, peace of mind, better communication and relationships, more satisfying sex, development of potentials, an end to addiction and bad feelings, and, in a word, happiness. Of claims for the attainment of such goals there is no end. At dinner parties, in bars, on planes and trains, and almost everywhere that people congregate, the familiar refrains are heard of dramatic changes and significant improvements. All these stories have the effect of reinforcing our beliefs about malleability: people really can change, life really can be better.

This book is about the ability of people to make changes in their personal lives, and specifically about the ability to make these changes through a variety of methods loosely called psychotherapies. Although psychotherapy is not synonymous with the American search for self-improvement and is not the only means available for achieving this end, it offers an ideal vehicle for examining widely held beliefs about human malleability that underlie it. By studying the growth, practice, and results of psychotherapy we can address such questions as why Americans have so completely accepted therapy and therapeutic thinking, how malleable human beings are, and the consequences of holding great expectations for change.

Psychotherapy, as I use the term, means any systematic course of action under expert guidance designed to alter a person's thoughts, feelings, attitudes, behavior, and relationships, without drugs or surgery. This broad definition encompasses not only professionally conducted therapies like psychoanalysis, behavior therapy, marriage and family counseling, gestalt therapy, and Transactional Analysis, but also encounter groups, Transcendental Meditation, est, Silva Mind Control, Co-Counseling, Weight Watchers, Alcoholics Anonymous, and similar activities. Many professionals are discomfited by being grouped together with est and Actualizations trainers, encounter group leaders (many of whom do not have professional training), and meditation teachers, arguing that the only real behavioral experts are those with training and licenses in psychology, psychiatry, social work, or psychiatric nursing. But such a view is unnecessarily restrictive. There is little difference between the types of people and problems seen by professional and non-professional helpers: e.g., some who are dissatisfied with their lives consult professional therapists while others go to est or encounter groups; similarly, some people trying to rid themselves of addictions consult behavior therapists or psychoanalysts while many others go to Synanon or Take Off Pounds Sensibly. I believe, and will attempt to demonstrate, that there is a great deal of similarity between professional counseling and other people-comforting and people-changing endeavors, a view which is gaining increased acceptance in at least some professional circles. Most of my emphasis in the following chapters is on professionally conducted therapies, because they have generated most of the research evidence from which conclusions can be drawn, but I also consider some of the other activities. Later I consider the question of whether professionals are any better at people-changing than those without graduate training and licenses. The results, I believe, will surprise many; they certainly surprised me.

This book consists of three major sections. In the first, chapters 2 through 6, I describe therapeutic ideology, demonstrate the extent of its triumph in America, and attempt to understand how this was accomplished. Our history and values, recent societal changes, and the aggressive sales tactics of therapists and their apologists are all considered. The second section, chapters 7 through 11, contrasts common beliefs about therapy-induced change with the best clinical and research evidence as to what therapy actually can and can't do. We find that the ability of counseling to alter behavior and resolve problems has been greatly exaggerated, but that it is relatively successful in providing other desired ends. For example, although therapy is now used with almost every known human complaint, it has proven its effectiveness with only a small number of them; the changes made are usually modest, very far from what we think of as a cure or resolution, and often not long-lasting; and participation in counseling can harm as well as help. On the other side, most people get something out of counseling, even if not exactly what they hoped for: they report benefits in terms of support, validation, increased understanding, and feeling better (at least for the moment). Clients and former clients generally feel good about their counseling, seek more of it for themselves and recommend it to others, and become friends and supporters of the therapeutic enterprise. I attempt to explain the reasons for these results. I also discuss some of the surprisingly large prices paid by all of us, including those who have never been to therapy, for our acceptance of therapeutic thinking. In the last section, I use material presented earlier, as well as information from other sources, to challenge American notions about human malleability. I conclude that people are very difficult to change and also that they are not as much in need of changing as is commonly thought. Most people are basically healthy and resourceful, quite capable of dealing with the trials and tribulations of everyday life on their own or with the help of their friends, and are not, as we now seem to believe, in need of constant monitoring and fixing up by behavioral experts. In the appendix I briefly discuss appropriate uses of professional therapy, comparing it with other sources of help for personal problems, and offer some pointers for those considering such counseling.

The alert reader may have guessed from the preceding remarks that this work does not fit into the usual categories of books about psychotherapy. It is not a chapter-by-chapter account of different counseling schools, pointing out the strengths and weaknesses of each (though there is some of this here), nor is it a criticism of all schools other than my own, intended to prove that mine is best (although there is some of this as well). My interest has been less in this or that model of counseling than in critically examining all therapies and the assumptions on which they are based, and to discover what their results can tell us about human plasticity.

You should know that this is a critical work, focusing on limits as well as possibilities. I am as interested in what can't be done as in what can be. Small changes, failure to change, and harm done by trying to change are all part of the picture, and a disservice is done to all by focusing only on successes, especially dramatic and quick successes, as so many books, therapists, and former clients do. Critical works about therapy are rare. Although there is no shortage of criticism of specific therapies or groups of therapies, or about something called "pop psychology," it is invariably in the service of asserting that some other counseling approach is superior. Thus critiques of newer methods such as Primal Scream and est are usually based on the belief that the further a therapy deviates from psychoanalysis, the less good it is. On the other side, many criticize psychoanalysis only to show how much better is their method (e.g., behavior therapy or family therapy). What remain untouched by such discussions are the assumptions that underlie all therapies and the limits that apply to all of them. The impression usually conveyed is that the desired changes are certainly possible, but only by using the author's or speaker's favorite method. There is an important reason for the lack of examination of the limits of therapy and the limits of change. Many of our hopes for ourselves, our children, and our futures are closely tied to our beliefs about the possibility of change, specifically about the ability of therapy to change us. To question these beliefs is to rock a very large and very shaky boat and risk upsetting many people.

I have not hesitated from asking the questions that seemed worth asking and from following the data where they led. Because of this, I think it fair to warn readers there may be material in here that is not easy to accept. I know, for I have had my own share of difficulty with some of it. Nonetheless, I believe it is time for us to take a careful and critical look at change and therapy, and to consider substituting ideas grounded in reality for mythology. Above all, it is long overdue for psychologists, or at least this psychologist, to try to make clear to the public the limits of what is known and what can be done.

Before going on, it seems reasonable to mention the sources I relied on for my information. There are four major ones.

1. My own experience as therapy consumer (a total of about five years in a number of change processes) and therapy provider (over twelve years in a variety of settings using many different methods and formats).

2. Conversations with and observation of other counselors since my days as a graduate student. I have spent much of my time in the company of other therapists and tried to take advantage of the opportunities thus provided to learn not only about their work and

how they think of it, but also to observe how they live their lives and to assess what their personal therapy has done for them. While preparing this book I interviewed a dozen experienced counselors of various persuasions to determine if there was sufficient support for impressions I'd gathered informally or from reading. Comments from and about these interviews are included in several places.

3. The now vast research literature on the effects of therapy. This literature is contained in a large number of psychological and medical journals, and as far as I know there has been no attempt to keep it secret, but the general public and even many therapists seem ignorant of what is in it.

4. Interviews conducted by me and several assistants of 140 men and women about their therapy experiences. Most of what my respondents said supported what is found in research reports, and their statements, quoted and summarized throughout the book, help give personal meaning to the statistics; and some of what they said makes possible new interpretations.

To minimize distraction, there is no scholarly paraphernalia in the text. Sources for quotations, and in some cases further discussion, are found in the notes. Since the clients I interviewed were promised anonymity, I have changed names and other identifying information.

The Therapeutic Sensibility

"Psychiatry has always had this in abundance: enthusiasm harnessed to a belief, often without rational basis, in the possibility and imminence of change."

— JONAS ROBITSCHER

TO BEGIN OUR EXPLORATION OF PSYCHOTHERAPY and how it contributes to our age of human change, it is important to discuss what I call the therapeutic sensibility. This is a series of little-examined assumptions held by most counselors, professional or not, regardless of the type of therapy they do. This belief system has an enormous influence on most of us and in important ways has become our sensibility, our way of viewing the world and ourselves. It is probably not unfair to say that it has become as important as the tenets of Christianity once were. It is our acceptance of this ideology, and not just the mere fact of greater participation in counseling, that makes me agree with sociologist Phillip Rieff when he says that our age is witness to the triumph of the therapeutic. What follow are the salient characteristics of the therapeutic worldview.

The World is Best Understood in Psychological Terms

Psychology has become one of the most important ways of understanding both the internal and external world. Other explanatory models — such as the supernatural, the moral, the rational, and the economic — have been largely supplanted by it. Psychological man reigns supreme. When we think of ourselves and others, we think in terms of psychological characteristics: anxiety, insecurity, complexes, inhibitions, self-esteem, identity, suppression and repression, obsessions and compulsions, depression, unconscious desires and conflicts, emotional traumas, unexpressed hostility, and on and on.

We use such concepts to account for all manner of things — physical illness, job and athletic performance, relationship conflicts, divorce, crime, drug addiction, and even political goings-on. Referring to Budget Director David Stockman's indiscreet revelations to a journalist, a respected magazine put this headline on its cover: "Schizophrenia Made Stockman Do It." Schizophrenia is apparently spreading, afflicting things as well as people: several recent reviews stated the books under discussion were "schizophrenic." Paranoia is also spreading, having reached the Middle East, where Israel is said to have come down with a bad case. All sorts of maladies are cropping up all over the place. Passivity used to be thought of as a trait of some people. But psychology moves on and now, so states a therapist on the *Phil Donahue Show*, "passivity is a disease" in need of treatment.

When someone important is assassinated, mental health experts are called upon by the media to explain the slayer's state of mind and, indeed, the state of mind of the whole nation. Are we, the question is always asked, a sick society? Perhaps we have all come down with some sort of emotional influenza. Our legal system, as we surely need little reminding after the Hinckley verdict, has become a strong outpost of therapeutic thinking, allowing culprits to escape punishment if the experts can persuade the jury that these individuals were insane or suffering from some other mental defect at the time of their crimes. But the media often make the diagnosis long before a jury is selected; a few days after the attempted assassination of President Reagan in 1981, the cover of *Time* proclaimed the act to be a "moment of madness." The acts of politicians, especially presidents, are often explained by reference to their emotional state (witness the many psychological explanations of Lyndon Johnson's and Richard Nixon's Vietnam policies), and it has been seriously proposed that presidential candidates should be subjected to psychological testing to determine their fitness for the job. Even our pets have been included in the new order of things. An article in *Time* on famous dog trainer Barbara Woodhouse says that the only dogs she can't train are "the canine schizophrenics and psychopaths." Woodhouse does not share the belief of some people that modern dogs are "naturally neurotic" but does believe they become "hyperactive and schizophrenic" when fed too much protein.

Even where other ways of conceptualizing the world remain, say in talks and writings by religious authorities, they have been heavily infiltrated by the psychological. One has only to spend a few minutes browsing in a religious bookstore to see how widely represented are the works and thoughts of Freud, Rogers, Maslow, May, Fromm, and other secular counselors. Not long ago, psychiatrist Karl Menninger, apparently not as up to date as his colleagues, asked *Whatever Became of Sin?* The answer is simple: it was psychologized away. Under the new arrangement, some of what used to be considered sinful — for example, masturbation — is now thought to be good for you, and most of the rest — such as gluttony and crime — is considered to be sickness, symptoms of mental disturbance. The only "sin" we seem to care about is failing to fully actualize all our potential, and that clearly is primarily a psychological matter. Evil has suffered a fate similar to sin's. As the Devil complains in Jeremy Leven's wickedly funny novel, *Satan,* "psychotherapy worries the hell out of me. . . . It keeps turning evil into neuroses and explaining away people's behavior with drives and complexes. . . . Modern psychiatry is putting me out of business."

It has gotten to the point where even material reality, as it is usually understood, is in danger of disappearing as an explanatory concept. We are told by some therapists that it is not your circumstances (material and social reality) that are important but only how you construe them (psychology). There is a real world, but it isn't out there — it's in our heads. Change your head, the way you construe things, and you change the only world that matters. When you change what's inside, you can change everything, even seemingly insoluble social problems like poverty, hunger, crime, and international violence. Psychologist Will Schutz puts the mind-over-matter proposition, at its extreme, this way: "The laws of nature only function if we want them to. All around us people are defying natural laws. . . . We are not required to follow any laws. We are running this show." Apparently, according to this notion, if Newton had not wanted the apple to fall and had been sufficiently instructed in the proper methods, it would not have fallen and we would not have been limited by gravity ever since. Of course for those of us who know these methods and are willing to take responsibility, gravity should be no obstacle.

Genetic and physiological explanations are regarded with indifference or hostility by most therapists except psychiatrists who, being physicians, are equally receptive to psychological and medical models. Nonpsychiatric counselors do not like to think that someone's genetic makeup may put limits on what he can do or predispose him to act or feel in certain ways. Similarly, they do not want to believe that a problem might be caused by a hormonal imbalance or a lesion in the nervous system; they prefer to see causes in psychological factors such as unresolved Oedipal conflicts, sibling rivalry, and failure to take responsibility. So it isn't surprising that even medical problems are now being explained as due to psychological causes, and this includes everything from headaches and backaches to cancer.

We have all been greatly affected by the psychological model of the world. Our everyday language is full of expressions reflecting its influence, and the language we use determines how we perceive and think about the world and ourselves.

What You See Is Not
Necessarily What There Is

With the exception of some behaviorists, therapists generally agree that observable behavior is only the tip of the iceberg. There is much more than meets the eye; there are depths you can barely imagine. Much of the responsibility for this way of thinking rests with Freud. Everything — except for his cigar, which, he claimed, was only what it appeared to be — has hidden meaning, expressing unconscious symbolism, motives, conflicts, and compromises. What seems like the innocent pleasure of sucking on a Popsicle is really the expression of a desire to suck on something else that isn't so innocent. What sounds like a joke is really the expression of hostility. What looks like confidence is really a compensation for a lack of confidence. What seems like a straightforward conversation is really a game, a devious way for the participants to influence each other and prove their power. What Freud began now permeates the world of mental healing. There are always hidden purposes and operations.

This assumption has led to an increased amount of introspection. Human beings need accurate and reliable maps of their world. If things are what they appear to be, the construction of such maps is easy. But if things are not what they seem to be, map-making becomes a difficult art. Maybe your influenza has nothing to do with flu bugs; there are, after all, always bugs in the air. Perhaps you have the flu at this time because you haven't worked out issues around dependency and being sick is the only way you can get cared for. Maybe you don't like your husband as much as you think; maybe you stay with him primarily because of some unresolved issues with your father or because you're terrified of being alone.

There is nothing wrong with psychological explanations or with believing in hidden meanings. Such things can be useful. There are many instances where an explanation based on unconscious motivation, systems theory, or some other psychological model is more accurate and helpful than a more obvious explanation. The only problem is that there is no certainty anywhere. There are so many possibilities, so many maybes and perhapses, so many ways of understanding what's happening. If things can be the opposite of what they seem and if what seems trivial can be fraught with significance, how can one ever figure out what is going on? So one is forced to look everywhere for signs and portents, for clues about what this act or feelings really signifies. Many enlist the aid of therapists, the Sherlock Holmeses of the psyche, to unravel all the possibilities and contradictions, and often simply to get validation for their way of looking at things. When the construction of maps is so difficult and the maps so often unreliable, one needs to stop frequently to ask for directions.

A corollary of the hidden depths rule is that one should talk about — communicate and share — what is in these depths. What is wanted is personal revelation, the details of life that in previous times would have been discussed, if at all, only with a confessor or spouse. The justification is that talking about such things will help prevent and overcome problems and keep one moving in a healthy direction. Freud's injunction that patients say everything that came into their minds, no matter how trivial, nonsensical, or shameful, was the beginning of the repeal of reticence. But Freud applied this rule only in the consulting room; he had no idea that people would soon be saying everything that came into their minds when they were out in public.

If there is something beyond what meets the eye, we want to know about it. These wants frequently become demands, both in and out of therapy. In his book on encounter groups, Carl Rogers has this to say:

> As time goes on the group finds it unbearable that any member should live behind a mask or front. The polite words, the intellectual understanding of each other and relationships, the smooth coin of tact and cover-up . . . are just not good enough. . . . Gently at times, almost savagely at others, the group *demands* that the individual be himself, that his current feelings not be hidden, that he remove the mask of ordinary social intercourse.

Other therapies such as the Synanon games have been even more clamorous in what Rogers calls the "ripping away of facades."

People have taken the rule to express themselves to heart and are doing it with a vengeance. Strangers "open up" to one another; lovers, friends, and spouses tell each other in gruesome detail what is transpiring in their psyches and genitals; and hardly a days goes by that we are not subjected to the personal revelations of public figures. All of which tends to reinforce the psychological world-view, the need for talking about oneself, and the usefulness of therapy. If Woody Allen, John Denver, Betty Ford, Valerie Harper, Jerry Rubin, and a host of other celebrities — athletes, movie stars, authors, politicians and their spouses — can admit their problems and acknowledge going for help, then why can't you? If famous people can be on the *Tonight Show* with Johnny Carson and right there, in front of Johnny and Doc and Ed and millions of viewers, talk about their alcohol and drug habits, their depressions, their feelings of insecurity and alienation, and their sexual hangups, then maybe that's the proper way to talk to friends, relatives, and even strangers.

People Are Not Okay As They Are

It is generally agreed among counselors that people suffer from lots of inadequacies and deficiencies, and are not as healthy, productive, creative, free, and happy as they should be. Most therapists are not willing to go as far publicly as the one who wrote a book titled *Your Life Is a Mess* — by which he means "A real mess. A no-good, rotten, stinking mess. A miserable mess." — but neither do they have a high regard for people as they are. Even those programs that say "I'm okay, you're okay," and "You're perfect just as you are" don't mean it. What they *do* mean is that you're enslaved by the notion that you're not okay or not perfect; you need their course or book to be able to shed your false beliefs and see that you really are fine.

Just as the main preoccupation of doctors is with disease and sickness, so the main preoccupation of therapists is with pathology and problems, with how people are *not* okay, with how their lives are *not* working. These are the things therapists presumably know about, can measure, diagnose, and treat, so it is not surprising they should see them everywhere.

Mental health researchers have done many studies to determine the extent of emotional pathology. Probably the best known of these is the Midtown Manhattan study done in 1950. A representative sample of over 1,500 New Yorkers was interviewed and rated on a scale of psychological health impairment. Less than one-fifth were rated as "well" while almost one-quarter were called "impaired," meaning they were evaluated as having "severe" symptom formation or as being "incapacitated." The rest of the sample was diagnosed as having "mild" or "moderate" symptom formation. While those who have visited New York may be inclined to accept these findings as valid, a second consideration is required. Is it really possible that only 20 percent of New York's inhabitants are well and that 25 percent are seriously disturbed? The findings of this study are not unusual; other studies in other places have concluded that over 50 percent of the population are having serious emotional problems.

Psychologist Sheldon Korchin's comments on the Midtown survey are worthy of attention:

> Why are "impairment" rates so high, when in actuality most of the people were carrying on life tasks with reasonable adequacy? A failing in this and comparable psychiatric surveys lies in the emphasis on symptoms and impairment without sufficient attention to sources of psychological strength and competence.

The truth is that mental health researchers and clinicians see problems and not strengths because that is what they are trained to see and because it is in their interest to do so. The more pathology, the greater the need for more studies, more therapists, and more therapy.

The diagnostic bible of the mental health field, the *Diagnostic and Statistical Manual of Mental Disorders*, includes just about every conceivable behavior, thought, feeling, and situation imaginable. Aside from psychoses and neuroses, there are categories for personality disorders (e.g., explosive personality, obsessive-compulsive personality, inadequate personality, immature personality, and "unspecified" types of personality disorder); alcoholism; drug dependence; learning disabilities; sleep disturbances; transient situational disturbances (e.g., adjustment reactions of infancy, childhood, adolescence, adult life, and late life); nonspecific disorders, such as marital maladjustment, social maladjustment, and occupational maladjustment; and, finally, nonspecific conditions (not the same as nonspecific disorders), which is for things that can't be classified elsewhere. Given that therapists are trained to view people in terms of these categories, the wonder is not that they find so much pathology but so little. Everything from being anxious to having problems at any stage of life or on the job or in a marriage is a reason for a label and for therapy.

That therapists tend to see pathology even in its absence has been demonstrated in a number of studies. In one of them, eight eminently normal people gained admission to different psychiatric hospitals after complaining of nonexistent symptoms. These pseudo-patients behaved normally on the wards but not one of them was discovered. They took copious notes; this was entered on their records as "patient engages in writing behavior." Eventually they all got out on good behavior; each was discharged with the diagnosis of schizophrenia "in remission." This study was replicated using different "symptoms," and the results were identical.

In another study, therapists and therapy students listened to what they were told was a recording of a first therapy session. Actually, the "client" was a professional actor who played a relaxed, confident, and productive man who was enjoying life and was free from psychological problems but who was curious about therapy. After listening to the tape, the therapists were asked to rate the "client's" mental health on a list of standard diagnostic categories, one of which was "normal or healthy personality." Forty-three percent of the therapists rated him as psychotic or neurotic and 19 percent thought he had mild adjustment problems. Only 38 percent evaluated him as healthy.

Because of the emphasis on pathology and problems, and the relative neglect of strengths and health, therapists exaggerate the extent of pathology and the need for therapy. Therapists simply don't know much about health or normal living. They certainly don't get classes or training in these subjects. But some norm of health is necessary. Jurgen Ruesch and Gregory Bateson indicate how therapists come to think of health. "Since the psychiatrist's attention is focused on deviation, and since he has little or no training in normal psychology, he tends to construct a hypothetical norm by averaging the exact opposites of those features he sees in his patients." In other words, health comes to be defined as an absence of conflicts, hassles, frustrations, and feelings of insecurity, anxiety, and guilt. Since almost no one is likely to be healthy by such standards, therapists come to think that everyone is unwell and in need of therapy or more therapy.

Some of the newer programs have made their own contribution to this way of thinking. Who can truthfully say that he is everything he could be, that he is "actualizing all of his potential," that he is performing at his peak and using all of his talent and brain-power? As long as he can't say he is, he can't be considered to be a fully functioning and actualized person, and may be receptive to the sales pitch for an activity that will unblock and quicken his growth.

The tendency to focus on what is wrong and problematic, rather than on the total situation or on what is good and problem-free, has become part of the modern sensibility. To some extent this tendency is due to our increased expectations and the absence of strong mean-ing in our lives, and to some extent it is due to the influence of therapeutic ideology. The result is that we have put ourselves in a permanent no-win situation. We have accepted a fantasy model of well-being and mental health, and therefore of life, that probably cannot be attained by anyone. So we have plenty of deficits to attend to, meaning both that we stay in a constant state of discontent and in continual need of assistance to try to make things better.

Individuals Need to Be Liberated from the Ties That Bind

The emphasis of most therapies is on the individual self. Individuals are basically good, compassionate, and creative but their natures have been distorted and their potential blocked by repressive and oppressive traditions and institutions such as religion, family, sex-roles, and society in general. These have placed conditions of worth, limits, restrictions, and obligations on people, causing guilt, inhibi-tions, and generally making them crazy, and it is from these things that people must free themselves if they are to be whole, free, and well.

Put slightly differently, the therapeutic outlook is antitraditional. It seeks to liberate the individual from the types of traditional ties that have given hassles, disappointments, and frustrations, as well as meaning, structure, and comfort to people since the beginning of time. Phillip Rieff, one of the most respected interpreters of Freud's work, say that Freud "was not impressed by the clerical strategy of confirming faith by strengthening the individual's iden-tification with the community." He saw communities of belief —

whether religious or political — as part of the problem, not the solution. "What is needed is to free men from their sick communities. To emancipate man's 'I' from the communal 'we' is 'spiritual guidance' in the best sense Freud could give to the words." Freud held to his antireligious, antitraditional position even though he acknowledged toward the end of his life that the cures of psychoanalysis could not compete with those of Lourdes because "there are so many more people who believe in the miracles of the Blessed Virgin than in the existence of the unconscious."

Carl Rogers, one of the best known of living counselors and one whose influence has spread to education, religion, and other areas, holds that we are born good, motivated by a tendency toward actualization that would almost invariably result in positive and constructive action were it not for the intervention of others. The representatives of society — the usual therapeutic list of suspects: parents, teachers, and clerics — are not sufficiently accepting and empathic and they withhold their love when children behave in what adults take to be unacceptable ways. Thus children learn that some parts of them are bad and start hiding these, which to Rogers is the start of emotional problems. The therapist must provide high levels of empathy and unconditional acceptance so the client can reclaim the buried parts of himself.

Given this view that the institutions of society cause all our problems, it follows that Rogers, who speaks for many therapists, is hostile toward tradition. In an interview in 1972 Rogers agreed that therapy is "basically subversive since it opposes what society stands for. . . . Therapy theories and techniques promote a new model of man contrary to that which has been traditionally acceptable." The new model stresses spontaneity, expressiveness, open communication, and a willingness to live without fixed belief systems. When asked if people could be secure with an "open self," Rogers said he doubted it and added that the "closed self" — more traditional ways — may have survival characteristics. For example, a study of air crews that survived internment in prisoner of war camps and a study of successful persons in pilot training showed that they tended to be "closed" — religiously orthodox, secure in their families, and firmly clinging to their values and beliefs. The failures were more like Rogers's ideal — people closer to their feelings, more open and flexible.

Despite this evidence and despite Rogers's own doubts that people can feel secure without something fixed to hang on to, he clings to his antitraditional stance. "He said that he hoped man could learn to be secure in a process of change rather than just in something fixed." And he continues to promote his model of human functioning as being appropriate to almost every single area of life.

Rogers's views on tradition are not unusual; they represent the norm among those who do therapy. As a group, counselors are much more liberal, antitraditional, than the general population and other professionals. Far fewer believe in God, far more give atheist or agnostic as their religious position, and far more call themselves "strongly liberal" in political matters.

Whether there is a tendency for already antitraditional persons to become therapists or if something about clinical training and work makes people more liberal than they were is not clear, but there is no question that the training counselors receive hardly promotes respect for traditional values. Many therapy students take courses on family therapy — where they learn about families in trouble, how they got that way, and what to do with them — but few take general courses on families: their history, functions, and strengths as well as their weaknesses. Harry Specht, dean of the School of Social Work at the University of California at Berkeley, did a survey of all the social work graduate schools in the country and found that not one had a required general course on the family. So what do therapists learn about families? They learn about their faults and problems, the ways they harm, oppress, and limit. They do not learn what a healthy or typical family looks like, the ways in which a family provides security, comfort, love, and direction.

Courses on groups are common in therapy programs, but their focus is on artifically created therapy groups whose purpose is to undo the damage supposedly wrought by traditional groups. Counselors do not learn much about the real groups in which people spend much of their time — clubs, neighborhood gatherings, work groups, teams, church groups, and friendship circles. Of such things little is heard.

The antitraditionalism of therapists is probably most clearly visible in their attitudes toward religion. Psychologist Allen Bergin sought to determine what the important psychology reference books and textbooks had to say about religious belief. He found these books had little to say on the matter. "An examination of 30 introductory psychological texts turned up no references to the possible reality of spiritual factors. Most did not have the words *God* or *religion* in their indexes." Is this simply a matter of benevolent neutrality or neglect? Not exactly. As one researcher who is interested in religion says, "In psychology, anyone who gets involved in or tries to talk in an analytic, careful way about religion is immediately branded a meathead: a mystic; a touchy-feely sort of moron." In all my years of clinical training, the only times I heard religion mentioned were in negative ways. Cases were presented in which the patient was brought up in a strict Catholic, Jewish, or other tradition, which obviously explained his guilt, depression, or whatever else was bothering him. Therapists dealing with sexual problems are especially hard on religion, seeing it as a major cause of all sexual difficulties.

Therapists' animosity toward religion and toward tradition in general has provoked less comment than one might expect, but it has reached such proportions that it was singled out for attack by the president of the American Psychological Association. In 1975 Donald Campbell said that

> present day psychology and psychiatry in all their major forms are more hostile to the inhibitory messages of traditional religions' moralizing than is scientifically justified . . . our fields are apt to invoke tradition and religious heritage only to explain malfunctions, be it neurotic individual guilt or collective social prejudice.

Given that therapists don't learn much about families, communities, and religions except for their negative aspects, it is easy to understand why they believe such institutions don't have any redeeming virtues and that people need to be liberated from them. The fact that therapy in groups has become increasingly popular does not detract from what has been said. The single most common form of therapy is still individual treatment. And much of group therapy is really individual counseling in a group setting, aimed at individual liberation. The focus is on the individual, with the group acting as an audience (witness psychodrama or Fritz Perls's work) or as an aid in giving feedback. Even therapy which takes account of what is called group process is still aimed at the individual. The main exception is family therapy, which takes the family as a unit and tries to work out a solution for the unit rather than for only one of its members.

Antitraditionalism is not unique to mental healing; it is found in most contemporary thinking. But since therapists as a group are more liberal than almost any other professional group and because their influence is vast, both in and out of the consulting room, they are in a unique position to affect the rest of us in the direction of their biases. Although most modern thinking pushes individual fulfillment, self-expression, and immediate gratification of desire, therapists are the ones who show us how to achieve these goals. In short, the therapy movement is an important spearhead of the drive away from traditional values and toward greater acceptance of the culture of modernism and the therapeutic worldview.

Everyone Needs and Can Benefit from Therapy

Since we all have problems and none of us is as good as he or she could be, it follows that we all need some therapy. This idea is now so entrenched that it no longer seems interesting. As comedian Sam Levenson says, "We have reached the stage when people no longer question the fact that we can all use a bit of psychotherapy." Whatever the situation, whatever the problem, therapy can be helpful. Everybody should have some and improve himself.

Another way of putting the therapeutic attitude is that counselors believe people are incapable of living their lives and dealing with difficulties and problems without therapeutic assistance. All of us are thought to need psychological assistance to lead decent lives. The sentiment is well expressed by a behavior therapist on his cassette recording devoted to having better relationships:

When we consider the amount of time and effort spent seeking after intimacy . . . it is amazing how little formal training any of us gets in coupling skills. Often, more time is spent in learning how to drive an automobile than in acquiring relationship enhancement skills. This reflects something important about our values. The damage someone can do to another's personal property with a car is different from the havoc we allow ourselves to wreak upon one another during the period from junior high days to the times preceding our second or third divorce.

Apparently the important message is that if we don't get sufficient "formal training" — that provided by counselors — we can look forward to wreaking more havoc on each other and several divorces. As I discuss in chapter 6, such scare tactics are commonly used in the selling of therapy.

Therapists themselves are huge consumers of counseling. A study of over four thousand mental health professionals found that 74 percent had been in therapy. Over a third had been in counseling more than once, and the average time spent in treatment was four and a half years. Although this may seem like a lot, it actually understates the case since therapy was defined narrowly and did not include encounter groups, meditation, and other therapeutic activities in which the counselors participated. Therapists believe that therapy is good for themselves, even though they are not always satisfied with the results, and they see it as good for everyone else. Rarely do they suggest that someone should not be in counseling, or should get out of treatment, or that therapy might not be able to help. Of five hundred people who came to one psychiatric clinic for evaluation, therapy was recommended for all but four, and this pattern is by no means unusual.

An extreme example of the therapy-as-goodness idea comes from a professional who had developed a new form of treatment for seriously disturbed — autistic — children. He was said to be producing his share of successes and I went to observe a session. While talking with the therapist, I was surprised to hear that he was now applying what to me was a brutal form of treatment to mildly distressed adults. When I mentioned that I thought the therapy was used only as a last resort for those children whom nothing else had helped, he replied that that was the original idea, "but then I saw its usefulness for adults. I think everyone needs it. I have a vision that someday the whole country will be doing it. One day, half of us will administer it to the other half, and the next day we'll switch." He wasn't joking.

American therapists are particularly optimistic. They believe there are few limits to human potential and to what therapy can do. Freud was not a contributor to this kind of thinking. He thought psychoanalysis was limited in its power and applicability, that the needs of the individual and those of society were always in conflict, and that humans possessed a drive toward self-destruction, the death instinct, that limited the positive changes anyone could make. But this part of Freud has not survived in America. Hopefulness has swept all before it and reigns supreme.

Because of this peculiar way of viewing the world, it was not until the last ten or fifteen years that therapists, and not all of them, have even been willing to consider the possibility that change can be for the worse, that therapy can fail not only by not producing change but also by producing the wrong kind of change. The findings, to be explored in detail in chapter 9, do indeed indicate that counseling makes some people worse, but this has been hard to see and admit because of the positive thinking engaged in by those who do the counseling.

Not content to have the whole country in counseling for personal problems, therapists also believe that therapeutic thinking and advice are required elsewhere as well, in areas as varied as athletics, child-rearing and education, physical health and medicine, and social and political policy. As we will see, they have already moved into these and many other areas, and are planning even bolder moves in the future.

The message conveyed to the public is not just that therapy can sometimes be helpful, but that it is capable of producing truly great changes in the individuals, couples, families, and other groups it works with. People go from fragmentation to wholeness and integration; from sadness to gladness; from powerlessness to pulling their own strings; from being effects to being causes; from staleness and boredom to creativity and joyfulness; from isolation and hostility to closeness and love. Counseling can, we are constantly told, remake us, transform us, change our lives. We can have, be, and do whatever we want. There are no limits to therapy's power to change us.

We will come back to the claims therapists make for their methods, so we need not belabor the point here except to note that many therapy consumers and even many who have never been to counseling take these claims seriously. Their expectations rise and they want a lot from therapy or whatever they are doing. Many therapists complain that their clients have "outrageous" or "unrealistic" expectations of what therapy can do for them, and these expectations are usually blamed on the clients' upbringing and societal pressures. Rarely do counselors stop to consider what part they and their colleagues have had in generating such notions.

As we shall see, the assumption that there are powerful methods available that can change almost anything is a common one in modern society and leads to consequences such as increased unwillingness to tolerate anything that is not as good as it might be and increased guilt over not making use of or deriving full benefit from these methods.

The Therapist Is an Expert and Knows Best

There is an interesting paradox in the mental health field. On the one hand, individual freedom is the paramount value. On the other hand, therapists, like politicians, another group that likes to talk a lot about freedom, believe they know what is best for the people they deal with. In practice, therapeutic freedom often means freedom from everything except the therapist's guidance.

That this is the case is not difficult to understand. It follows from the idea of deficit. If people are not thinking clearly or are upset, how can they know what's right for them? Therapists have skill and knowledge that others lack; they can see through superficialities to the heart of the problem and can therefore make a better determination about what's right for the client. Besides, despite the rhetoric to the contrary, therapists don't seem to hold most people in high regard. They see people as pretty much screwed up, very confused and unable to tell what is bothering them or what they want. The theory of human functioning most influential among therapists is psychoanalysis and it holds that the most important sources of our behavior are unconscious; by definition, we are unable to know much about what we are about. A woman comes to counseling saying she wants to have closer relationships with men, but the therapist knows her unsatisfying relationships are just a manifestation of the messed-up relationship she had with her mother when she was two and that is what needs to be worked on. Given that we are all so confused and damaged, it stands to reason that someone has to do our thinking for us.

The idea that the therapist knows best is by no means confined to psychoanalysis and other traditional methods. Carl Rogers, whose client-centered therapy was a reaction against analysis and who consistently denies that he in any way directs the treatment, says that his therapy aims at "the greater independence and integration of the individual. . . . The aim is not to solve one particular problem but to assist the individual to *grow*." But suppose the client wants only to solve a particular problem and has no interest in growing? Too bad for the client. As one well-known therapist made very clear to me when she accosted me at a conference several years ago, clients don't know what they want and neither do I. Deep down, they really want to grow, to "have the world opened up to them and their horizons expanded," but they come with problems because that's all they do know about. It's up to the therapist to help them understand what they really want.

Not taking clients seriously is a common phenomenon in counseling. The termination of treatment is one of the main battlegrounds between the wishes of the client and the supposedly greater knowledge of the therapist. Many of my respondents ended treatment against the advice of their therapists. The clients thought that they had gotten what they came for or else that even though they hadn't achieved the desired results, more therapy wouldn't help. The therapists, on the other hand, thought that more therapy was indicated, either to continue working on the problems the client first brought in or to deal with other areas that the therapist saw as needing work. It is abundantly clear from these stories that the counselors did not believe in the clients' freedom to make their own decisions.

Here is an example of the struggle between leader and participant from an unexpected source, for est stresses the autonomy of the individual almost more than any other therapy. Several years ago two friends and I took the est training, apparently the last training in which Werner Erhard himself directly played a significant role. The three of us, as well as some others, were restless and disgusted by the last day. Late in the afternoon we did a "process" in which everyone became enlightened. According to Werner, we all "got it." We were then treated to a lecture on the meaning of being enlightened. Among other things, it meant that we knew we were the cause rather than the effect of our experience. We were free and could run our own lives. It had been many hours since we had eaten or gone to the bathroom and I was very hungry. Finally one of the trainers announced a bathroom break, which surprised many of us; we thought we were going to get a supper break. I decided enough was enough and said I was going to eat. The trainer in charge said I couldn't do that. I replied that since I was enlightened, I would do what I wanted; I was hungry and would eat. At this point, Werner took over and demanded that I follow the rules. I said that he apparently hadn't meant what he said about being enlightened, and, that being the case, I was leaving the training for good. My two friends joined me in this decision. Werner seemed to lose control of himself and started ranting about what bad people we were — for breaking our agreement to abide by the rules — and the harm that would befall us if we didn't complete the training; he was vague, but implied that all sorts of damaging things might happen. Freedom and enlightenment are apparently fine, as long as the leader is in charge of them.

It will be tempting for some readers to conclude that this happened only because Werner Erhard is not a professional therapist, but such a conclusion would be an error. Professional counselors do the same things all the time. I have heard the same threats of damage that would occur if the client left and even the ingenious claim that the desire to quit is itself indication of just how badly more therapy is needed.

Of course therapy itself is not the only place where therapists think their expertise should prevail. As already indicated, they now present themselves as knowledgeable in many areas having nothing to do with therapy, and they expect us to follow their advice. And increasingly they are getting what they want. In more and more areas, we accept the idea that counselors know more than we do and are better at resolving problems, so we are willing to turn to them and at least consider their advice even when it sounds strange and at odds with our own inclinations. We become, in short, more and more dependent upon therapeutic assistance.

This, then, is the sensibility that has become such an important part of all our lives, including the lives of those who have never gone to counseling. Because so many of our actions — personal, social, and political — are determined by the tenets of this ideology, it is worth knowing to what extent they make sense and are valid. And that, in brief, in what this book is about.

Before moving on, however, we should look at some of the evidence of the extent to which we have bought the age of psychology. I have already mentioned the ways our language has been invaded by the therapeutic, but that sign, though significant, is only one of many. Every day the mass media reinforce the use of this language and teach us about psychology and therapy. A steady stream of personal advice, complete with testimonials of individual change and improvement, gushes forth from our newspapers, magazines, radios, and televisions. Think of how barren many of the talk shows and magazines, especially the women's magazines, would be if no more stories about how to improve this or that aspect of your life were allowed. Psychological research and new treatments are often considered front-page news. In the past few years, therapists have been given their own radio programs and now in Boston, New York, Washington, Los Angeles, Seattle, San Francisco, and other cities across the country they hold forth for several hours a day giving advice and encouragement about all sorts of personal issues. Psychological books are regular best-sellers. Six of the fourteen best-selling nonfiction books of the 1970s were of this genre, including *Your Erroneous Zones, The Joy of Sex,* and *The Sensuous Woman.* The trend continues in the 1980s as books on self-improvement grace and in some cases top the best-seller charts. Each month millions of copies of *Psychology Today* are sold, a magazine started only fifteen years ago to report the latest in psychological ideas and research.

Professional therapy is a mushrooming business. Every year millions of Americans take their problems and hopes to psychiatrists, psychologists, and other professional healers. The proportion of Americans who had consulted a mental health expert more than tripled between 1957 to 1976, from four to fourteen percent. Among the college educated, the group most likely to seek such help, the increase was from nine to twenty-one percent. That the trend will continue is suggested by the fact that far more college students than ever before are now receiving some kind of professional counseling.

Other therapies, many not conducted by professionals, also do quite well. They wax and wane in popularity, often seeming old fashioned only a few years after their arrival, but there is no question they attract many participants. Consider a few statistics:

- Over five million people have taken part in encounter or sensitivity groups in the last fifteen years.
- Transcendental Meditation has been taught to more than a million students, about the same number of people who have participated in marriage enrichment programs.
- Silva Mind Control claims over half a million students since 1966, while the newer and better-known est claims three hundred thousand.
- There are now more nonprofessional therapeutic programs than anyone can count, from drug, alcohol, and smoking projects to those with names like Arica, Actualizations, Co-Counseling, and Recovery, Inc.
- Weight control programs, most using psychological principles and exercises in addition to diets, enroll millions of people a year.

Another indication of the triumph of the therapeutic is the very large number of people now doing therapy, far more than there were just a few years ago. The phenomenal growth of the therapy professions is illustrated by one set of figures: in 1968 there were 12,000 clinical psychologists in America; now there are 40,000. We now have about 280,000 professional counselors (psychiatrists, psychologists, clinical social workers, marriage counselors, psychiatric nurses, and so forth). That may not seem like a lot in a country of over 220 million people, but some comparisons with other occupations give a different perspective. There are more professional therapists than librarians, firefighters, or mail carriers, almost twice as many therapists as dentists or pharmacists. Lawyers and police outnumber counselors, but in each case the ratio is less than two to one. The practice of psychotherapy is not exactly a Mom and Pop operation.

The number of people doing therapy is actually much larger than even the above figures indicate. Unlicensed counselors probably outnumber licensed ones. There are, for instance, over 130,000 paraprofessional counselors in our mental hospitals and clinics. They go by various names — psychiatric technicians, mental health workers, alcohol counselors, to give only a few — but therapy is largely what they do. Many of our 300,000 clergy also do therapy, often called pastoral counseling. Transcendental Meditation is said to have had 10,000 instructors during its peak, most of whom would not show up on a tally of professional healers. Weight reduction programs, as well as activities designed to deal with drugs, smoking, and child abuse problems, employ many thousands of nonprofessional counselors.

Perhaps the most compelling evidence for the triumph of the therapeutic is supplied by what is becoming the most common question put to those who report any kind of personal or interpersonal problem, whether to friends, colleagues, or in calls to experts on talk shows: "Have you talked to a therapist about this?", or more delicately, "Have you considered getting professional help?" When we put together the figures and examples from the last few pages with what has been said earlier about the expanding influence of behavioral experts on how we think of and conduct ourselves in both the private and public spheres of our lives, there is little doubt that the age of psychology and the therapeutic is upon us.

American Values
and the Beginnings of Psychotherapy

> *"Psychological man is, I suggest, more native to American culture than the Puritan sources of that culture would indicate."*
>
> — PHILLIP RIEFF

AMERICA HAS BEEN AND IS the world capital of psychological-mindedness and therapeutic endeavor. One indication is that we have far more therapists than any other country. Of the estimated 90,000 psychiatrists in the world, a third are Americans. Half of the 4,000 members of the International Psychoanalytic Association practice here. It is said that New York City has more psychoanalysts than any European country. And far more than half of all clinical psychologists in the world are Americans. In 1968, when there were 12,000 clinical psychologists here, no other country had more than 400. Obviously, we also have far more people attending therapy. Well-known British psychiatrist Antony Storr writes that "for the last three decades, European visitors have been constantly astonished at the number of middle-class professional and academic colleagues who have been, or are, 'in therapy.' " And Americans who go abroad are often surprised that so few people in other countries are in therapy and that psychological self-help books which sell so well here do much less well in other countries; in fact, many aren't even published elsewhere. Numbers are not the whole story. Many psychotherapies were created outside the U.S. — including psychoanalysis and behavior therapy — but flowered only in America. And many more therapies, such as encounter groups, Parent Effectiveness Training, est, and Weight Watchers, are peculiarly American.

The growth of the therapeutic enterprise is not simply a consequence of modernization or technology. Other modernized and technological societies have not followed the therapeutic route. To explain the American obsession with personal change and psychotherapy, it is necessary to examine certain American beliefs and values. These, I suggest, along with recent changes in our society, are what made possible and perhaps even necessary the triumph of the therapeutic.

Several American characteristics have made this country particularly receptive to therapeutic notions.

Primacy of the Individual

From the start, America was more focused on the individual — his rights, property, and ambitions — than were other countries. Ties to tradition, family, community, and religion were transformed and usually weakened by the simple fact of immigration, and the situation in the new land caused further changes in the traditional social arrangements. The individual emerged as the primary element in society. In the early 1820s, one European visitor, Henry Addington, observed that

> the social ties sit looser upon them than upon any other people, and like well-boiled rice they remain united, but each grain separate. Yet an American is an excellent father, husband, neighbor, and performs all his family and social duties to admiration. But in spite of this his nature is essentially solitary, and he casts off his social ties with greater facility than another man, and leans less on others for his comforts and necessities.

By the middle of the 1880s, the glorification of the individual was in full swing, with Emerson and Thoreau celebrating self-reliance and nonconformity, and Whitman celebrating himself. What one critic has called the idea of the imperial self — the unfettered individual — was being developed. The American hero — from Daniel Boone to the characters of Melville, Twain, and Hemingway — has usually been an isolated man wandering about on his own.

It is not my intention to suggest that Americans did not value their families, communities, and religions — they did and still do. But the individual was raised to an unprecedented position. Americans were hardly an unruly bunch of nonconformists a century ago, and it is certain that much of the glorification of the individual was more fantasy than a reflection of reality, but the idea of individual primacy was accepted and kept well fertilized, ready to blossom in more propitious times.

As freedom did flower, many made a disconcerting discovery: the price of individualism is high. Alexis de Tocqueville, probably the most perceptive of our foreign visitors in the 1800s, said it well:

> Thus not only does democracy make every man forget his ancestors, but it hides his descendants and separates his contemporaries from him; it throws him back forever upon himself alone and threatens in the end to confine him entirely within the solitude of his own heart.

Leading an unfettered life, being true to oneself and one's own values, sounds virtuous but it is a tough way to live. It means great uncertainty about what one's self and values are and what to do about them; it also means uncertainty about whether one has made or is making the right decisions. One of the main functions of culture and tradition is to eliminate uncertainty and choice, or at least to keep them within tolerable bounds. If you accept tradition and it says that engaging in certain occupations, leaving your spouse, or moving to California is wrong, then you don't have to trouble yourself about these things; you just follow the rules. (For the sake of simplicity, I omit the plight of those who can't accept the common beliefs or who can't follow what they believe.)

But if you think you are free to decide how to manage your life — the first tenet of individualism — you have to make decisions about these and many other things. And since your decisions and your values may differ from those of the people around you, you are to that extent cut off from them. Uncertainty, constant decision-making, and isolation are some of the prices we have to pay for our individualism.

Having discovered that individual freedom, no matter how highly touted and prized, is also an annoyance, Americans have always been on the lookout for someone who would tell them how to live or at least give them some pointers on how to decide for themselves. And they have also sought ways of joining together with others to combat the separation inherent in their way of life.

Duty to Better Oneself

The moral obligation to better oneself is part of the ethic of individualism. Each of us is given certain talents and potentials and it is only right that we develop them to the fullest extent possible. Historian David Potter observes that a man "must justify the gift of equality by making full use of the opportunities it offers him." More than perhaps any other people, we have believed in the malleability and perfectability of people. Men and women can improve themselves and they have a duty to do so.

No better example of self-improvement can be found than Benjamin Franklin, the American model of the self-made man. In addition to everything else he did, Franklin developed a system of moral bookkeeping. He found that his efforts toward self-betterment were of little avail without a definite plan. In order to break bad habits and establish better ones, he prepared a little book listing thirteen useful virtues, including temperance, order, resolution, frugality, industry, and humility. To each he gave a week's attention, daily setting down in his book the success achieved in its practice. He went through a course in thirteen weeks and then started over again, four courses a year. Franklin would not have been surprised by the diaries and assignments of many modern therapies. It is important to recall that Franklin was an inspiration to millions of Americans in the nineteenth century. Washington may have been the father of the country, and Jefferson an intellectual genius, but Franklin was the man to emulate.

Americans rarely saw a contradiction between self-betterment and the interests of society. Adam Smith's formula — what is best for the individual is also best for society — was calmly accepted and defended by many intellectuals, including Emerson. Self-improvement — or self-actualization, as we now call it — has usually had a moral tone in American life. We were bettering ourselves not only because we were concerned with ourselves, but also because such a course was in the best interests of everyone, was right, and was what God intended. This tone accounts in large part for the seriousness and self-righteousness that pervades many therapeutic enterprises. Even books on bettering your sex life or making more money often sound as if the salvation of souls is at stake.

Unbounded Optimism

This country was settled by people who hoped and expected that life could be better. Our vast resources, isolation from enemies, the relative absence of traditional barriers to success, and the hard work of the settlers all served to reinforce the optimism. Things did get better for many.

The sense of fate was weaker here than elsewhere. The very act of immigration was itself a challenge to fate. And in this new land, with new rules and opportunities, it was not difficult to believe that what happened to a person was more a result of what he did than what the gods decreed. Tocqueville noted that Amercians were "apt to imagine that their whole destiny is in their own hands." There seemed to be no limit to what you could do for yourself. Almost anyone could go from rags to riches and a poor boy could become President. Of our confidence and optimism, Robert Heilbroner says:

> We are naturally sympathetic to ideas which stress the plasticity and promise, the openness of the future, and impatient with views which emphasize the "fated" aspect of human affairs. We strive to see in the challenges which beset us not obstacles but opportunities. In a word, we are an optimistic people. . . .
>
> As few peoples on earth, we were permitted the belief that we were the sole masters of our destiny, and as few peoples on earth have been, we were.

We could master our fate, make a better life, if only we wanted to badly enough. "Where there's a will, there's a way" could be our national slogan. People can become richer, happier, healthier, or anything else they desire. This kind of thinking is an important component of both the therapies of the late 1800s and those now popular. It is difficult to imagine therapy flourishing in a society that does not place a high value on human plasticity and the possibilities for constructive personal change.

The Right to Happiness

An almost sacred American belief is the right to the pursuit of happiness, or as it later came to be felt by many, the right to happiness. Max Lerner writes that

> America is a happiness society even more than it is a freedom society or a power society. The underlying strivings may be toward success, acquisitiveness, or power, toward prestige or security. But what validates these strivings for the American is the idea that he has a natural right to happiness.

Happiness is of course tied to individuals rather than to groups. Emerson, who had such an important influence on American thought and our first experiences with therapy, defined happiness as *self-realization*. It is the individual who has a right to be happy, a state he may achieve if he develops himself within the spiritual laws of the universe.

The fact that we believe we have a right to be happy should not be taken to mean that we have achieved that goal more than have others. In fact, Tocqueville thought we achieved it less frequently:

> In America I saw the freest and most enlightened men placed in the happiest circumstances that the world affords; it seemed to me as if a cloud habitually hung upon their brow, and I thought them serious and almost sad, even in their pleasures.
>
> The chief reason for this contrast is that the former [peasants in Europe] do not think of the ills they endure, while the latter [Americans] are forever brooding over advantages they do not possess. It is strange to see with what feverish ardor the Americans pursue their own welfare, and to watch the vague dread that con-

stantly torments them lest they should not have chosen the shortest path which may lead to it.

We wanted and expected so much — and still do, a point I shall return to later — that almost nothing could satisfy our cravings.

Whatever the results, people who believe they are entitled to happiness tend to be receptive to almost anything that promises to relieve them of affliction and annoyance, deficiency and incompetence, or whatever else they believe is in the path of their feeling better. The bearing of crosses is not for them and neither is the acceptance of tragedy or of personal limitations. They want ways around such things. The right to happiness serves as a constant spur to find methods of overcoming barriers and limits. For our ancestors, religious devotion and the accumulation of wealth were the usual means. In our time, psychological development has to a large extent supplanted them as the main way of securing happiness.

Belief in Solutions

Our confidence and our belief that we could achieve happiness were supported by our faith in the power of technology. For a long time, it appeared that whenever there was a pressing, or even a non-pressing, problem confronting us, technology came to the rescue. Historian Daniel Boorstin comments:

> Among the novelties of the American experience, none have been more striking than our innovations in technology, in standards of living, in the machinery of everyday life. . . . Do you want an adhesive that will not require moistening to hold the flaps of envelopes? Do you want a highway surface that will not crack under given variations in temperature? Do you want a pen that will write under water? Do you want a camera that will produce an image in twenty seconds? Or, perhaps, do you want it in full color? We can provide you all these things.

Boorstin notes that Americans have tended to take the technological problem — the potentially soluble problem — as the prototype of all problems. We have a knack of turning anything that bothers us into a problem, a problem being something for which there must be a solution. We have great faith in solutions and have refused to accept the possibility of insoluble problems, the very idea being a contradiction to many of us. As the Seabees put it in World War II: "The difficult we do right away, the impossible takes a little longer." We have been less than eager to hear that fixing a road and fixing a person may be different things, that changing a tire and changing a habit are not exactly the same, and that there may not be any cures or solutions for things like violence, criminal behavior, and schizophrenia. Everything that bothers us, we believe, can be changed for the better. As one therapist writes, "Somewhere there is a technique that is just right for you." All we need to do is find the right techniques and we can take care of everything.

These, then, are some of the salient beliefs that have been with us at least since the nineteenth century, a period that saw the beginnings of what would later be called psychotherapy. Self-help material was in evidence from the start. A new genre of books and articles gushed forth after 1800, full of domestic and child-rearing advice, followed by a flood of books on how to be rich and successful. And in the late 1820s, phrenology made its appearance, imported from England. Historians have not been kind to this doctrine and it is now known, if at all, as the reading of bumps on the head, but it was far more than this: it was a full-blown system of thought, applicable to all areas of life. Historian John Davies writes that, "As psychologists do today, phrenologists told their age how to be happy, how to choose a profession, how to select a wife, how to raise children." They also offered advice on education, the diagnosis and cure of insanity, the rehabilitation of criminals, and on health and medicine. Phrenology was very popular in the 1830s and '40s, both among intellectuals and common people, more popular than it was in Europe. This is not surprising because in its vulgar form it fit in well with the American beliefs just discussed. It saw man as good, was optimistic for the chances of personal change, and seemed practical in that it offered specific methods for inducing constructive changes. Despite its widespread influence, it had only a one-generation career. Phrenology ran out of steam before the Civil War and by the end of the century was little more than a faint memory for most people. But its main message remained: methods could be derived for making people happier.

Meanwhile, work on the edifice of psychotherapy continued in other quarters, to one of which we now turn. After the Civil War physicians were sought out by patients with an interesting problem. These patients were educated, affluent, and successful, complaining not of clearly defined symptoms but of vague and unclassifiable ailments, of inability to concentrate, unaccountable fatigue, and irrational fears. The medical profession regarded such complaints with skepticism. The patients weren't really ill; it was "all in their minds."

But something was troubling many middle- and upper-class Americans, and finally some doctors took it seriously. One of them, New York neurologist George Beard, gave the name neurasthenia to the problem and in 1881 published his magnum opus on the subject, *American Nervousness*. What he described was very different than the restlessness and agitation noted by Tocqueville and other visitors. It was not hyperactivity but depletion, nervous exhaustion. A few of the symptoms Beard listed:

> insomnia, flushing, drowsiness, bad dreams . . . nervous dyspepsia . . . sweating hands and feet . . . fear of lightning, or fear of responsibility, of open places or of closed places, fear of society . . . fear of fears . . . fear of everything . . . lack of decision in trifling matters . . . a feeling of profound exhaustion . . . vague pains and flying neuralgias. . . .

Beard had taken a radical step. He had admitted into the list of legitimate medical complaints a host of feelings and behaviors that medicine had previously been unwilling to accept. The way was being paved for the acceptance of Freud.

But Beard was no revolutionary and could go no farther. Like many others, he blamed the problems on American civilization. America led the nations in nervousness because it led the nations in civilization. When it came to treatment, Beard was true to the somatic and mechanistic teachings of the time; he relied on medical therapy — drugs, injections, and electrical stimulation.

The time during which nervousness appeared and in which Beard practiced was another one of the many periods of upheaval in American life. The value of religion had been greatly undermined for many middle-class citizens. Though they all professed to believe in God — as do most Americans even today — religion was no longer able to provide direction and comfort. When Nietzsche announced that God was dead in the hearts of his European contemporaries, he could just as well have been talking about Americans. The thinking of many Americans continued to shift from the supernatural to the concerns of everyday life; from a belief in happiness after death to a desire for happiness in this life; from a belief in the intervention of God in human affairs to a belief that men could and should take command of their own lives; from a belief that man was small, base, and limited, compared to God, to the beliefs that man was good, worthy, and important, and should develop himself as he saw fit.

A vacuum had been created. Religion was not working as therapy. The nervous patients expected results here and now, and could not be mollified by messages of patience, stoicism, or rewards in the world beyond. Neither did medicine have much to offer them. Psychiatry was concerned with psychotics in institutions; it had nothing to say to those who suffered only from nervousness.

The last quarter of the nineteenth century was a time of seeking and searching, and as such, was similar to our own time. Healers and healing systems rose and fell in a never-ending stream of neurologists, psychologists, physiologists, and self-styled experts of every description. More than a half-century of looking to experts for advice about marriage, child-rearing, and how to be successful had prepared the way for the new advice. Dr. Sylvester Graham promoted vegetarianism, open windows, cold baths, and the crackers that bore his name. A Horace Fletcher pinned his hopes on the healing properties of cellulose in raw vegetables and slow and thorough mastication. Fletcherism became a fad. Psychologist William James tried the regimen for three months and gave it up because "it nearly killed me." There were also those who believed in the healing power of the sun shining through blue glass.

New systems of mental healing appeared, combining Christian theology, spiritualism, suggestion, Transcendentalism, and smatterings of Hindu and Buddhist esotericism. Probably the best known of these approaches was Mary Baker Eddy's Christian Science. Many of the rest are simply lumped together under the rubric of New Thought or mind cure. All claimed to cure every ailment under the sun and were characterized by what William James called a "moon-struck optimism."

Mind cure was in large measure a revolt against the old religions, especially Calvinism. As one of its leaders put it:

> The "old thought" was undeniably pessimistic; it dwelt on sin, emphasized the darkness and misery of the world, the distress and the suffering. The new dwelt on life and light pointing the way to the mastery of all sorrow and suffering.

Although the many schools and cults differed in a number of ways and were often at war with one another, some common threads are discernible. Man was basically good. In fact, man was mind, an individualization of Divine Mind. When man opened his mind, he was in direct contact with the mind of God. The problem was that man relied overly much on his conscious mind. What was needed was greater reliance on the subconscious — also called the subliminal self and the superconscious — for it was the channel to the Divine Essence. By surrendering to the nonconscious or spiritual aspect of one's mind, one could have whatever one desired. There was an unlimited supply of everything one might want. Series of exercises were provided by most of the schools, and by most of the journals and books they published, to help the troubled person achieve his ends. The exercises included proper breathing, relaxation, autosuggestion, and visualization of desired states and objects.

A few quotations from mind cure writers give the flavor of their enterprise:

In just the degree in which you realize your oneness with the Infinite Spirit, you will exchange disease for ease, inharmony for harmony, suffering and pain for abounding health and strength. . . . One need remain in Hell no longer than one chooses to; we can rise to any heaven we ourselves choose. . . .

The New Thought came as the corrective to this abject submissiveness [of Calvinism]. It substituted self-realization for self-sacrifice, and development for self-effacement. It is nothing if not an affirmative thought, and this positiveness has come to stay. . . . The tendency of radicalism in the New Thought is to exalt the finite self to the first rank.

The principle is, to affirm and persistently maintain as *true now* that which you desire. . . . If necessary, you are warranted in denying whatever apparently stands between you and this ideal. By thus giving the mind unqualifiedly to one idea you exclude every doubt, fear, or negative thought that might arise in protest.

In short, mind cure was rooted both in religion and in the new hope that suffering was unnecessary, that by cultivating the right attitude and doing the right exercises, people could really be the masters of their fate.

New Thought or mind cure is important for at least two reasons. First, by emphasizing the nonconscious aspects of life and the idea that many physical problems were mental in origin, it paved the way for the acceptance of psychoanalysis. Thanks to George Beard and New Thought, Freud received a warmer welcome in America than in any other country. This is not to say that Freud liked mind cure. Though he knew little about it, he promptly condemned it. He didn't like its connection with religion and its use of suggestion. Having abandoned suggestion and hypnotism earlier in his career, he didn't think anyone else should use them. Such procedures, he said, did not result in permanent cures. New Thought seemed to Freud to be a simpleminded fad "of questionable good" which would soon fade away. It was Band-Aid therapy, dealing only with superficial symptoms, unlike psychoanalysis, which went after the unconscious causes of symptoms and resulted in long-term improvement (a claim to be repeated countless times by analysts for the next seventy years whenever new treatments arose). Although Freud was probably unaware of it, New Thought did concern itself with the unconscious, but what the curists saw was very different from what he saw. For Freud, the unconscious was the seat of the most primitive and unsocialized impulses, the source of much human conflict and suffering, which had to be brought under some kind of control by the conscious mind. In contrast, the curists believed the unconscious to be the higher and better faculty, the source of man's spirituality and goodness. The American tendency to see a silver lining in every cloud was at work and in time would give psychoanalysis a more optimistic tone than Freud intended. Much later, following the precedent of New Thought, it would spawn a host of therapies based on the idea that there was nothing to be feared in the depths of the unconscious or in life itself, nothing that necessarily led to conflict or tragedy, and it would transform the gloominess of European existentialism into a cheery, uplifting approach to self-improvement.

Despite these differences, New Thought did well by Freud. Not only did mental healers prepare Americans for his theory and therapy, but they also publicized his work after his visit here in 1909.

The second reason for mind cure's importance is that it provided the tone, the philosophy, and even many of the specific methods of a number of the therapies that would follow, including some that are popular today. Its positive and optimistic tone is peculiarly American and formed the basis for what was later to be called positive thinking, the most popular exponents of which are probably Norman Vincent Peale and Joyce Brothers. New Thought's denigration of consciousness was worlds apart from Freud, who saw consciousness as weak but all-important, but was close to many of the modern activities such as encounter, meditation, and Est. Mind cure was modern in still other ways: the notion that mind was more powerful than body; the use of meditation and relaxation exercises; the goal of self-realization, later to be called self-actualization; the idea that one could have whatever one wanted by visualizing or suggesting it; and the claim that its methods were simple and scientifically based.

These statements by contemporary therapists and writers could easily have been written almost a century ago by the curists:

If you are in poor health, you can remedy it. If your personal relationships are unsatisfactory, you can change them for the better.
If you are in poverty, you can find yourself surrounded by abundance. . . . Each of you, regardless of position, status, circumstances
or physical condition, is in control of your own experience.

When we concentrate on a thought, the thought becomes true because our bodies transform it into action. . . . "Negative thoughts,
negative suggestions, have no influence over me at any level of
mind."

Ultimately, what you believe is what you become. . . . What's real
is that there are no limitations to what you can be and do.

Love, power, riches, success, a good marriage, exciting sex, fulfillment are not impossible dreams. They can be yours if you want
them. . . . There is nothing esoteric about the techniques that I
recommend. They are scientifically based, absolutely straightforward. . . . And you can use this knowledge to get whatever you
want out of life.

In the late 1800s and the early years of this century there was
widespread interest in emotional problems and the many ways of
treating them. After 1905 there was a great deal of publicity about
the "growing menace" of mental disorder. Alarms and salvation,
the usual proclamations of those trying to sell something, were the
order of the day. Statistics were presented "proving" that mental
illness was increasing faster than the population (interestingly, California was said to have the highest proportion of the insane). High
suicide rates — with San Francisco leading the nation — were offered as evidence of the growing problem. A number of prominent
Americans — including William James; Jane Addams; Woodrow
Wilson; Senator William Beveridge; Frederick Taylor, the father
of scientific management; and John Watson, the behaviorist — were
known to have suffered from one form of nervous disorder or another. Several journalists, including Floyd Dell, Lucian Cary, and
Max Eastman, wrote about the therapy they received for their
problems.

The news was carried in books, magazines, and newspapers. Articles on psychological problems and treatments were found in old,

genteel magazines like *The Atlantic* but more often in the new magazines for which the muckrakers wrote, magazines such as *McClure's* and *The American.* The Emmanuel Movement, one of the spearheads of the mental health movement, published its own journal with the formidable title of *Psychotherapy: A Course of Reading in Sound Psychology, Sound Medicine and Sound Religion.* Emmanuel's founder, the Reverend Elwood Worcester, preached that America faced a crisis of nerves and national character, pointing to the "alarming increases" of insomnia and nervousness, that "most prevalent disease of modern times." But, as we might expect from looking at our own times, most of the articles on nerves and mental cures were carried by the women's magazines such as *Good Housekeeping* and the *Ladies' Home Journal.* The former, in 1911, even printed a recipe by a psychic on how to become beautiful by thought.

Of books there was no end. There was a flood of material: Mary Baker Eddy's *Science and Health,* which constantly appeared in new editions; *The Healing Power of Mind; As a Man Thinketh; Twice-Born Men; The Science of Being and Christian Healing; The Christian's Secret of a Happy Life; What Men Live By*; and one of the biggest sellers of the time, *In Tune With the Infinite.* These books were distributed widely; all were best-sellers. And there were many others.

Although there were many skeptics who tried to disprove both the alarms and the claims for miracle cures, they were drowned out in the rising tide of optimism. Glowing reports of new methods and new developments appeared regularly, with every book and every practitioner claiming that his way could heal just about anything.

Magazines eagerly printed almost any hopeful medical news: the speculation that insanity might be caused by a toxin and cured by an anti-toxin, that insanity was not a "disease" but an inability to adapt to environment. Some physicians urged that the old words "chronic and incurable" be abandoned. Psychiatry, they insisted, despite lack of improvement in recovery rates, was on the threshold of a golden age.

All of which should sound familiar enough to the modern reader. That was about psychosis. About milder forms of emotional suffering, another familiar perspective was being established: if only you thought the right thoughts, did the proper exercises, had the prescribed attitude, you could have, be, or do anything. America was well on its way to becoming the therapeutic society.

A sign of things to come was the great success in the early 1920s of the French psychologist Emile Coué. He had developed a system of healing called self-mastery by autosuggestion. The patient had only to repeat continuously the appropriate words — usually "Every day and in every way, I am becoming better and better" — and health and happiness would be his. Coué claimed his method could cure many ailments and even grow hair on bald heads. If an expectant mother said over and over again every day, "My child will be a girl," she could determine the sex of her child. She could also determine the child's career by practicing autosuggestion during her pregnancy. "If she wants her unborn son to be a great architect she should visit great buildings and surround herself with pictures of architectural masterpieces and above all she should think beautiful thoughts." Delinquency, crime, vice, and other social problems could also be reduced or solved by use of his methods, said Dr. Coué.

It was only fitting that Coué should come to America. His trip here in 1922 received great publicity and he attracted large crowds on his cross-country lecture tour. A magazine devoted to autosuggestion came out, containing many successful case histories. Coué institutes were established in cities across the country. And many people were seen walking along muttering to themselves, "Every day and in every way . . ." Couéism became a national fad.

Although Coué's methods were condemned by the American Medical Association and some members of the scientific community, they found favor in many places. The president of the American Museum of Natural History said that "American high-speed life needs the calming effects of Couéism." A doctor at New York's Presbyterian Hospital said that Coué had gotten people to believe in their own regenerative powers. Pastors preached the virtues of autosuggestion and a number of individuals gave testimony to their cures. Although some called Coué a miracle worker, he merely said:

"I am not a miracle man. I do not heal people. I teach them to cure themselves."

Couéism soon faded, but the idea of autosuggestion remained, surfacing in many of the healing systems that have arisen in recent times; Coué's methods are an essential ingredient in Silva Mind Control. And here is Joyce Brothers, writing of a success story in 1978:

> "Every morning when I shave," Avery said, "I look at myself in the mirror and I say over and over, 'You're going to succeed.' I've said that every morning for the last twelve years. And it works. I have succeeded." Avery had instinctively found the most effective psychological tool for increasing his initially very low success potential. He thought himself into success.
>
> You can too.

And many of the contemporary methods for dealing with pain and disease have their patients repeat, among other things, "Every day and in every way . . ."

The Acids
of Modernity

"Psychotherapy can be viewed as a social institution created to fill the gap left by the decay of other institutions that gave meaning to life and a feeling of connectedness to others."

— JEROME FRANK

AMERICA HAS UNDERGONE a number of dramatic changes in the last two hundred years, and particularly in the last three decades. My thesis is that these changes, combined with the beliefs already discussed, are what make us so receptive to the psychotherapeutic sensibility. These societal changes are the topics of this and the following chapter. I begin with some comparisons between traditional, rural America — epitomized by the time before we became a nation, the colonial period, but many strands of which persisted until the turn of this century — and contemporary life. Although, as the title of this chapter indicates, modernization has corroded many of the institutions and beliefs that guided the lives of our forebears, I do not intend to suggest that things were better in times gone by. Life in America in the late 1700s and for a long time thereafter was far from what most of us would consider tolerable; it was short, dirty, dangerous, and lacking in most modern amenities. By no stretch of the imagination could it be considered the good old days. It was hardly better than what we now have. But it was different, and therein lies the tale.

The Loss of Unity,
Simplicity, and Consistent Identity

Compared to our time, life in traditional America was limited, simple, unified, and understandable. In colonial times, almost everyone lived in little towns or villages of fewer than 1,500 persons. The largest city in 1770 was Philadelphia, with a population of less than

28,000; the only other two places that might be called cities, New York and Boston, each had fewer than 22,000 inhabitants. These cities were not like modern ones; they were basically clusters of "neighborhood villages where face-to-face intimacy combined with family status to place people in their accustomed niches." Transportation was primitive, confined to footpower, sailpower, and horsepower, as was communication: there was a postal service but most colonists never sent or received a letter. Progress in transportation and communication soon came, but America remained a predominantly rural society until 1920. That was the first time the census reported more citizens living in towns of over 2,500 inhabitants than in places with smaller populations.

Life in traditional America was confined to family and community. Everyone, with the exception of a few trappers and traders, lived with families, their own or someone else's. Even young adults did not live alone or with their peers. Peter Laslett's description of life in England during an earlier period applies as well to traditional America. The "whole of life," he writes, was framed by a "circle of loved, familiar faces, known and fondled objects." Most communities contained a host of relatives; and those who weren't related acted as if they were. There was little alternative to this type of close-knit existence; there was nothing else to turn to. People needed and depended on one another for everything — for help in dealing with the crises of life, such as childbirth, illness, and death; for help in getting the work done; and for entertainment, protection against enemies and natural disasters, the care of the sick and aged, and the control of crime.

The boundaries between various aspects of life — work, recreation, child-rearing, worship — were not nearly as rigid as they are today. The various aspects were not really various. Work was usually carried out in or around the home, as was entertainment, and the same known faces were encountered wherever one went and whatever one did. Families were not walled off from the community in the modern way; the community tended to act as everyone's extended family. Everyone knew everyone else and minded everyone else's business. Since all of life more or less blended together, with relatively smooth transitions between what we now think of as different aspects of living, one didn't need different personalities or styles for different parts of it. Those around a man knew him in his work and leisure, his health and illness, his good times and bad times. In short, he was known as what we might call a total person; it was hard to keep secrets even if one wanted to.

People were much more understandable to each other than they now are. Everyone in the community did pretty much the same kind of work, believed the same things, lived the same kind of life. It wasn't hard to understand where others were coming from.

The rules of life were simple, obvious to all, and enforced by all the powers that existed — family, church, neighborhood, and courts. The duties of husband and wife, parents and children, neighbors, boarders, and co-workers were clearly spelled out. One could comply or not, but at least the rules were clear, as were the consequences of noncompliance, and the alternatives were limited.

A sense of coherence — "a perception of one's environments, inner and outer, as predictable and comprehensible" — was easier to come by than it now is. The world and one's neighbors made some kind of sense, even if one didn't like the sense they made. Technology was not changing the world every year and neighbors were not adopting a new life-style every month. Life was hard but it was also structured, understandable, and predictable.

To put it mildly, things have changed. Science and technology have drastically transformed the outer world, and the transformations continue at an accelerating rate. The average American living in a large city probably comes into contact with more people in one week than the average colonist did in his whole life. Even if the modern citizen lives in a rural area, the mass media and the telephone bring him into instant contact with people, places, and events all over the world, and this happens every single day of his life.

Life is more complex and fragmented. Different skills are needed to negotiate different aspects of life, and the boundaries between the different spheres have grown more rigid. Other people are not as understandable as they used to be. We see them in only some of their roles, not as total persons, and we often have no idea of what their work or play consists of.

Options abound in every area, and this is one of the most important changes wrought by modernization. Just think of all the different kinds and brands of appliances you can choose from, and homes, cars, furniture, clothes, and so on. But these are not the important things. There are different jobs and careers, different marital and nonmarital arrangements, different sexual preferences and styles, different values and belief systems, and what we call different life-styles. The rules of life are many and flexible. There is no longer only one correct way. As we say, different strokes for different folks. But greater freedom and more alternatives mean that a sense of coherence barely exists for many of us. We can neither predict nor understand what others, or even ourselves, will do.

One consequence of the changes I've mentioned is that the development of personal identity — a coherent sense of self — is much more difficult than ever before. Identity has been much in the news lately. People talk of finding and expressing themselves, of doing their *own* thing, of developing and actualizing themselves. At the heart of all these phrases is identity, that which is to be found, developed, expressed, and actualized. The reason for our near-obsession with identity is simply that its development and even its very existence have become problematic.

In traditional times, one did not so much develop an identity as slip into one that was already waiting. A place was carved out for one as soon as one was born. One followed the lead of the same-sex parent as soon as one was able. One was put to work at an early age, learning skills and manners from one's parents, siblings, and neighbors, and gradually grew into the type of work one would probably do for the rest of one's life. One inherited the religion, values, and beliefs of the family and community. Although the world wasn't static, it was reasonably stable. There was good reason to think that the world of the future would be similar to that of the present and therefore that the skills and knowledge one was learning, and the identity one was assuming, would be relevant in the years to come.

The development of a strong and stable identity was encouraged by two other factors. First, everyone was always in the company of others who had a strong stake in his being exactly who he was supposed to be and who wouldn't think twice about reminding him that he wasn't being himself. Second, there weren't a lot of alternatives.

There was one basic way of living and that was that. The pluralistic society had not yet been invented. A person was not confronted daily with authorities and experts who questioned or condemned his way of life and portrayed the benefits of other life-styles, a term that would have made no sense at that time.

Modernization has made great changes in this situation. No longer is identity created and enforced by the community; it has become a private affair. There is much more room for people to create their own identities. There are choices everywhere; virtually nothing is forbidden or closed off. And everything keeps changing. People must be prepared to live in a world that doesn't yet exist, and therefore for which the rules and values of yesterday and today may not be relevant.

It is not only that there is more external information to integrate and a changing environment to cope with. There is also more internal information to make sense of and deal with. In the past, much of inner life was suppressed. One knew who one was and internal rumblings not consistent with that view were usually kept out of awareness. As Allen Wheelis notes, "modern man has become more perceptive of covert motivations. . . . Areas of experience formerly dissociated from consciousness have become commonplace knowledge." We did not invent anxiety, depression, or disguised hostility, but we are more aware of them. Paradoxically, as we have lost our sense of identities, we have discovered more of the elements of ourselves out of which identities may be formed. Being less sure of who we are, we can't know what to exclude from awareness. We feel that we should acknowledge and attend to each thought, motive, feeling, and fantasy, for it may offer clues as to what we are about. But having all this material available makes it more difficult to establish a firm sense of identity. We are overwhelmed by parts but have lost the center. Compared to our ancestors, the elements we need to integrate are far more numerous and less homogeneous.

No longer is it possible for most people to slip quietly into an identity their parents and community laid out for them, if for no other reason than that no one can lay it out anymore. The period for getting ready to participate in the adult world — for developing skills and finding oneself — has lengthened considerably in the last two centuries. Children used to be viewed as miniature adults, not fully participating in the adult world only because they lacked knowledge and physical strength. Then childhood came to be seen as a special stage of life with its own special requirements. Later, toward the end of the nineteenth century, adolescence was invented, carrying the state of not being ready to enter adult life to the age of nineteen or so. Recently, some have suggested an additional stage of life called youth, which lies between adolescence and adulthood. According to Kenneth Keniston, one of the advocates of this stage, the main characteristic of youths is "that they have not settled the questions whose answers once defined adulthood: questions of relationship to the existing society; questions of vocation; questions of social role and life style." Imagine how a colonist in the 1700s or someone in the 1930s would have reacted to such a description of people in their twenties. Not being an adult now can last until the late twenties or even into the thirties. It is possible that we have reached or are reaching a time when there will be nothing that can be called adulthood, if by adult we mean someone who has come to some firm conclusions about the issues Keniston poses.

Until quite recently, it was thought and expected that one settled down early in life — in a place, a family, a job, and a way of life. In colonial times, such a settling down was expected to take place before the age of twenty. In modern times, there has been more flexibility; one might not settle down until after college or professional school. But the idea remained the same: there comes a time when you put down roots and live the life you have been preparing for. Doing so would of course be conducive to the development and maintenance of a stable identity.

For millions of contemporary Americans settling down is more a figure of speech than a reflection of reality. We change our residences more often than any other people. This is more than just an interesting fact. Moving means uprooting, and the more one is uprooted, the fewer the roots and the less chance of a stable sense of self. We also frequently change jobs, marital status, and life-style. All of which is both a reflection and cause of our diffuse identities.

Those who make commitments — to a career, a spouse, a place — often sense them to be tentative. Even those who want to make a lifetime or a long-term commitment know at least intellectually that they may feel differently later. Feelings change, better opportunities open up elsewhere, jobs become obsolete, neighborhoods change. Who is to say what you'll feel and be thinking and doing in ten years? New possibilities keep appearing and one has to be open to them.

The fact that we live a lot longer than our ancestors also has effects on our commitments and identities. Life expectancy has more than doubled between 1790 and 1970, from thirty-five to over seventy years. The average woman in colonial America raised her children and then died. Now the average woman knows she has many years to look forward to after the children are gone; she may want to return to school or work, find some other way of expressing herself, or reassess her relationship with her spouse. The now well-known stage of life called midlife, and its attendant crisis, occurs at an age that most colonists and even people in the middle of the nineteenth century didn't live to experience. Commitments and identities that are serviceable for ten or twenty years may not work as well for thirty or forty years.

The potpourri of alternative ways of living thrown out by the media, combined with a longer life-span and therefore more time to experiment, can be unsettling.

A man of fifty-two went to a therapist because he had started to think his life had been wasted. "I was successful but I worked like a dog and didn't have much fun, not compared to what my kids and others were having. I had many impulses and fantasies in my life, like taking a year off and sailing around the world, but I always suppressed them. Maybe I fooled myself. Maybe I'd be happier if I weren't so compulsive, if I could be less rigid and take more time to enjoy myself. It would certainly be a big change and I'm not sure I could do it but I want to explore the idea. I'd hate to die thinking my life had been a waste." What this man was proposing to explore was no less than his identity.

A woman of thirty-eight was very clear about the issue: "My marriage was pretty good and so was sex, even after seventeen years. But I'd only been to bed with one other man and it seemed that sex had opened up so much since then. I wanted to sleep with other men, see what that was like and what I was like with them. I wanted to try different things, maybe even making it with a woman. I wasn't getting any younger; if I wanted to experiment, this was probably my last chance. But I was ambivalent. It wasn't easy to think of myself in a new way. What was I — an adulteress, a swinger, a lesbian, or a responsible married woman and mother?"

The whole notion of a fixed identity, of a personality and life-style basically fashioned and accepted by early adulthood, has been challenged by the dynamics of modern society and by some segments of the mental health establishment. Psychiatrist Robert Lifton suggests that the idea of a stable identity derives from an outdated view of the relationship of people to societal symbols and institutions and therefore is also obsolete. Lifton argues that the twentieth century has produced a new kind of individual whom he calls protean man, after the mythological creature who could change his form at will. As he puts it, the protean style "is characterized by an interminable series of experiments and explorations — some shallow, some profound — each of which may be readily abandoned in favor of still new psychological quests." In other words, no stable identity and no stable self-concept, just a lifetime of self in process, being one thing today and another tomorrow.

Earlier I said that adulthood in the old sense may no longer exist for many people. What I meant was that decreasing numbers of people seem to achieve a stable identity at any age. If this is true, it marks a milestone in human affairs. A stable identity meant that the person had arrived, had resolved certain basic issues, had answered many of the important questions of living. Durable identities were not cast in concrete; there was room for doubt, questioning, and alteration. And, as Erik Erikson has demonstrated, different stages of life generated new problems and new opportunities for reexamination and reintegration of identity. Nonetheless, some threads remained constant; there was some solid ground on which to stand, something one could get hold of.

Now, for increasing numbers of people, there is no solid ground, no threads that remain constant, nothing to get hold of. Our language reflects the change. In place of words such as character, personality, and being, we now talk about self — of which there may be many inhabiting a single human form, all of which are mutable — and process and becoming. Fewer people expect to arrive anymore; they just want to be, or expect to be, in process all of their lives. Lifton quotes one of his patients, a young teacher: "I have an extraordinary number of masks I can put on or take off. The question is: is there, or should there be, one face which should be authentic? I'm not sure there is one for me. . . . I tend to think that for people who have these many, many masks, there is no home." Which is reminiscent of Saul Bellow's character Augie March: "I touched all sides, and nobody knew where I belonged. I had no good idea of that myself." The uncertainty and homelessness portrayed in these two examples are representative of the psyches of many modern Americans.

There is no question that stable identities were confining; they did prevent certain types of exploration and experimentation. You knew beyond a shadow of a doubt that divorce or giving up your job or leaving your family to meditate in Nepal was not for you, period. Some doors were definitely closed. Many people appear to be quite happy to be free of such constraints. Without a constant identity weighing them down, they are free to try on many new faces, styles, and behaviors. Some of the best-selling novels of recent years have been celebrations of the self as process, including Herman Hesse's *Steppenwolf* and *Siddhartha*, which sold so well on college campuses in the 1960s, and Richard Bach's *Jonathan Livingston Seagull*, the third largest selling book of the 1970s. Jonathan well exemplifies the rootless, always searching self. "Home I have none. Flock I have none." He is banished from his flock after consistently violating its rules. But he doesn't care, for he believes that other gulls are stupid, spending their lives eating, mating, and being together. Such a pedestrian life is not for Jonathan. He seeks to fly, to be free, to find himself. He spends his whole life finding and perfecting his true nature, first alone and later under the guidance of an eastern guru named Chiang.

For many others, however, the price of liberation has been high. One of the virtues of stable identities is that although they limited some types of freedom, they created a different kind of freedom — freedom from more choices and decisions than a person could deal with. Many people today are overwhelmed by all the choices they have to make and rarely have a moment of peace. They feel empty and at a loss to make any sense of their lives. They do not like not knowing who they are and where they belong and are unnerved by the "continuous psychic recreation" they experience.

Therapy serves both groups — those who want to experiment and those who want to stop the bus and get off, that is, to find a home and a way to live. That so many people are trying to get a better sense of who they are or could be, questions that people in traditional society rarely wrestled with, is an indication of how far we have come. It is truly a brave new world, and so far millions have not found satisfying ways of living in it.

Modernization also causes a tremendous increase in loneliness. As already noted, people in traditional America lived their whole lives surrounded by familiar others. Such an arrangement is not without a price; it could be claustrophobic and some, like Daniel Boone, headed west to get away from it. But its virtue was that almost everyone had a strong sense of community and belonging. People may or may not have been happy but few were lonely.

The proportion of the population living in homes with six or more persons has declined from 50 percent in 1790 to 16 percent in 1940 to 6 percent in 1980. There has been a corresponding increase in the number of people living alone, from less than 4 percent in 1790 to 11 percent in 1940 to 22 percent in 1980, and in couples living alone, from 8 percent in colonial times to 30 percent now. To be sure, not all individuals living alone or with one other person feel lonely; some wouldn't have it any other way. But in general, the fewer the people in the home, the greater the chance of loneliness. And this is only part of the story. The close-knit villages and neighborhoods of colonial times — the community as a kind of extended family — served as a protection against loneliness, whatever one's living situation. Such communities are no longer much in evidence.

Modernization begets aloneness, which often begets loneliness. A number of institutions have grown up to deal with the problem, and some of them are ably discussed in Suzanne Gordon's *Lonely in America.* Therapy is one of those institutions. Some people go to counseling to learn the skills and develop the confidence needed to meet and get along with others. Social skills and shyness groups and workshops are now available in most metropolitan areas. A number of books also deal with the issue: e.g., *Contact: The First Four Minutes; Shyness: What It Is, What to Do About It; It's Up to You: Developing Assertive Social Skills; We, the Lonely People: Searching for Community;* and *How to Make Friends with Someone of the Opposite Sex.*

Others go to counseling to enjoy the sense of community that often exists there or with the hope of meeting someone special. Therapy groups and workshops have a number of advantages for those looking for friendship, romance, and sex. Although therapy also has a number of defects as a remedy for loneliness, so do all the other methods. Marriage is not for everyone and neither are singles bars and clubs. Communal living, as many young Americans discovered in the 1960s and '70s, can be too much of a good thing. We value privacy far more than our ancestors, and enforced togetherness can be a pain. So it appears that, as more of us feel lonely, therapy will continue to be a popular way of dealing with it.

The Loss of Meaning, Faith, and Control

As we have seen, modernization involves a weakening of the traditional beliefs and institutions of society, the things that had provided meaning, support, and comfort, the things that made it possible for people to endure the vicissitudes of life. This makes for a huge problem because people need to believe their lives have purpose, they need to have faith in something that makes sense to them, and they need to believe they have some understanding and control over internal and external events. They need, in short, some source of meaning and comfort, something to help them weather the storms of life. By destroying traditional sources of meaning, modernization tends to leave people feeling alone, lost, and impotent. Fortunately, however, modernity has its own resources and offers new systems of meaning and control — things such as science, progress, and nationalism — although it is by no means clear that these are as powerful and as comforting as those they supplanted.

The conditions of colonial life in America starting breaking down in the early 1800s. New conditions and new systems of meaning arose. Although there are several worthy of consideration, I will discuss only nationalism or the American way of life.

It is well to recall that Americans did not feel a strong sense of identification with their country until about the time of the Civil War. Before then, the closest ties and identifications were with family, local community, and sometimes to region. Indifference to national politics was the rule. In 1787 less than one-third of those eligible voted on whether to ratify the national constitution. And "almost every state and every political faction and interest group attempted, at one time or other between 1790 and 1860, to weaken the power of the national government or to break up the Union directly." It was only after the War between the States that the majority of Americans started to feel a strong identification and loyalty to their country and to derive a sense of meaning from their attachment to it.

Religious beliefs and local ties grew less important. In their place stood nationalism and the American Way, the latter attaining such importance, despite its vagueness, that some scholars called it a civil religion. Being an American meant something; Americans had a common faith by virtue of being American, and they took pride in it. Their land was the greatest of all lands, the country of unlimited opportunity, where life would always get better and better, a country with a manifest destiny. Their way of life was something to brag about. Increasingly, the federal government came to be seen as the symbol and embodiment of the American Way. Such a situation is not to be taken lightly. In a country where the influence of primary groups and transcendent meaning systems had seriously declined, the state and belief in the country came to be the great respository of the social bond, the glue that held society together and gave a collective meaning to its inhabitants. Almost more than any other institution, the state and its ideology provided the framework and meaning of life. It supplied the heroes (the Founding

Fathers, Lincoln, Franklin Roosevelt, and many others); the devils (robber barons, Fascists, Communists); the rituals (the Pledge of Allegiance, the national anthem, national elections, Independence Day); and the hope without which people cannot live (the hope that life would continue to get better). Should the state lose the loyalty and respect of its citizens, what then would give meaning and a sense of community? The question is crucial because since the end of World War II the government and the American way of life have steadily lost influence.

America emerged from the war as the richest and most powerful nation in the history of the world. We had pulled ourselves out of the Great Depression, had soundly beaten the Axis powers, and were the sole possessors of atomic weapons. There seemed to be no limit to what we could accomplish and little reason to doubt that this indeed would be the American century, as Henry Luce called it. It was a heady feeling, shared by the majority of Americans. The golden age of peace, prosperity, power, and progress was at hand.

This feeling didn't last very long. Since 1945 we have suffered one setback after another, and even our successes were somehow never good enough. The result was the replacement of optimism and faith with cynicism and pessimism. The undermining of faith in America began much earlier than the assassination of the Kennedys and the Vietnam war. I can do little more than briefly mention some of the events which undid us. Soviet acquisition of nuclear weapons reduced our sense of omnipotence, as did their Sputnik. What was called the loss of mainland China was another blow. The Korean war, which we couldn't win, was another indication that no matter how strong we were, we couldn't have everything our way. The national hysteria that was both exploited and aggravated by Senator Joseph McCarthy was a sure sign that our confidence and sense of security had been eroded.

All of this was only the beginning. Inflation and recession reminded us that we were not as much in control of the economy as we had hoped and thought. We began to realize how much our lives were influenced by giant bureaucracies that we couldn't direct and often couldn't even understand. Our education system, once a source of pride, was found to be full of problems.

Things were turning out to be different than we expected. In 1959 Robert Heilbroner wrote of

> our contemporary feeling of unease and confusion. We feel ourselves beleaguered by happenings which seem not only malign and intransigent, but unpredictable. We are at a loss to know how to anticipate the events the future may bring or how to account for those events once they have happened. The future itself is a direction in which we look no longer with confidence but with vague forebodings and a sense of unpreparedness.

Life ceased to make sense for many of us. When writer Joan Didion said that "the world as I had understood it no longer existed," she echoed the feelings of many. Two of the biggest insults we endured were the Vietnam war and the rebellion of the students. How the war sapped our will and confidence is a story that has been told too many times to need repetition here. The behavior of college students in the late 1960s and the related advent of the counterculture are equally important as reflections of the decline of faith in America. Here were the students, even if only a small minority of them, at our best universities, the children of the educated and affluent, objecting not only to the war and the way the schools were being run, but also to everything Americans held sacred — affluence itself, capitalism, most middle-class values, our whole way of life.

Futility, confusion, and a growing realization of the lack of meaning and control — these are the legacies of the period since World War II. The meaninglessness of the assassination of the Kennedys and Marin Luther King, the absolute absurdity of them, combined with the inability of anyone to stop such occurrences, only served to add gravity to feelings already present. And the beat has gone on. Bad news is everywhere. Our water and air are foul, and there seems to be nothing we can eat or drink that does not cause cancer, meaning that the costs of technology and our way of life are greater than anyone imagined. The economy has become a chronic problem and crime seems to be getting worse. It has been a while since anyone took pride in our education system, which apparently is producing less knowledgeable students each year. We still have some faith in science and technology — after all, we did put a man on the moon — but we have become more aware of their costs and also of their limitations, their inability to help us in the things that count the most. And, to add to the confusion and frag-mentation, there have been interminable lists of nonnegotiable demands put forth by just about everyone — women, ethnic mi-norities, old people, young people, homosexuals, prisoners, mental patients, and so on.

We have become increasingly estranged from our government, our way of life, and our communal future. Surveys over the last twenty years have found increased dissatisfaction with the way the country is being run and with its major institutions and professions; greater pessimism about its future; greater concern about stability and order; and a growing feeling that people have lost control of the institutions that are supposed to serve them, a sense that no one cares about their opinions. The following statement by an account-ant who has been doing tax returns for middle-class professionals for the last three decades is eloquent testimony of the changes in our society: "It was very different in the fifties. People had their gripes and fears but the general feeling I recall was that they were willing to pay their fair share, a term I heard a lot then. What they thought their fair share to be and what I figured out for them were usually close. They believed in the country and didn't want to shirk their duty. This feeling has all but disappeared. I haven't heard anyone say anything about their fair share for a long time. Now no one wants to pay anything. They think they are being ripped off and feel resentful regardless of their income or the amount of their taxes. Many say they'd rather throw the money in the gutter than give it to the government."

Contemporary distrust of society is reflected in the arts. Critic Lewis Lapham notes that the movies of the 1970s "assume an absence of society. The characters seem to wander in a void, with-out connections to family, friends, church, neighborhood, political organization, or any kind of government." When it is evident at all, "the apparatus of society appears as an instrument of destruction."

The paradox of modernity is that in delivering on its promises of greater material comfort, more leisure, and more freedom, it ends up with people who are no happier, who feel less able to control events, more easily disappointed and frustrated, and who can't seem to get enough of anything to make them feel good.

When there is no meaning, no central thread around which we can understand and organize ourselves, everything becomes problematic and unsatisfying. It becomes hard to put up with anything — trouble at work, problems with the children, any kind of disappointment — because there is no context or perspective. Particulars take on an exaggerated importance because we have no way of seeing them in a context. What Irving Kristol writes about freedom applies as well to well-being and satisfaction:

> People feel free when they subscribe to a prevailing social philosophy; they feel unfree when the prevailing social philosophy is unpersuasive; and the existence of laws or judiciaries have precious little to do with these basic feelings. The average working man in nineteenth-century America had far fewer "rights" than his counterpart today; but he was far more likely to boast about his being a free man.

We feel content and well, able to endure the usual frustrations and disappointments of life, when our lives make sense to us, when we have an idea of how things fit together and how we fit into the general scheme of things. Having more possessions and knowledge can also help, but only when the sense of coherence remains. Without it, there can never be enough of anything to make us feel good.

A thirty-five-year-old woman comes to therapy suffering from what she calls a "mid-life crisis." She is married, with two children, is successful in her career, and she doesn't have to worry about money. But she says, "I'm not satisfied with anything in my life. Nothing makes me feel any better. . . . I thought I would feel better when I got the house of my dreams. I've had it for almost a year now, it's what I always wanted. We even have a woman in twice a week to do most of the housework. I have plenty of time for my work, where I'm doing very well, and the kids are hardly any trouble at all. I know I have everything and ought to be content but I'm not. Sometimes I feel like running away or having an affair or giving up work and becoming a housewife. But I don't think it would make any difference."

Meaning, control, and hope are what therapy offers to many people. All change processes provide ways of viewing and understanding the world and one's place in it. Some of the briefer, symptom-oriented treatments may give only a way of understanding the problem for which the client seeks therapy, but many offer a great deal more: a framework for viewing all the important aspects of life — mental processes, emotions, relationships, work, love, and so on. There is no question that many people derive a sense of meaning from being in therapy and are pleased by this result, whether or not the problem they brought to therapy is resolved. And for some, as we will see later, therapy itself becomes the central meaning of their lives.

Meaning itself brings a measure of control. We feel more in charge of events when we have an adequate understanding of them. But many of the current therapies promise even more. They say you can be in complete control of your life. An advertisement for the est training features a flying superman called Captain Well-Being saying: "Is life kicking sand in your face? Then listen to me . . . The wholeness and satisfaction in your life is determined by YOU, NOT your circumstances. And THAT is the essence of the EST training." It doesn't make any difference what anyone else does — you can still be in charge. You don't have to feel angry or guilty or confused or helpless or hopeless. You can feel precisely what you want to feel. You can have what you want — a place to park your car, a new career, a better social and sexual life, more money, or anything else. Nothing is out of control once you are in control of yourself.

Concerns about control and mastery have become obsessions. In a recent book, Will Schutz, one of the chief theoreticians of the new therapies, summarizes the principles and methods of the self-realization programs, and limitless control is what they're all about. A few passages:

Each of us is running her or his own life. . . . Once we accept responsibility for choosing our lives, everything is different. We have the power. We decide. We are in control. . . . If I choose everything, and if there are no accidents, then life becomes a soluble puzzle.

That such simplistic and unrealistic notions are widely accepted should tell us something about how people view their lives. Many fear not only that they are not in control but that they have no control at all. Even more seem to fear that life is not a "soluble puzzle."

The giving of hope has been implied in much that I have said. Most people apparently cannot feel comfortable without some kind of hope in themselves and their future. Therapy provides hope in two ways. On one level, there is the hope that your problem can be resolved. As long as you can believe that even one person lost weight, became less depressed, experienced more joy, found himself, or got along better with his family, there is reason to believe that the same can happen for you. I think this is one reason people read so many self-help books even if they don't follow the advice in them. Just knowing that the advice exists and that it has helped someone is enough to keep hope alive. If you ever decide to work on what's troubling you, there's a chance you'll reach your goals.

Behind this kind of hope is a more important one, the hope that changing the problem will lead to contentment or happiness. One couple expressed this idea clearly. Since their marriage, they had been involved, together and separately, in over fifteen types of counseling. I asked why so much therapy.

SHE: "Because I think there's something more, something we haven't quite reached. We get something from almost everything we attend and often feel an awful lot better. But I still don't feel, you know, fulfilled."

HE: "It sounds a bit silly to put it into words but I'm looking for something . . . like a transformation. To see the world differently and be differently. I usually get one or more things from any therapy work I do but I want more than specifics. I want an enlightenment experience like the ones I've heard and read about, where everything becomes radically different."

With the loss of traditional communities and beliefs, and with the more recent erosion of faith in the substitutes offered by modernity — nationalism, progress, science — we are thrown back on ourselves, ending up with one of the great paradoxes of our times. On the one hand there is pessimism and resignation, a sense of political, social, economic, military, and even scientific limits, and a feeling of despair about the future. But on the other hand, there is boundless enthusiasm and optimism about the prospects for individual change and betterment. We seem to have lost the old American hope in building a utopian society and even in our ability to make improvements on a large scale. Rather than abandon our commitment to progress, however, we have shifted the arena and redefined the terms. Maybe America doesn't have a manifest destiny, maybe we won't be the richest and strongest nation on earth, maybe we can no longer have bigger cars and houses, and maybe we won't make as much money as we hoped, but that doesn't mean we can't change our lives. We can have better bodies and health, better habits and personalities, better relationships and sex. We are not giving up our hopes for satisfying, meaningful, exciting lives. If we can't get them one way, we'll try another. The millennial impulse lives on; only the means have changed. An example is provided by the radicals of the 1960s. When they failed to change the political and economic policies of society, many moved to the personal realm. Eldridge Cleaver became a born-again Christian, Rennie Davis a follower of Maharaj Ji, Jerry Rubin a devotee of everything therapeutic, going through more than twenty programs in less than five years, and many others became therapists and therapy clients.

In his study of suburban youth in the 1970s, Ralph Larkin observes that the weakening of traditional institutions "has led to radical individualism. Students at Utopia High find that the one thing they can believe in is the self. . . . The self seems to be the mooring of last resort." The phrase "mooring of last resort" is apt. I do not believe people willingly turn inward: they do so only where there seem to be no other reasonable alternatives. We have to believe that something makes sense, that someone is in charge, that something is worth believing in. Since we have given up on so many things that used to fill these needs, many feel that the only thing left is themselves. But the burden they have taken on is awesome and difficult, far more so than therapists usually acknowledge. Everyone now has to be something of an expert on the construction of universes and meaning systems, on finding his own sources of purpose, comfort, control, and community. In short, we must all become experts on how to live, a task most previous generations were spared. And therapy has become one of the most popular ways of dealing with this complex and demanding issue.

Affluence, Attitudes, and Expectations

"Don't settle for so little in your life! You deserve a lot!"

— SONDRA RAY

TO THE SOCIAL CHANGES discussed in the last chapter must be added a number of others, most occurring since World War II, that have contributed to our general concern with individual change and our specific susceptibility to the psychotherapeutic enterprise.

Greater Affluence

Participation in therapy on a mass scale is possible only in a society which has a large surplus of money available after meeting more basic needs. Tom Wolfe notes that the rise in affluence in America has been so large and obvious that few even bother to comment on it. "Wartime spending . . . in the 1940s touched off a boom that has continued for more than thirty years. It has pumped more money into every class level . . . on a scale without precedent in any country in history." One figure says it all: per capita income after taxes more than doubled between 1939 and 1969, even after adjusting for inflation. In the postwar period, we have had more money than ever before to spend as we wished.

Although this does not explain why some people choose to spend their money on self-improvement, it does mean that increasing numbers could consider spending money in this way. Our affluence is so great that going to counseling requires few sacrifices in other areas for most middle-class people, and we subsidize, through government plans and insurance programs, therapy-going for many who could not otherwise afford it. Despite the complaints of therapy consumers and therapy critics, virtually everyone can get counseling at a price he can afford to pay.

The struggle for survival, a struggle that has preoccupied the mind and taxed the strength and will of the overwhelming masses of people since the beginning of time, is over at last, at least for most Americans. We no longer have to concern ourselves with where the next meal is coming from or about obtaining adequate clothing and shelter. This point may seem too obvious or trivial for words, especially to those born after 1945, and that in itself is a measure of how much things have changed.

The change was monumental. We were now free. Having bettered our condition, just as the capitalist ethic encouraged us to do, and freed ourselves from the battle for survival, we are left to face the question of what to do after we have bettered our condition. We are free to consider the quality of our lives, or more prosaically, what else we might want. Much time and energy has gone into the consumption and accumulation of material objects; buying a piece of art or a car or even a pair of running shoes can take days or weeks of research and shopping. And much of our attention has gone in other directions. As Abraham Maslow, one of the leading theorists of humanistic psychology, predicted, as the more basic human needs are fulfilled, those involving self-expression and growth become prominent. Tom Wolfe offers a more cynical view: "The old alchemical dream was changing base metal into gold. The new alchemical dream is: changing one's personality — remaking, remodeling, elevating, and polishing one's very self . . . and observing, studying, and doting on it."

Affluence, even the relatively lower levels of it that many are currently experiencing, adds a different perspective to life. The state of one's self-esteem, how well one expresses oneself, and questions about how happy one is are not important issues to someone who is struggling to make ends meet — he doesn't have the time, energy, or inclination to consider such things — but they can become matters of concern and even urgency for someone in more comfortable circumstances. Millions of people today seek therapy for personal and interpersonal discomforts that less affluent societies would regard as trivial.

There is yet another way that affluence promotes going to therapy, and that is by disproving the commonly held assumption that prosperity leads to greater contentment. It is easy to believe that once you have more money everything will be better, that the problems and hassles of today will simply disappear and that you will feel more comfortable and happier. But this happens only rarely. True, it is nice to be able to eat in expensive restaurants without having to think about whether you can afford it, and to plan a vacation without first consulting your checkbook to make sure there are sufficient funds, and to get that bigger home or the fancier car, but nicer is not the same as happier. The old problems do not vanish. Most remain and are joined by new ones attendant upon having more money and a higher standard of living. You still get anxious when dealing with authorities, you still are given to depressions, you still are not confident of your abilities, and now you also have to consider whether the fancy new car is safe in the old neighborhood, whether you deserve the goodies that have come your way, where to invest extra money, and so on.

Since the old equation of money equals happiness has proved to be an illusion, the questions become pressing: What does bring happiness? or, How can I be happier? More than a few who seek answers to such questions end up in therapy.

Greater Tolerance of Diversity

One myth dear to the hearts of many Americans is that the past was a time of rugged individualism while the present is a time of conformity. In the good old days, according to this bit of fantasy, there were men of principle (women don't count for much in this particular story) who knew who they were and did what was right, no matter what anyone thought. More recently, still following this myth, we have become a bunch of conformists, without principles and unable or unwilling to follow our inclinations. When confronted by alternatives, we merely follow the crowd.

Despite the popularity of this theory, it is wrong. The past rather than our own time was the period of great conformity. Tocqueville noticed it and so did most of the other foreign visitors in the 1800s who put their thoughts on paper. Political scientist Andrew Hacker is closer to reality than the popular notion when he notes that up until recently, "the majority of Americans spent their lives in circumscribed settings which, if not literally feudal, nonetheless enforced regimens that tolerated little deviation from established local standards."

No matter how you measure it, Americans have become far more tolerant of diversity than ever before. When we think about attitudes toward those who look and believe differently, toward divorce, adultery, abortion, heterosexual cohabitation, homosexuality, or almost anything else, we are far more accepting than our ancestors. You can deviate all you want from established local standards and probably not suffer too much. Americans have always been relatively tolerant of religious diversity but not of a lack of religious belief: a person had to believe in something. But this has changed: atheism and agnosticism are now calmly accepted. Being a member of the Communist party brought ruin to many in the 1950s. Now no one seems to care one way or another what you belong to or whether you belong to anything. This is not to say that every single person accepts every kind of diversity. Such a condition has never existed in any society and never will. It does mean that the sanctions against diversity have become increasingly negligible and that tolerance is now a rule rather than an exception.

While a number of factors are responsible for this liberalization, two deserve mention here. The first is higher education. College students are significantly more tolerant than the rest of the population on most issues. The percentage of the population between eighteen and twenty-four years old attending college in 1970 was thirty-two, compared with one in 1870 and eight in 1938. There is also now, for the first time in our history, a large number of people over the age of twenty-four attending college. The second factor is the mass media. Both the media and the colleges are heavily populated by members of what critic Lionel Trilling called the adversary culture, intellectuals opposed to the current order of things and champions of deviant behavior and unpopular groups and causes. By vividly calling attention to those who are different, reporters and professors challenge our thinking and biases. They help to make understandable, reasonable, and respectable different attitudes, behaviors, and ways of life. The media also provide a powerful forum for others in the adversary culture to tell us what is wrong with the way we raise our children, work, make love, and conduct the rest of our lives.

The increased acceptance of diversity is important in two ways. First, on the positive side, it has made people willing to acknowledge and explore and express parts of themselves that in previous times would have been suppressed. For example, now that you understand that homosexuals are basically like other people and not sick or crazy, you are free to admit and explore your attraction to same-sex persons and determine if you would enjoy their company more than people of the opposite sex. Or, now that you know that many people get divorced and that this doesn't necessarily affect their children adversely, you are freer to consider whether you really want to stay with your spouse, something your grandparents would never have allowed themselves to think about. Of course, people often seek professional help with these and similar deliberations.

On the less positive side, greater tolerance has had the effect of making many people less sure of themselves. They find little support and legitimacy for their own ways. When society accepts everything, it supports nothing. It used to be that the standards of right and wrong learned early in life could be counted on to remain stable for the rest of life. Not so anymore. What was considered evil, wrong, or sick only a few years ago is now thought to be normal, healthy, or at least okay for those who want to do it. Not only are once-bad things now considered to be acceptable, or even laudable, but the whole notion of right and wrong has come under attack. To make value judgments is widely thought to be a sign of intolerance, inhibition, and uptightness.

One of my favorite places for learning about the effects of tolerance is Phil Donahue's show. Donahue has a variety of guests, including many who champion unconventional ideas and behavior. In the last year, the guests I saw included a man who thought that spanking children was immoral and unhealthy; several women who had murdered their husbands; a married couple, each partner of which was having outside sexual encounters with same-sex partners; children who had "divorced" their parents and parents who had "divorced" their children; a lesbian couple, one white and the other black, one of whom had been artificially inseminated with sperm from the brother of the other partner; a family, the mother of which had committed suicide with their knowledge when she learned she had cancer; a woman who had been involved in an incestuous relationship with her father; and a transsexual couple. Although some members of the audience were outraged by each of these guests, they usually were in the minority. The rest of the audience seemed to have a hard time of it. They had been taught that what they heard was wrong but were now being asked to understand and accept, or at least not to condemn. Many in the audience wanted to do this and were careful to apologize for any judgments they made or implied. At the same time, it was clear that they couldn't quite accept what was presented. They were torn between past and present.

The struggles of Donahue's audience are just a small example of what goes on in most our lives almost daily. The media are constantly challenging our ways of looking at and evaluating the world. And challenges to traditional ways often come from closer quarters as well. We hear that a neighbor or friend has given up his successful career and is now living on a commune or selling artwork on the street. A woman at work leaves her family because she wants to find herself. Your fourteen-year-old daughter announces that she wants to have sex with her boyfriend, or maybe that she's already done so. You discover that your son's best friend is stoned on drugs most of the time.

What is right and what is wrong? The modern answer is that everything is permissible as long as you're not hurting anyone. But this means there may be little we agree on because what's right for you may not be right for me. Both the sense of identity and the sense of community — always based to a large extent on agreement about right and wrong — fade. Gone are the days when a way of thinking, believing, or living received support from all the powers around you.

I recall the reaction of several couples who attended a sex course I participated in several years ago. The course, typical of many given in the early 1970s and still being given today, focused on the unusual and unconventional — homosexuality, bisexuality, masturbation, and multiple relationships. One presenter talked enthusiastically about his five "primary relationships," none of which was hurt by his many casual affairs. The people who confronted me during a break wanted to know why nothing had been said about their lives. They were heterosexual, monogamous, and in long-term relationships. They said they were familiar with the other arrangements, being constantly bombarded with information about them from the media. But what about themselves? Were they a deviant sect? Why was there no support for their way of life?

The remarkable thing is that almost everyone has these feelings now. No matter what one's preferences or patterns, there is a sense that they do not receive as much support as they should. People are left wondering whether some other way, some other arrangement, might not be better for them. And whatever they try, there are still so many other attractive possibilities beckoning on the horizon. Perhaps we have exaggerated the ability of people to live comfortably with diversity. The kind of recognition and support they seem to want comes only from universal or near-universal validation, emanating from all the powerful institutions of society, and that is no longer available. Which means that everyone feels at least a little at loose ends. And this is one reason why group therapy has become so popular. People meet in groups with others like themselves — women, men, divorcees, parents without partners, expectant parents, singles, addicts, former mental patients or former convicts, and so on — to give and receive the support they don't get elsewhere. One of the great comforts of participation in such groups is revealed in the often-heard remark: "It's so helpful to discover that I'm not the only one who [thinks, feels, believes, or behaves] this way." Many other people go to individual counseling to sort out all the alternatives facing them or to get more comfortable with whatever alternative they have chosen. (And of course there are a number of nontherapy resources people turn to in order to deal with the threat of all this diversity, usually organizations that clearly spell out what is right and what is wrong: e.g., fundamentalist religious groups, cults, and extremist political movements on both the right and the left.)

Greater Tolerance of
Emotional Problems and Psychotherapy

Although personal problems are as old as the human race, there has usually been strong pressure against admitting to them. One simply should do one's best with the strengths and weaknesses one was given. There was some help available, of course: support, understanding, and advice might be received from one's family, neighbors, and local religious authority. But there were limits: if one was too bizarre, one might be taken for a witch or thought to be a laggard or very sinful. As Allen Wheelis says: "This intolerance amounted to a pressure against the emergence or admission of neurosis. . . ." This caused the suppression of many problems and forced people to try to live with or despite their difficulties and keep on going no matter what the cost. "It forced, also, some curable neurotics into suicide, and it locked up and made custodial cases of some who, in a different setting, might have recovered."

A step forward was taken when medicine came in with labels such as "mental illness" and "neurosis," which gave a degree of respectability to emotional problems. It was far better to be thought of as sick than as one who communed with the Devil. Public tolerance of mental illness has grown steadily during this century. Among the many reasons for this change in attitude were the work of Freud and others demonstrating the continuity between mental health and illness; studies revealing the widespread incidence of mental health problems in both civilian and military populations; and the increased education and sophistication of the American populace, which have resulted in a greater acceptance of many things once considered beyond the pale of respectability.

Although the medical model of psychological distress was an advance over traditional ideas, it had problems of its own. Despite the increased tolerance it brought, mental illness remained something tainted and shameful for many people. Illness of the mind, after all, was not easy to comprehend. It didn't seem like real illness or other medical problems. Also, mental illness covered everything from vague feelings of discomfort and discontent to the bizarre thoughts and behavior of psychotics. Not everyone was eager to be included in such company. Better to keep your mouth shut about your feelings of inadequacy or your problems with your spouse.

The medical model and the stigma attached to mental illness were slowly undermined. A fair number of respectable people were in psychoanalysis in the 1920s and 1930s, and everyone knew they weren't sick in the head. Books by therapists such as Jung, Horney, and Carl Rogers made it clear that much of therapy dealt with the ordinary problems of ordinary people. During World War II, millions of American men in the armed services had their first exposure to psychological tests and therapy. Although many made fun of psychology and resented its intrusion into their lives, they were nonetheless learning about it, and some thought it had something to offer them. The majority of therapists trained and working since the war were not physicians. They were psychologists, social workers, marriage counselors, and pastoral counselors. Since they had no competence in medical matters, it is not surprising that they advertised themselves as working with the usual problems of living rather than with mental illness.

Within a decade or so after World War II, the idea that therapy was only for the sick, the bizarre, and the deviant was definitely on the wane, at least in the middle-class consciousness. This did not mean that a majority of Americans were in therapy, then or now. But the idea that you could have problems for which you would seek professional help became plausible; one could imagine the possibility without horror and one could accept it for friends and colleagues. The demise of the medical model of emotional distress was hastened by the blow dealt it by maverick psychiatrist Thomas Szasz. In his book *The Myth of Mental Illness*, first published in 1961, Szasz argued that there is no such thing as illness of the mind, that the term was merely an inappropriate metaphor. Psychological problems, he wrote, should be "regarded as the expression of man's struggle with the problem of how he should live." Disturbed individuals suffer not from illnesses but from problems in living. And psychotherapy could be useful, not to help people recover from

illnesses, but to help them "learn about themselves, others, and life."
Szasz's book received a lot of publicity and quickly became a classic.
Emotional problems and psychotherapy were well on their way to
respectability.

Therapy soon received another boost. Not only was it an acceptable and presumably effective way of dealing with the problems of
living but it could also be used to enhance the quality of one's life:
it could facilitate growth and development, two words that soon
became clichés. No matter how well you were doing, you could do
better. A common saying of the 1960s, first applied to encounter
groups and then to almost every therapy, was "You don't have to
be sick to get better." It became commonplace to think that counseling — in groups, workshops, marathon sessions, as well as in
the traditional one-to-one format — was a place for already well-
functioning people to further develop themselves.

The change was radical. Before, you could demonstrate your
mental health or well-being by *not* being in therapy; now, being in
therapy would do the same.

It was not simply that counseling became acceptable or fashion-
able. In many circles, it became the paradigm for the preferred
style of life. What occurred in counseling, especially in many of
the newer versions that were constantly appearing, was what ought
to occur in life: the sharing of secrets; open, honest, and spontaneous
communication; confrontations of all kinds; taking risks; breaking
through inhibitions; and the development of potential. Rogers,
Glasser, Schutz, and Erhard were only a few of the mental healers
who promoted their systems of therapy as the foundation for better
family relations, business management, prison organization, education, and countless other activities. Where therapy had once been
considered an isolated activity for helping people to get on with the
rest of their lives, it now became for many the model for how life
should be lived.

Therapy acquired so much influence that it was used to give
legitimacy to other activities. To give but one example, most of the
organizations for single and divorced people that have sprung up
in the last twenty years seem to think they can carry out their
functions only under the umbrella of self-improvement. Their get-

togethers involve talks and workshops on topics such as "healing with mental visions," "assertive living," "getting free from Mom and Dad," "sex, love, and higher consciousness," and "the role of therapy in singlehood." Most of the groups whose newsletters I receive, from which the above titles are taken, are unwilling to have even a dance without a talk on psychology beforehand.

It is only fair to add that the change in attitude toward emotional difficulties and therapy is not universal. Many Americans continue to believe that therapy is the refuge of sickies who refuse to stand on their own two feet and live their lives. Despite this, the point stands. Counseling has become respectable in the minds of most Americans, especially the well-educated in most metropolitan areas. One of the main barriers to seeking psychological assistance has been overcome. The regular appearance of therapists in the media is both a reflection of the new accepting attitude toward counseling and a cause of still greater acceptance in the future.

Acceptance of the Need to Change

Since America was never weighted down with the tradition of many centuries, change has always been more welcome here than elsewhere. But in the past, the high value placed on change was complemented by the high value placed on stability. The contradiction between desiring change and desiring stability has been resolved on the side of change. Kenneth Keniston writes that one of the striking characteristics of contemporary youth

> is the enormous value placed upon change, transformation, and movement, and the consequent abhorrence of stasis. To change, to stay on the road, to retain a sense of inner development and/or outer momentum is essential to many youths' sense of active vitality. The psychological problems of youth are experienced as most overwhelming when they seem to block change. . . .

To many youths, adulthood is perceived as a period of little or no change and is thus equated with nonbeing or death, not being really alive.

Many adults have come to share this view. It is important to grow, develop, change with the times, go with the flow. Conflicts in and breakups of relationships are frequently attributed to the blockage of growth in one or both participants. People switch careers because "I wasn't growing anymore." To facilitate or continue one's growth is the reason many people give for seeking therapy. To be fixed in anything, to be closed, not to be moving is considered by many to be rigid, uptight, or inhibited.

There is an obvious parallel with technological change. In that area, Americans have long felt that anything new was automatically better. When Henry Ford was building cars, he wanted them to last as long as possible. But others in the industry realized they could exploit the public's desire for change and so the idea of a new model every year was born. Rather than taking pride in how long something lasts, how well it continues to function despite its age, we measure how up to date we are. Does our car, stereo, refrigerator, even our running shoes, have all the latest gismos and gadgets or, on the other hand, is it old fashioned and lacking all the modern conveniences? This is not simply the result of vanity. Products are constantly being changed. Whether they actually get better is debatable, but they do look different and are touted to be far better than last year's model.

People themselves seem to fear going out of style. And with good reason. The skills needed for coping in this society of vast change keep changing. How many people in the 1950s knew anything about computers, teaching machines, or sound systems? How many parents these days feel frustrated and out of date because they don't understand the math their children are learning? What is true of skills is also true of attitudes and values. The beliefs you held just ten or fifteen years ago — about the role of women, the position of minority groups, patriotism, divorce, political participation, and other important issues — may now qualify you for membership in the old fogies club. Given this, it is not surprising that people would get the idea that the most important quality is ability to adapt to change, to be able to take on new points of view, new attitudes, new behaviors. What is unacceptable today may well be acceptable tomorrow.

The need for keeping up with the times is complicated and aggravated by the perceived necessity for being self-sufficient. Individualism — self-reliance, self-sufficiency — has always been a strong theme in American life and thought, but in the past it was tempered by a strong commitment to and dependence on others. With the transformation of community, individualism has become dominant. People no longer feel strong ties to groups which collectively deal with change. One may well have to cope alone. You can't count on your family of origin because they are in Florida while you are on the West Coast. You can't count on the neighbors because who knows how long you'll be neighbors. Given the divorce rate, you can't even count on your spouse. So if you're a woman, it makes sense for you to learn how to support yourself, to be assertive, to live independently. If you're a man, it's reasonable that you learn to do all the things your father never bothered with because his wife took care of them. Everyone, it seems, should be competent in almost everything.

The current fad of androgyny can be viewed as a reflection of this situation. In older times, it was assumed that men were experts in some areas and women in others. Whatever the defects of that arrangement — and it clearly had defects — it at least limited the number of areas in which any one person had to be proficient. One didn't have to be good at everything because one could count on someone else, or a group of others, to take care of some things. Androgyny seems to hold that everyone should be good at everything. Both men and women should be proficient in "masculine" as well as "feminine" characteristics and activities. Both should be passive and active, strong and nurturant, task-oriented as well as emotional, intuitive and rational, and so on.

This means that we not only have to be more flexible, more ready to accept change, but that we have to be this way in more areas. Clearly this is overwhelming for many people. Many of them, as well as others who just want to make sure they're keeping up and staying flexible, turn to therapy, for it has become one of the main ways of dealing with change and its consequences.

Great Expectations

Expectations have always run high in America but in the last thirty years or so they have absolutely skyrocketed. We want and expect far more than ever before. Parents expect more of their children and of themselves as parents and spouses; children expect more from their parents; men and women have higher expectations of their jobs, their leisure pursuits, their sexual activities, and just about everything else. When our desires are not fulfilled, as is frequently the case, we are ready to complain, get assistance, try something else, or file a lawsuit to right the wrongs we think have been done to us. Almost everyone seems to feel entitled to all sorts of successes, adventures, and joys right now, without having to make any great sacrifices to get them.

One reason for the change in expectations is the declining power of traditional institutions and beliefs, which were largely instruments of restraint, teaching that one's grasp should not exceed one's reach and that rewards would come later. These days there are few instruments of inhibition, little reason for thinking that rewards will be achieved later or that there is any reason for holding back. The present is all that counts. The credit-card mentality which emphasizes immediate satisfaction of desires has replaced the traditional virtues of abstinence and restraint. "You only go around once," a recent advertisement announces, "so grab all the gusto you can." This idea is pushed by many, including the advertising industry, therapists, and politicians. We deserve more and will get more if only we buy their products, use their services, put them in office.

Phil Donahue, who has interviewed many therapists on his program and witnessed his audience's response to them, sums up the change in expectations this way:

> There's a growing belief that life need not be a vale of tears. There's a realization that the gloom and doom picture of life has been sold to us by a church that promoted suffering in order to sell salvation and by immigrants who really did suffer. With the dimin-

ished influence of religion and the ideas that men have to be in a rat-race and women have to be self-effacing and long-suffering, we are looking for something different. There's a new sense that life can be more fun and need not be the pain in the neck we've expected it to be. The new idea is that we only have one shot at life and to be miserable is to waste the opportunity. One can make his or her life more exciting and more interesting.

Your father may have worked himself to death and never been able to express his love for you, but that's no reason you have to be the same way. Your mother may have suffered silently or not so silently all her life, never thinking of herself and never developing her talents, but you can be different. You may not have done much with your life so far, but that's not a good reason for continuing in the same way. Or you may have had a rich and exciting life up to now, but there's no reason you can't have more.

The sense of fate, always weaker in America than elsewhere, has all but disappeared in recent years. With our science and technology, we have conquered diseases that in previous times destroyed entire populations. We have traveled on land and sea faster than any beast and we have flown higher and faster than any bird. We have even set foot on another planet. We eat strawberries in winter and light up the world at night, thus freeing ourselves from the cycles of day and night and of the seasons, cycles that have regulated the affairs of mankind since the beginning of time.

If we can defy gravity, ignore the seasons, conquer great distances, and do all the other things which we have done, it is easy to assume that we need not accept anything as given — not our frustration, our lack of ability or success, our pain, our unhappiness, or anything else. It is easy to assume that there are no limits to what we can accomplish and become. We begin to think we are like Jonathan Livingston Seagull, who knew "that he was not bone and feather but a perfect idea of freedom and flight, limited by nothing at all." We no longer have a way of setting limits or excluding anything. All the old systems of meaning had limits. X, Y, or Z was impossible because it was contrary to tradition, God's will, natural law, or something else. There is no longer a rationale for saying that any-thing is off limits or impossible. It has become easy to accept what previously would have been considered absolutely fantastic notions about what is possible for human beings to be and do. If someone says it is possible to live without guilt, to experience continuous joy, to love unconditionally, or to lose weight by eating papayas and pineapples after each binge, who is to say it's not true? If someone says that a weekend course or daily meditation or open marriage or twenty sessions with Dr. X radically changed his life, made him calmer, immeasurably happy, and able to clear up all the things that had been troubling him, who is to say it's not so?

The seductive idea that things could be other than what they are reigns supreme. Not only could they be better, they *ought* to be better. People believe they are entitled to more than they have, and therapists, along with many others, are quite willing to encourage great expectations. One book says it all: "I deserve love. I deserve to be trusted. I deserve freedom. I deserve friendship. I deserve respect. I deserve sexual pleasure. I deserve happiness."

Many people have benefited from the idea that their lives could be better. I think, for example, of some women who made changes in long-standing problems, who developed better relationships or greater confidence, went back to school or changed jobs, or devel-oped previously unused talent. Another example is of some older couples I worked with in sex therapy. They had problems with sex for years — in some cases for over twenty years — but either didn't know where to go for help or hadn't realized that things could be different. Once they understood that change was possible and help was available, they came for therapy and made important modifica-tions in their sexual behavior.

All of this fits in nicely with what Donahue said and what is being expressed by thousands of therapists, authors, and satisfied clients. But there is another side that needs attention. For many, unlimited expectations mean unlimited dissatisfaction and frustra-tion. Their standards are so high that they are forever focused on the gap between what they want and what they have.

In a later chapter we will discuss in greater detail the problems brought on by unrealistic expectations. Here it is important to note only that great expectations, whether realistic or not, bring a lot of people to therapy. Counseling is one of the main places we go when we feel that we're not getting as much out of life as we should, that we're not experiencing as much joy, that we're not fulfilling our potential.

The Selling of Therapy

"The biggest big business in America is not steel, automobiles, or television. It is the manufacture, refinement, and distribution of anxiety."

— ERIC SEVAREID

"There will be more psychologists than people in this country!"

— EDWIN BORING

MY THESIS SO FAR is that deeply ingrained American values, the weakening of traditional sources of meaning and support, and changes in attitudes and expectations have paved the way for acceptance of the therapeutic. But two more factors must be added: our penchant for relying on experts, and the aggressive efforts of these same experts to persuade us that we are in great need of their assistance.

Our belief in the superiority of specialization and our predilection for solutions and perfection pushes us to depend on experts. Even if we have some competence in a given area, we know there are others who know more. Our own efforts seem amateurish and inefficient. Why not let someone with special training do it or at least help us do it? The modern view is well expressed in a recent book: "The key to a successful adult life lies in surrounding yourself with experts, a master person for every need. We have gone beyond taking care of ourselves. We need others to care for our medical, legal, financial, emotional, and even our bodily survival." America is probably the most specialized and professionalized society on earth. We have more experts in more areas than does any other country. Thus, the county of Los Angeles is said to have more lawyers than all of England. Our culture is dominated by professionals who call us clients, tell us what our needs are and how to satisfy them.

Nowhere is our dependence on experts more evident than in the area of personal guidance. With increasing regularity, we look to those whom we assume to have special competence to tell us how to live. Experts in living are not new. There have always been people — witch doctors, wise men and women, astrologers, clerics, and physicians — with whom you could discuss your sins, feelings of unease, bad dreams, physical ailments, and problems with your spouse. There have also been other sources of advice and comfort, from *Poor Richard's Almanac* in the eighteenth century and *The Old Farmer's Almanac* in the nineteenth, to the "Miss Lonelyhearts" newspaper columns of this century, and more recently Ann Landers and Dear Abby. But reliance on experts has mushroomed in recent times. We have more such experts than ever before, we depend on them in more areas, and their presence and advice is ubiquitous.

It is a mistake, however, to think that the therapeutic enterprise flourishes only because we have problems and like to find experts to help us deal with them. Therapists themselves have been very active in promoting a demand for their services. This is not hard to understand once you accept the fact that whatever else counseling is, it is a business. Therapy differs from some other businesses in that what it sells is a want rather than a need. People do not need counseling the way they need food, shelter, and clothing. There could be very little demand for psychological services or a very large demand. Quite logically, mental health workers prefer the latter and have been more than willing to increase it.

Psychiatrist Jerome Frank, one of the wisest observers of the therapeutic scene, thinks that therapy to an important extent generates its own business:

> Ironically, mental health education, which aims to teach people how to cope more effectively with life, has instead increased the demand for psychotherapeutic help. By calling attention to symptoms they might otherwise ignore and by labeling those symptoms as signs of neurosis, mental health education can create unwarranted anxieties, leading those to seek psychotherapy who do not need it. The demand for psychotherapy keeps pace with the supply, and at times one has the uneasy feeling that the supply may be creating the demand. The greater the number of treatment facilities, and the more widely they are known, the larger the number of persons seeking their services. Psychotherapy is the only form

of treatment which, at least to some extent, appears to create the illness it treats.

Therapy advocates take offense at this kind of statement, arguing that the expansion of mental health services meets existing and previously unmet needs. In other words, therapists deal with already existing problems; they do not create new ones. This argument suffers from a number of difficulties and I think it is specious. Frank's position is closer to the known facts and, if anything, is an understatement. Readers will be in a better place to come to their own conclusions after reading this and the following five chapters.

The way in which therapists sell their services and therefore contribtue to increased demand for them can be broken down like this:

1. Continue the psychologization of life;
2. Make problems out of difficulties and spread the alarm;
3. Make it acceptable to have the problem and to be unable to resolve it on one's own;
4. Offer salvation.

This formula, or some variation, is applied both by individual clinicians and by organizations. You can hear it when therapists have lunch with those who refer clients to them, when they give lectures and interviews, when they appear in the media, and when they and professional organizations petition agencies, usually those of the federal government, that have money to give away.

Before looking at the formula in greater detail, I want to emphasize that it is not the result of a conspiracy or even consciously arrived at. Neither the outline nor the details are taught in professional and graduate schools, at least not explicitly. But trained therapists obviously want to make a decent living doing work they enjoy and they often find there is no great demand for it. They discover they have to do something to generate consumers for their talks, books, courses, and therapy. I suggest the kinds of things they end up doing, with or without full awareness, are what is described in this formula.

Continue to Psychologize the World

This is simply increasing the size of the pie. The idea is to find more and more places, issues, and events with psychological causes, cures, or implications. Is there unemployment and inflation in the land? Surely they must cause worry, fear, and depression, and therapists need to come to the rescue. In an example perhaps more comical than anything else, *Time* reports that as a result of our current economic problems, counselors are "talking more and more about money in sessions with troubled clients. . . . Some therapists have even taken on the role of financial adviser to their patients." Are there children not learning in schools? Surely this is a result of emotional difficulties such as hyperactivity, and counseling is the appropriate remedy. Are people frustrated, bored, and tense at work? Surely these things, now labeled jobs stress and job burnout to make them sound like official problems, require psychological assistance. Are divorce proceedings adversarial and expensive? Obviously what is needed is a new service provided by therapists: divorce mediation. Are more people exercising these days? Clearly they need help from behavioral experts lest they never discover what one book calls "the profound mental benefits that running offers," or they miss out on, as one article puts its, "the idea that athletics is somehow more than athletics, that it is a way to know ourselves, to balance the feminine and masculine aspects within us all."

To ensure that no one eludes the therapeutic net, counselors divide life into a number of phases or stages, with new ones being discovered all the time, each with its own requirements, problems, and experts. There are now specialists in pediatric therapy, adolescent therapy and, at the other end of life, in geriatric therapy. The portion of life in between is divided up in many ways, a recent addition being something called mid-life and its attendent crises, about which there are now countless articles, many books, and a number of experts.

We have barely begun to scratch the surface of the expanding influence of the mental healers. As I believe will become clear, they really do intend that all of life should be included in their sphere of influence. And they don't mind saying so publicly. Howard Rome, one of psychiatry's most prominent spokesmen and former president of the American Psychiatric Association, wrote in 1968 that "actually, no less than the entire world is a proper catchment for present-day psychiatry, and psychiatry need not be appalled by the magnitude of the task." A few years later, he added that "our professional borders are virtually unlimited."

Providing psychological services only for the sick and the seriously distressed was too limiting for many therapists. "Therapy is too good to be limited to the sick," say Erving and Miriam Polster, two highly respected gestalt therapists. They continue: "Psychotherapists who have been used to thinking of the individual, the dyad, and the small group have recently glimpsed the vast opportunities and the great social need to extend to the community at large those views which have evolved from their work with troubled people." Those who are mentally distressed need counseling, and so do those who aren't.

Obviously the role of therapy is being redefined. Some even advocate getting rid of the restrictive term "mental," substituting instead overall health. This would allow counselors to roam freely in all areas now coming under the rubric of health. In line with this vision, therapists have launched a blitzkrieg into areas usually considered the province of medicine. An article in the *American Psychologist* announces that "the most serious medical problems that today plague the majority of Americans are ultimately behavioral, and as such, fall squarely within the province of psychology." What is meant by this is that since the major infectious diseases of the past have been conquered, medical problems today are largely the result of people's behavior: smoking, overeating and overdrinking, too much stress, and insufficient exercise and rest. Psychotherapists rather than physicians are the experts of choice for people whose health is impaired or might become impaired in the future for such reasons. And so a new area of specialization was recently created, usually called behavioral medicine or health psychology. It has its own division in the American Psychological Association and is, I am told, growing by leaps and bounds.

Other definitions of psychology are even more expansive. A book entitled *The Professional Psychologist Today* says that the field is dedicated to "dealing with any problem of less-than-optimal behavior." The idea has gained momentum, and there are now a number of courses and books devoted to the promotion of "wellness," "optimal performance," "peak performance," and "optimal health." A talk in Berkeley was called "Beyond Perfect Health," a state we are told can be reached in "seven easy steps." The assumption here, an engrained part of therapeutic ideology, is that no matter how free of diseases or problems you are and no matter how well you are doing, it's not enough. Who's to say that you're really as well, as efficient, as effective as you could be, or that your performances are truly the best you're capable of. As Lewis Thomas warns, "Once you start on this line, there's no stopping." And that is precisely what makes goals of this kind so attractive to therapists.

Preventing emotional distress is another way of expanding the boundaries of mental health work and it is a topic receiving increased attention. The key assumption is that an ounce of prevention is worth a pound of cure. The idea is unexceptional, being the foundation of public health work. There is, however, an important difference between many medical problems, with which public health is concerned, and psychological problems. As the President's Commission on Mental Health notes, we lack the kind of understanding of the causes of emotional disorders needed for dramatic prevention efforts. Undaunted by this difficulty, many push for more preventative projects. These would include, according to the President's Commission, reducing the stressful effects of life crises such as death of a loved one, marital disruption, unemployment, and retirement, and also creating environments in which people could achieve their full potential.

One of the most vocal advocates of prevention is psychologist George Albee. Starting with the idea that "our social problems are all human problems, and we are the experts on those," he urges mental health workers to become "radical social activists proselytizing for changes in our society." Albee and others think that psychological problems are caused by a dehumanized and unsupportive society, which is tempting enough to believe after you've dealt with the IRS or another bureaucracy, and the way to prevent problems is to change the nature of society. Since society by definition includes all the people, groups, and institutions in the country, adoption of Albee's views would allow therapists to intrude into every single aspect of life.

This seems to be the goal of our mental healers, whether or not they use the rubric of prevention. Evidence supporting this assertion comes from a remarkable book, *Career Opportunities for Psychologists*, published by the American Psychological Association. In a chapter on careers in forensic psychology, we read that "our expectation is that in the future forensic psychologists will roam confidently and competently far beyond the traditional roles of the psychologist in forensic settings." The doing of therapy "need not be viewed as the primary function of the psychologist in the criminal justice system." What else will the confidently and competently roaming psychologists be doing? Among other things, they will be *"reforming* the criminal justice system. Areas suggested ripe for reform are (a) modifications of substantive criminal law; (b) modification of the police role; (c) bail reform . . . (e) prison reform . . . (h) psychologist and psychiatric testimony; and (i) employee selection, job analysis and description, and performance evaluation." There is almost nothing in the justice system that the authors don't see psychologists having a hand in. Undoubtedly social workers and forensic psychiatrists also have plans of their own.

The same book contains a chapter on a new specialty called public affairs psychology. The authors want to be involved in public policy, "especially as it may be proposed or expressed in the form of legislation, defined or clarified through administrative regulations, implemented through government agency actions or operations, or assessed or interpreted by judicial review." In other words, they want to help run the government. If you are wondering precisely what areas they want to help with, the authors supply a handy "minimal list of deserving social problem areas":

Employment, Social welfare and income maintenance, Human resource development, Energy resource allocation, Environmental
degradation, Crime and administration of justice, Transportation,
Housing, Education, Urban Life, Technology assessment, Minori-
ties and prejudice, Health Services, Old age and retirement, Population and crowding, Violence and social unrest, and Militarism and
war.

As Christopher Lasch, Thomas Szasz, and a few others note,
therapists want to diffuse the therapeutic sensibility and therapy
itself into every nook and cranny of human existence. Lasch's comment that they "would abolish the hospital only to make the whole
world a hospital" does not seem extreme after looking at all the
areas they want to encompass in their sphere of influence. To a very
large extent, mental health workers have been successful in what
Szasz calls the manufacture of madness. The idea of psychotherapy
for young people, even infants, old people, and all those in between,
for individuals, couples, families, and even whole villages, no longer
seems outrageous, and the idea of psychological consultation for
businesses, schools, courts, athletic teams, the military, and every
other organization you can think of no longer seems strange. Rather,
these ideas seem quite reasonable and logical, maybe even necessary.

Make Problems out of Difficulties and Spread the Alarm

We are already incredibly self-conscious and psychologically
minded. All the publicity about emotional problems increases both
qualities, making many things seem more serious than they are. If
you're forty and disappointed because life isn't turning out the
way you expected, we have a label for your situation. It's a mid-life
crisis, or if you really want to get technical, an adjustment reaction
to adult life, an official psychiatric problem. We also have labels
if you're recently divorced and feel uneasy about being single again.
Perhaps you are suffering from divorce trauma or maybe you're
having a life-style transition problem. Whatever your situation and

feelings, we have a name for it and therefore you can be sure it constitutes a real and legitimate problem.

What has been created is the psychological version of medical students' disease; everyone sees bits of himself in what any expert says or writes and makes what he or she sees into problems. Yes, it's true I don't always feel in charge of my life, that I sometimes feel guilty, that I'm not using all my potential, that life isn't always joyful. Such commonplace banalities are converted into important, significant issues that demand attention, work, and resolution.

Since there is some resistance to turning every feeling and event into a big problem, therapists feel obliged to spread the alarm, to scare people into giving up their resistances. In *Your Erroneous Zones*, Wayne Dyer informs us that "if you are growing you are alive. If you are not growing, you might as well be dead." Dead? Who wants to be dead? Maybe you better start growing. And here is Joyce Brothers: "The giant marriage wrecker is the most insidious one. Boredom. Sheer spirit-crushing boredom. . . . The chilling fact is that close to 75 percent of all marriages fall short of their potential because boredom creeps in." Where that refrigerated fact comes from is beyond me: I have never seen any data to support it. But surely Brothers's use of it, as well as such terms as "marriage-wrecker," "insidious," and "spirit-crushing," is enough to get many readers wondering if their marriages are in danger of being torn asunder.

While on the subject of mariage, an article in *Reader's Digest* tells us that although only one out of ten marriages achieves its full potential for happiness, every marriage can be enriched. To aid us in our enrichment, a test of marital potential is presented. It yields scores in ten areas, thus assuring that partners will be fully aware of every area where one or both is falling short. The test is to be taken once or twice a year, just in case anyone starts to feel too comfortable. Immediately after husbands and wives share their scores, they should devise "a marital growth plan." Couples are going to have trouble doing nothing about the distressed areas just discovered, a point acknowledged by one of the test's developers: "Once a couple know where their marriage stands . . . they are impelled to do something about it. The test says: Now you know

that your marriage can be better. The next step is up to you." By
this time, it should be obvious that therapy will be the next step for
many of the couples.

Tests on which almost everyone falls short and scare tactics are
all part of the selling of therapy. Here is how one therapist spreads
the alarm:

> How much of yourself have you really discovered? Are you sure
> there isn't more? *Much* more? Are there perhaps some talents you
> haven't tapped, haven't even realized? Are you using your mind
> as well as it was meant to be used? Are you still growing?
>
> Yes, I said *growing*. And by that I mean becoming more of
> what you really are. Because if you aren't growing, then you can't
> possibly be satisfied with your life. There are areas of yourself
> that are crying out for expression.

Sex is a good area about which to make people nervous, since
many people already have some doubts about how well they are
doing there. Here are a few statements from the experts about this
interesting aspect of life:

> The vast majority of us live in a state of sexual deprivation.

> Sex is life. . . . If sex is "right," then everything else is right. If
> sex is "wrong," then nothing else can be right.

> The couple that satisfies each other in only three or four ways
> barely know how to please each other. . . . If they don't get past
> the starting gate and move forward they may not stay satisfied
> much longer.

If you can't get people worked up about themselves, you can
probably succeed in making them worried about their children.
Here is how Stanford psychology professor Phillip Zimbardo and
Shirley Radl do this in their book for parents on *The Shy Child*.
After stating that "shyness does lots of bad things to people" — such
as causing "depression, anxiety, low self-esteem, and loneliness,"
and learning difficulties in school — they conclude with this:

Our primary concern is to help you to minimize the effects of shyness that may keep your children from reaching their full potential as human beings. Even when children are only moderately shy, they still miss out on valuable social experiences. And, when shyness is really severe, living in that psychological prison can ruin a life.

Aside from boredom, deprivation, living in psychological prisons, and having areas that are crying out for expression, there are many other serious consequences to not doing something about your problems, and therapists have been effective in exploiting concerns about them. Publicity for drug and alcohol treatment programs is often not very subtle: ruined careers, health, marriages, and lives are what you can expect unless you get help. Parents are made to feel they are endangering the development of their children unless they deal with them in ways that have to be learned from experts. Couples are told their relationships may deteriorate or end unless something is done to make them better. Sometimes rather strange analogies are drawn in order to make people nervous enough to get into therapy. In an interview at the Fifth World Congress of Sexuality, expert William Masters said that only an "infinitesimal percentage" of those with sex problems were in treatment. He then added, "If they had a broken arm, they'd jolly well seek help right away."

Make It Acceptable to Have the Problem and Be Unable to Resolve It on One's Own

We are constantly told that we are not alone: many, most, thousands, millions, the vast majority, 50 percent, or 75 percent of the population are similarly afflicted. For instance, William Masters and Virginia Johnson, the creators of modern sex therapy, have for more than a decade given wide currency to their idea that "at least half of all marriages in the United States are contending with major degrees of sexual dysfunction or disorder." As far as I know, there is no evidence to support their assertion or similar statements made all the time by other counselors regarding the prevalence of emotional problems. But that is really beside the point, which apparently is to make you feel that you don't have to be ashamed or consider yourself "weird" because of your situation. If millions of other people have similar problems, then it's not so bad that you do too. This is a necessary step in the selling of therapy because many people with problems are embarrassed and might try to hide their shame rather than seek help. But if they can be sold the idea that they are not alone in having the problem and being unable to deal with it on their own, they may be willing to acknowledge their distress and get help for it.

Counselors expend great effort in their public appearances and books not to blame people for having problems. Something else — modern society, religious teachings, repressive upbringing, lack of love or of instruction — is held to be at fault. This is an important part of the selling of therapy, helping potential consumers believe that their distress is not a sign they are bad or mad. They are suffering because others have not given them the right training or adequate opportunities or sufficient support. As I discuss later, however, this notion frequently changes when people get into therapy and they are held responsible for having their problems. Whether or not this happens, one clear message therapists get across to current and prospective consumers is that they and they alone are responsible for doing something about their difficulties. No one else is going to make things better, and problems will not go away on their own. You need not feel guilty or ashamed for having your problem, only for not taking action to correct it. You owe it to yourself and to those around you to get help. This idea fits in nicely with the American penchant for not letting things be and for wanting to *do* something to deal with problems, and is supported by the fear of all the terrible consequences that presumably will ensue if you don't change your ways.

Offer Salvation

All of the above is mainly to set the stage for and make you receptive to the therapy, book, cassette, or course that the therapist has to offer. When it comes to salvation, it seems that every clinician, every book, and every mental health program has a unique and extremely effective way of helping you. Because of the heavy competition, therapists find it useful to differentiate their products and services from those of others. In this sense, the selling of change processes is not much different from the selling of automobiles, detergents, and many other things. The point is to make a distinction even though there is no difference.

Meditation offers a good illustration. All schools of meditation require the student to focus on a constant stimulus, but they use different stimuli — phrases, words, puzzles, breaths, sights, or sounds. However, an impressive body of research indicates that the same results are achieved — what Harvard's Herbert Benson calls the relaxation response — regardless of what the meditator's attention is fixed upon. This strongly suggests that the essential ingredient is the act of focusing and not what is focused on. If all meditation is basically the same, people could be expected to choose the cheapest or most convenient type, or the one that is most aesthetically pleasing to them. If you want them to buy your brand of meditation, you have to make it appear special. You need, in a word, a secret ingredient. Transcendental Meditation, the most aggressive and most successful of the meditation schools, has its secret ingredient, the mantra, a word on which the student focuses. Mantras, we are told, are specially chosen by the instructor for each student and such individually tailored mantras work better than ones the student could select for himself. This despite what the research indicates. So TM sounds different and special. This apparently has been quite an attraction and one of the main reasons for TM's great success. Many people who already knew how to meditate, something that can easily be learned from a book or a brief demonstration, took the TM course thinking they would be getting something better there. And why shouldn't they think this? TM's publicity was aggressive and well done, and TM — not meditation in general but *Transcendental Meditation* — received numerous testimonials from well-known therapists and other public figures. It was easy for those who hadn't derived benefits from other meditation to believe they might reach their goals if only they had the right mantra.

Whatever program, method, or book is chosen, the prospective consumer is led to believe that dramatic changes can be expected, and moreover that they will come in a short time without much effort. Est, for example, says it will "transform the level at which you experience life so that living becomes a process of expanding satisfaction." It's not clear what that means, but it certainly sounds good. Usually the claims are more specific. Adelaide Bry is a therapist who has written books about several change-processes. In one of her books she tells us that life need not be "a time of quiet desperation." Instead, "it can be a time of infinite and joyous possibility" if you make use of her new method, visualization. Here are a few of the things she says you can "realistically expect" from using this method:

- To improve the quality of your life in exactly the areas that need improvement.
- To be healthier, wealthier, and — believe it! — wiser.
- To expand your creative talents.
- To help you get well when you're sick.
- To deepen your feelings of love.
- To experience other dimensions of yourself so that you can go beyond all your present limitations.

According to Arthur Janov, whose Primal Therapy created such a stir in the early 1970s, his methods produce "a tensionless, defense-free life in which one is completely his own self and experiences deep feeling and internal unity. . . . People become themselves and *stay* themselves." Clients become more intelligent; are better coordinated; enjoy sex more; work better but do not overwork; lose their depressions, phobias, anxieties, as well as their compulsions to take drugs and alcohol, to overeat, and to smoke; and they are "never moody." There are special benefits for women: increased breast size for flat-chested women and the disappearance of premenstrual cramps and irregular periods. In a way, says Janov, "the post-Primal person is a new kind of human being," one who "is truly in control of his life." (Before readers rush off to sign up for Primal Therapy, I should mention that I am unaware of any independent research demonstrating the validity of these claims.)

Other counselors tell us their approaches are "pleasant," "un-complicated," and that "the easiest thing to be is yourself." And not much time is required. A book called *Psychological Fitness* offers a "unique three-week psychological shapeup program" that "is the start of your fresh, more exciting life." Clinical psychologist Joseph Bird and his cotherapist promise more in less time. Your life will be changed "almost totally" by their book. "All that is required of you is that you test the formula in its pages — a matter of a few minutes a day for a week or less." But even that sounds like a long time compared to what psychiatrist Robert Goulding, past president of the American Academy of Psychotherapists, has to offer. He told the *San Francisco Examiner* that he "can cure most phobias in 15 to 30 minutes. . . . Therapy doesn't have to be hard or long. It doesn't have to be painful."

Success, effectiveness, and spectacular changes are what we hear about. Successes are big news. Failures are not, unless there is evidence of scandal, e.g., that results were faked. It goes even further than this because, as psychotherapist Albert Ellis notes, the successful cases therapists present are most often "unusually good successes." The modest, partial, and later-relapsing "successes" are not much heard about. Because of this, Ellis observes, the public "may well gain the impression that failures are nonexistent," or at the very least, that the methods discussed are marvelously effective.

Strictly speaking, however, it's not true that therapists don't talk about failures. They do . . . but usually other people's failures. A common theme is that "my" method or genius succeeds where others have failed. Behaviorists heal psychoanalytic failures; family therapists succeed where individual counseling failed; meditation or est works where more traditional methods were of no avail. Counselors gleefully report how many of their patients have been through other programs without benefit. Janov claims that the great bulk of his Primal Therapy clients have had previous treatment ranging from psychoanalysis, gestalt, rational-emotive, to just above every other kind. Masters and Johnson say that 85 percent of their couples have failed in other therapies, and it is becoming increasingly common for weight loss programs to mention how many of their successes failed elsewhere.

The point of such comparison is to demonstrate the effectiveness of the counselor doing the talking or writing. What is easily missed is the fact that a lot of failures are being mentioned.

Another way of discussing failures also leads to viewing therapy as very successful. This is when the therapist's own past failures are mentioned, but only as a contrast to present successes. Thus Heinz Kohut, one of the latest psychoanalytic gurus, in writing about his new treatment methods, which he would have us believe are very effective, says that for some fifteen years he felt "increasingly stumped" by as many as half of his cases. Yet there was no acknowledgment of this fact in his papers written during that period. It is easy to focus on present successes and forget about past failures and just as easy not to ask why the failures weren't admitted when they were relevant.

This pattern has a long tradition in mental healing. Before he developed psychoanalysis, Freud believed in hypnosis and suggestion. In *Studies on Hysteria*, he and his colleague Breuer claimed 100 percent success in treating hysteria with hypnosis. Each hysterical symptom "immediately and permanently disappeared" after the hypnotized patient brought forth the memory of the event which had caused it and expressed the accompanying emotion. Obviously we were well on our way to stamping out hysteria. But the new wonder cure turned out to be not so wonderful after all. Only a few years later Freud was saying that most patients couldn't be hypnotized and that hypnosis rarely resulted in long-term cure. So much for the permanently disappearing symptoms. By this time, however, Freud was using the psychoanalytic approach, the new best way of treating neurosis, and everyone could imagine that all was well.

Clients engage in a similar kind of thinking. Thus Adelaide Bry, therapist, author, and apparently perpetual client, has this to say after taking est:

> I, like so many others, have had high moments after encounter groups, meditation, and other brief or extended mind-expanding experiences. But these feelings were always short-lived.
>
> My own experience with est, and that of the professionals and graduates I interviewed, is that most people continued to experience growth and change over a long period of time.

Bry forgets or never knew that participants in encounter groups and other "mind-expanding experiences" said the same things about them that she is now saying about est. Many reported that while past counseling had resulted in no change or transitory change, whatever it was they had just completed had really done the trick.

It's very easy to overlook the fact that when counselors and clients in 1986 and 1990 discuss past failures, in order to contrast them with the current successes, they will be referring to what we are doing right now.

The exaggerated claims and hoopla that attend the introduction of new therapeutic methods also contribute to the image of therapy's great effectiveness and help bring in customers. Since new methods are added all the time, and since these receive a disproportionate share of publicity, we constantly hear of great things. Every new approach claims unprecedented success. The bad news is longer in coming and the public often doesn't hear about it when it does arrive. The life cycle of new treatment methods has not varied at all in over a hundred years. As an article in the *American Journal of Psychiatry* puts it, "the initial enthusiasm and the report of remarkable results are tempered by the application of more critical study and evaluation resulting in less impressive statistics." As far as I have been able to determine, there has never been an exception to this statement. No psychotherapy's initial claims of remarkable results have stood the test of time and independent investigation. There are a number of reasons for initial successes, including that the innovator's interest and enthusiasm may itself be beneficial. But enthusiasm also seems to put blinders on therapists and researchers so they don't see what they don't want to see. The criteria of success are often too loose, meaning that the results are more a function of the loose standards than of the interventions. Anyone still breathing at the end of treatment is considered to be cured or greatly improved, which tells us nothing at all about the usefulness of the therapy. Enthusiasm also leads to other kinds of errors. For instance, a review of the high recovery rates reported for hospitalized patients in the early 1800s found that the statistics included repeated recoveries of recurring problems in the same patient. Thus one patient who improved and relapsed and then improved again would be counted as two successes. Since some patients relapsed and improved many times, there were more successes than there were improved patients. Needless to say, this does something to the statistics. There is also the fact that enthusiasm is both contagious and intimidating; it may be impossible for many clients to acknowledge to their therapists a lack of progress or a backsliding.

A recent illustration of what often happens with new methods is provided by the issue of controlled drinking. Conventional wisdom has held that total abstinence is the only worthwhile goal for those physically dependent on alcohol, but in the early 1970s two young therapists, Mark and Linda Sobell, published a study apparently demonstrating that their behavior modification approach was very successful in retraining a small group of alcoholic men as social drinkers. Follow-up studies at two and three years after termination of treatment concluded most of the men were "functioning well." The study was hailed as a breakthrough, supplying what was thought to be the first scientific demonstration that controlled drinking worked. The Sobells were accorded widespread publicity and recognition, and their work had a tremendous effect on the thinking of health care professionals regarding the treatment of alcoholism; for many, controlled drinking became a feasible goal, and indeed a more attainable and safer one than abstinence. Then, almost ten years after the Sobells' first report of their results, a reevaluation of their work was published in *Science*. The three researchers who conducted this study carefully reexamined the Sobells' evidence and did a thorough ten-year follow-up. Their analysis showed that the Sobells had misinterpreted their data: the controlled drinking project was an almost total failure from the start. Only one of the twenty patients succeeded in becoming and staying a controlled drinker, and he apparently was mistakenly classified as physically dependent on alcohol in the first place. The sobering conclusion is that there was "no evidence" that the alcoholics "had acquired the ability to engage in controlled drinking safely after being treated in the experimental program."

Another example of the history of new methods concerns biofeedback, the amazing claims for which received widespread and uncritical attention in the 1970s. Here is what Barbara Brown, one of its most visible proponents, had to say:

Nearly every human being is a potential candidate for biofeedback . . . biofeedback still appears to be the closest thing to a panacea ever discovered. . . . Probably no discovery in medicine or psychology compares in breadth of applications or in scope of implications to the biofeedback phenomenon.

Biofeedback was thought by some to be an all-purpose treatment, applicable to medical, dental, and psychological problems, especially problems related to stress. Unlike controlled drinking, biofeedback was not an absolute failure. It does have its uses. If nothing else, it can help some people relax, and there's nothing wrong with that. But it has not lived up to most of the claims made in its behalf. As a recent review of the research puts it, "On the whole, the clinical effectiveness of biofeedback-assisted relaxation procedures is not overly impressive." Although positive results have been reported in many studies, biofeedback has not been shown to be superior to other relaxation procedures such as general relaxation training and meditation. In fact, if what people want is a feeling of calm and peacefulness, they would do about as well just sitting in a chair and relaxing, without any formal procedures or training.

But what therapists, clients, and the public usually hear about is the good news. Obviously this is of great help in the selling of therapy.

Therapists are not alone when they set out to sell their services: they have powerful allies. An important group of allies, which one author calls the friends and supporters of psychotherapy, consists of satisfied therapy consumers. They usually miss no opportunity to give testimonials to counseling in general and especially to the specific approach that did so much for them. Even if you are skeptical about the claims made by counselors and public figures, it's easy to become a believer when your neighbor, friend, or colleague reports great benefit gained. Since, as I discuss later in more detail, satisfied clients tend to spread the message while dissatisfied ones tend to keep quiet, chances are that any news you hear will be good news.

The mass media, where most of our beliefs about therapy's effectiveness are learned and nurtured, are another powerful ally. Although the popular media in America have a well-deserved reputation for muckraking, it is also true that in certain areas they are primarily interested in news that is encouraging and optimistic, e.g., in reporting tools for overcoming physical and emotional handicaps. We are regularly offered tidbits about new medical and psychological treatments for all manner of ailments. We are told that experts have discovered a new method for treating cancer, alcoholism, depression, and so forth. Only at the end of the story — if even there — do we hear that the research has so far been done with laboratory animals or on a small and highly select group of people. If one-half, or even one-tenth, of the new cures worked as well as we are told they do, there wouldn't be any disease or problems left uncured or unresolved. Most people are in no position to know that the overwhelming portion of the research will turn out to be useless: that it will be found to be unreproducible, to be inapplicable to the population for which it is intended, or to have terrible side effects.

An illustration of the strength of the media's positive bias is given by Curtiss Anderson, once an editor of *Ladies' Home Journal*. Some time ago, the *Journal* had done a series of articles on women who had dieted, lost lots of weight, and gone on to fulfill their dreams: marriage, children, and homes in the suburbs. Anderson decided to do a follow-up, which was approved by chief editor Beatrice Gould, who thought it would show the women "living happily ever after." But this is not what was found. According to Anderson, "Ninety-nine percent had blown right back up to their old weights. They'd lost their husbands, been divorced, and they were angry again." Anderson thought he had an important story on the meaninglessness of the *Journal's* stories and of diets. But it was never published. "Mrs. Gould was appalled. She didn't want to hear about it. 'I don't believe it,' she said. 'I don't believe it's true.'" The *Journal*, of course, like so many other of what are called women's magazines, continues regularly to run stories about people who have lost weight, become more independent and assertive, found happiness, and so on. And nary a negative sound is heard.

Mrs. Gould was exhibiting the strong tendency toward cheeriness that characterizes certain parts of the media, especially women's magazines and talk shows. The idea seems to be that people get enough bad news elsewhere which should be balanced with hopeful reports. It's not that depressing and difficult subjects are avoided. Far from it: drug abuse, child-beating, suicide, divorce, sex problems, you name it and you see it or read about it. All of these subjects are acceptable, but the push is to treat them in an uplifting way by presenting suggestions to prevent or resolve them. Therapists who are interviewed are essentially given carte blanche to sell their books and methods however they choose. So no matter how widespread and terrible the problem, we end up on the note that there is something to alleviate or resolve it. It is rare for the therapist's methods and success stories to be questioned, mainly because there is no one to question them. Talk show hosts and reporters are not therapists or therapy researchers. Phil Donahue and Merv Griffin are in no position to say that when they tried the suggested approach with ten people, the results were far less beneficial than what the therapist claims. Even if they or members of the audience doubt the claims, they have no solid base from which to criticize. They can say that it sounds too good to be true, but this does not exactly a strong argument make. Also, time and space limitations encourage absolute statements and work against qualified ones. It is much quicker and easier to say "It works wonders" or "It's very helpful" than to make a thoughtful statement about what kinds of results are obtained by what kind of people with what kind of problem; who benefits most, least, and not at all; and who is harmed.

The pushing of the positive is not restricted to the popular media. It also occurs where you might not expect it, in professional literature. What is wanted is interesting results, meaning positive results. Failures to replicate previous research are published, but not in proportion to their occurrence. Criticism is allowed, as long as it doesn't go too far. As a result, therapists are not forced to think seriously about what they are doing and accomplishing. Reading their own journals, therapists have their positive biases confirmed and reinforced, and then go out with renewed vigor to peddle that optimism to the media and the public, both of which are only too ready to accept it.

Most of the selling of therapy takes place on the local level, on an individual basis, for the prosaic motive of survival. The great majority of counselors I have talked with say they don't like having to sell themselves; they do not necessarily think that therapy is the solution for all the ills of the world and are often embarrassed by the media appearances and claims of other counselors. They wish that without any salesmanship enough clients would show up to keep them in business. But competition is intense and they have to do something. One day I talked with a colleague who was upset about the comments made on television by several forensic psychiatrists. It's disgraceful, he complained: there's no scientific basis for what they do. They're just out to expand the scope of psychiatry and make a quick buck, and in the process they're making a laughing-stock of the profession. Yet two days later this colleague was out doing his thing, telling an audience of doctors and nurses that psychological treatment rather than medical care is what most of their patients require. When I ask how this is different from what the forensic therapists do — isn't he also trying to expand the scope of therapeutic work and where is the empirical support for his claims? — he is perplexed; he can see no similarities between what he does and what the forensic experts do. He comes up with many good reasons why his work is important and beneficial, and with as many showing why their work is silly and even harmful. Rationalizations come easily to all of those, including therapists, who have something to sell.

To get a better idea of how the formula for the selling of therapy is actually carried out, let's look briefly at a therapist trying to establish himself in private practice. He must find some way of standing out, otherwise clients will go to already established therapists rather than to him. One way of standing out is to be very good at your work. If the therapist has demonstrated his effectiveness to his teachers or colleagues, they may refer to him. But this route is not open to many, especially in an area with lots of therapists, all of them about equally effective. So what else can be done? One possibility is to specialize. Therapists of all persuasions dealt with their clients' sexual problems, but in the 1970s a new army of specialists arrived, sex therapists, who claimed to be better able to resolve these problems. They received a tremendous amount of publicity, both because of the new methods some of them used and because of the simple fact that they specialized in this interesting area of life. What is true of sex therapists is also true of the many stress specialists who have appeared in recent years. In both the areas of stress and sex, as well as many others, the increased publicity has made people more aware of the issues. For some, this has meant turning hassles and difficulties into problems and for others it has simply meant realizing that help is available. In each case, the result has been more people going to therapy.

If specializing is good, creating a new specialty is even better, for in a new specialty there are unlikely to be many competitors, at least for a while. Creating a new specialty usually means creating a new problem, a new area for which psychological methods are thought appropriate and effective. Some new areas that have been opened up in this way: "learning to love again" after divorce; conflicts in dual-career marriages; transition crises, such as the birth of a child (the crisis of becoming a family) and the children leaving home (the empty nest crisis); and psychological aspects of serious illness such as cancer and even not so serious illnesses. Most of these examples involve the continued psychologization of the world and are attractive for just that reason. A whole industry, for example, has grown up around death and dying as psychological issues. There are now specialists who give therapy to terminally ill clients, their families, and friends. They also conduct training courses for lay people and professionals, especially for physicians and nurses, who are thought not to be sufficiently informed and sensitive about such matters. The media have been very responsive and given much time and space to the new experts because they have basically come up with a new twist to an issue that concerns all of us. Lewis Thomas's observations on the new death business are telling:

There are so many new books about dying that there are now special shelves set aside for them in bookshops, along with the health-diet and home-repair paperbacks and the sex manuals. Some of them are so packed with detailed information and step-by-step instructions for performing the function that you'd think this was a new sort of skill which all of us are now required to learn. The strongest impression the casual reader gets, leafing through, is that proper dying has become an extraordinary, even an exotic experience, something only the specially trained get to do.

A related way of standing out is to come up with a new treatment, presumably more effective than conventional ones, for dealing with familiar problems. Many sex experts and stress experts have done this. Another example is the use of jogging to treat depression, to get in touch with your spiritual side, or "to balance the feminine and masculine aspects" of your personality. Hypnosis can hardly be called a new treatment, having been around for several hundred years, but it is now enjoying one of its vogues, being touted as a useful remedy for almost anything that ails you. Following in the wake of the women's movement, feminist therapies and therapists have become common for women suffering from all kinds of emotional upset. The message is that a feminist-oriented therapist will better understand and be more helpful than someone else. An increasingly popular "new" treatment is the combination of several methods — such as nutritional analysis, guided imagery, gestalt, and movement therapy — under rubrics like "comprehensive" and "holistic." Such combinations have been particularly popular among humanistic therapists. The advantage of combinations is an important one. For prospective clients, and for referral sources and the media, they sound new — after all, gestalt therapy plus Bioenergetic Therapy is not the same as either one or the other — and the labels of comprehensive and holistic are difficult to resist. Closer examination may reveal that what is offered is not substantially new, but since such examinations are rarely done, there is an excellent chance that our therapist will get referrals and publicity he would not otherwise have received.

Publicity is of course all important. Once our therapist decides what he is selling, he needs to get the word around. Probably the most common way of doing this is to make the rounds of possible referral sources — physicians, lawyers, clergy, and other therapists — and tell them of what you have to offer. If you can persuade several lawyers that their work will be easier if their divorce cases spend some time with you for divorce therapy, you are in business. Another common way of selling your services is to advertise publicly by offering courses or workshops, through organizations with large mailing lists. Extension divisions of major universities are a prime target because their catalogues often reach many thousands of people. The point is both to give the course and to use the catalogue to advertise your specialty. People often come to such events for help with their own problems, and it is not uncommon for some to find they want more help than they can get in the course. If they are impressed by the leader, they may ask for an appointment. Those who have no desire for further assistance from him may remember to mention him to friends or to their own clients. And many more who do not attend the particular course or workshop will nonetheless have been made aware — simply by reading about it in the catalogue — of the leader and his work.

The fortunate few are those who are noticed by the media. Journalists frequently check the mental health listings for newsworthy items. If you are interviewed, you're on your way. The interview is likely to bring referrals and attract the attention of referral sources. Furthermore, media coverage makes you an established expert, leading to requests for more interviews or for talks and more workshops.

So far the discussion has centered primarily on the ways in which individual counselors try to sell their services, but organizations do much the same, and for similar reasons. The media advertisements for programs dealing with problems ranging from drug abuse, alcoholism, obesity, smoking, family relations, depression, and other matters are now so common that no further comment is required. And similar things go on when organizations apply to government and other agencies for money for services or research. Whether at the individual or organizational level, the message is pretty much the same, namely the four-part equation that is the subject of this chapter.

Advertisements for therapy do more than just increase the referrals, fame, and fortune of a particular practitioner or the funding of a particular agency. They redound to the benefit of the entire mental health enterprise. They continue the psychologization of the world, help make problems out of difficulties or things that were barely noticed before, and spread the word that a solution, a psychological one, is available for whatever is troubling you. In short, the promotion of any therapy or therapist reinforces the therapeutic worldview.

The messages we get about therapy, regardless of the source, are seductive. For all the reasons discussed in the preceding chapters, we are receptive to what counselors have to say. When they tell us that we have problems we don't have to put up with, that we could be happier, healthier, and more successful, we listen. They are addressing our main fears and desires. And when they alleviate the guilt we feel for being in the situation and capitalize on our concerns and fears about being there, and then offer a way out, many of us will go for it. The rational parts of our minds may rebel at some of what is said, especially the fantastic claims of therapeutic effectiveness, but for increasing numbers of us there is the suspicion and the hope that maybe there is some truth to what is presented. The counselors usually have impressive credentials and training, and say their work is scientifically validated. They present so many success stories; surely these are not fabricated out of whole cloth. And then there are the testimonials, often from public figures we admire and trust; surely they wouldn't lie. Quickly or gradually, you begin to believe that this book or program can do what it says it can. The questioning, doubting part of you is easily put to sleep or at least told to mind its own business. Hope conquers all and soon you may find yourself enrolling in the program, calling for an appointment, or buying the book. The selling of therapy is one of the most successful examples of salesmanship in modern times.

It is not, I should add, that I have anything against therapists making a living or advertising their services. They have as much right to these things as anyone else. But we should realize that the

selling of hundreds of thousands of individual therapists and organizations has a cumulative effect. We are day and night innundated
by their messages — indeed, some of the counselors appear so
regularly in the media that we think we know them — and the net
effect of this over the years is to change the expectations we have
of ourselves and the way we look at life.

Bias, Chaos, and
Difficulties in Determining What Works

"Therapists are not in agreement as to their goals or aims. . . . They are not in agreement as to what constitutes a successful outcome of their work. They cannot agree as to what constitutes a failure. It seems as though the field is completely chaotic and divided."

— CARL ROGERS

As WE HAVE SEEN, therapy in its many forms is widely used in our society and many claims have been made and accepted for its efficacy as an instrument of human change. Unfortunately, what is thought to be true of counseling and what has demonstrated to be true are far from being the same. We will turn to the evidence regarding therapy's effectiveness in the next two chapters, but first it is necessary to discuss the basis of our knowledge of therapeutic outcome, or how we know what we know, because many of our erroneous beliefs are the results of using the wrong kinds of information and asking the wrong questions. We will see that most of our information comes from highly biased sources and that designing good research to answer important questions is difficult because of the chaos and lack of agreement about almost everything in the therapy fields.

The bulk of our information about the usefulness of therapy comes not from scientific research but from the personal experiences of two groups of people, clients and therapists, both of which accentuate the positive and minimize or deny the negative. We read about, hear, and see former clients tell how therapy saved their marriages, their careers, even their lives, opened up new vistas and transformed them. And even more amazing stories come from therapists about clients they worked with. Successful case studies have become a staple of American life. They are everywhere, and since cases illustrating failure or even worse are hard to come by, it's no surprise we end up believing what we hear.

What's wrong with believing what former clients and therapists tell us? After all, they're the ones most intimately involved in counseling, so they should know. Maybe they should, yet there are reasons to be wary of what they tell us. Research reports are fairly consistent on one point: therapists tend to see more improvement than anyone else, with clients following a close second; the results of objective indicators and the evaluations of independent judges are often less favorable. Both therapists and clients are highly biased, and I take up their prejudices separately.

Clients tend to talk only about therapeutic successes. Those who get little or nothing from their experiences tend to forget or distort the facts, or to keep quiet. Some examples follow.

I overheard a conversation in which one of my assistants asked a friend of hers to give an interview about her experiences with therapy. The friend replied she had nothing to offer.

ASSISTANT: "Didn't you tell me you were in therapy with Dr. X?"

FRIEND: "Yeah, but nothing much came of it."

The friend, who later did give an interview, assumed that only positive reports were wanted and worth talking about.

We usually began our interviews of experiences with therapy by asking for a chronological list of treatments. A large number of respondents left out one or more programs, almost all of which they felt were not beneficial. A number did something like this: "I was in individual counseling for a year, then in a group, then . . . that wasn't important, then there was marriage counseling." When asked what it was that wasn't important, invariably the answer was a therapy that produced little or no change. It was like pulling teeth to get negative statements of any kind. Respondents were quick to give positive evaluations but required prodding and constant reassurance that we were interested in all their therapy encounters, whatever the outcome, before they would give less favorable responses, even when their main evaluation was negative.

A friend whom I had already interviewed offered to do some interviews for me. At the end of our talk on how to conduct them, I warned her about the positive bias and mentioned some ways of dealing with it. She suddenly exclaimed, "Oh, my God," and started laughing. She just recalled that she had forgotten to tell me about one of her therapies, the only negative one she had. I asked her to tell about it then. Details came slowly and with difficulty. At the end of a thirty- or forty-minute interview, she still could not remember the therapist's name.

Several respondents called days after their interviews to say they had forgotten to include one or more experiences, all of which they were unhappy about. They prefaced their reports with "I don't know if this is relevant" or "I don't know if you're interested in this," and what followed was given sheepishly, as if it indicated something wrong with the client.

The strength of positive feeling toward therapy and the need to defend it is illustrated by a woman who sent in a questionnaire about her counseling experiences. Her last sentence reads: "I hope you're not going to write a vitriolic book attempting to cash in on the 'anti-shrink' fad," a sentiment voiced by others as well. She did something interesting in writing about the treatment she had for two years. One of her presenting problems was "nervous stomach," which improved during counseling. She rated therapy as "very helpful," and in answering a question about change maintenance, wrote "All [underlined four times] changes have been expanded." But in answering another question she noted, "Only my nervous stomach has reappeared." I suspect she then realized she had trapped herself: reappearance of the stomach problem does not square with her claim that all changes had been expanded. She wriggled free with this: "As you know, no doctor can attribute [reemergence of stomach disorder] to *purely* emotional reasons."

The tendency to accentuate the positive was not new and should not have surprised me as much as it did. I had heard it all before. Over the years in many settings I have heard or overheard hundreds of people talking about their counseling experiences. The positive reports ranged from the wildly enthusiastic to the mildly encouraging, but the negative ones were so few I can count them on the fingers of two hands. If therapy is as effective as these reports indicate, why are there still so many problems around and why do so many of the people giving the positive reports still have the same problems they said were resolved? I have witnessed a similar tendency in my own clients when I ask about previous counseling for the same difficulty they bring to me. Even when the problem had changed not at all in earlier attempts, they work hard to find something positive to say. The therapist had been very understanding, the client had gained a new perspective, he learned to communicate better, his mind was eased, anything at all so as not to have to say treatment was a failure.

Psychoanalyst Allen Wheelis notes that "few analyzed persons are critical of psychoanalysis." When treatment doesn't help, it is rare for the patient to face this fact. If it is accepted, usually the patient "will blame himself and exonerate psychoanalysis. The most common outcome, however, is simply to pretend that the analysis was successful."

A particularly clear example of the positive bias is given in a study of five women treated for low sexual arousal and lack of orgasm. A large number of outcome measures was used, including rating scales, questionnaires, physiological indicators, and interviews. *None* of the behavioral, questionnaire, or physiological measures showed evidence of change. Yet in post-therapy interviews, patients said things grossly discrepant from what was recorded on these measures, including those they had filled out themselves. They all expressed positive attitudes toward the therapists, increased capacity for sexual arousal, increased knowledge and understanding of sex, and general improvement in their sexual relationships. Glowing reports of continued improvement and satisfaction with the therapy continued for two years in telephone interviews. Since similar results and discrepancies were found in an earlier study, the researchers warn that "these studies imply that previous outcome and follow-up data obtained during interviews may be highly misleading."

Of the many reasons why clients exaggerate the effects of therapy, three will be noted here. The first has to do with the basic nature of counseling: it is, for most people, a very personal, even intimate, matter. You open up to the therapist, confiding thoughts, feelings, and fantasies you've shared with perhaps no one else. You confide your deepest fears and hopes and hurts. And the therapist is often supportive, understanding, sympathetic. You trust him, believe he cares for you and has your interests at heart, and that he does his best for you. By its very nature, this kind of relationship is hard to criticize. Sure you may make jokes and utter muffled complaints to friends about how much therapy costs or how your therapist answers your questions with questions of his own, but it's usually understood that these comments are not meant to be taken as real criticism. It's hard to say that this kind of relationship or process is useless or harmful, just as it's hard to say that praying is useless even when your prayers aren't answered.

A second reason is that counseling almost always produces some results, even if not the ones you wanted. A lot goes on in therapy. There are usually new insights and perspectives about yourself, a heightened sense of self and power, a feeling that you are not alone. These things are appreciated and clients rate therapy positively because of them. An alcoholic man told me that est had done wonders for him. When I asked about them, he said he felt an incredible rush of power and confidence after he graduated and this enabled him to stay away from alcohol. On further questioning, it turned out that his abstinence lasted exactly three days, after which he immediately resumed his drinking and his usual ways of feeling. But he still thinks est is wonderful and recommends it to everyone he knows. When people ask what est did for him, he tells them it changed his way of looking at himself and made him feel more in control of his life. Only he, his wife, and I know how brief was the transformation.

Another example of how things get confused in the minds of both clients and therapists comes from a counselor's report about a group she led for preorgasmic women (those who have never had an orgasm but would like to). The therapist said, "It was a good group, it went quite well." I asked how many of the women were now orgasmic. "Well, none of them . . . but it was successful. The women made changes, they're more comfortable about sex and themselves; they all said they felt good about the group."

What makes this example so sad is that preorgasmic groups have only one goal: getting the women to have orgasms, usually by masturbation. This is what they are set up to do and this is what prospective clients are told about them. Everything done in the groups — whether looking at one's genitals, exploring them by hand, discussing sexual feelings and patterns with the other members, or other assignments — is seen as a means toward this end. Yet the therapist rated the group as successful because some of the means had been achieved and because the women said they "felt good" about the treatment. The clients also thought the group beneficial. I know this because the therapist kindly allowed me to listen to a tape of the last session. One client proudly announced, "I was able to look at my genitals, something I could never have done before." Another said something similar about being able to masturbate. Almost completely forgotten was the obvious fact that no one had had even one orgasm.

I have no reason to doubt that the women did get something from their group. But it seems important to say that what they got was not what they came to therapy for. No one, as far as I am able to determine, came into the group looking for a good group experience, to learn about other women's inability to have orgasms, to learn to look at their genitals or how to masturbate. Yet these means were given by the leader, and once achieved, became sources of pride and satisfaction even though they did not lead to the desired goal. There is probably not much wrong with taking pride in achievements that aren't exactly what you were looking for except that doing so tends to make therapy appear more successful than it is in accomplishing its goals. In this case, the message spread by the therapist and almost certainly by the clients is that counseling was successful and beneficial. It was, in certain ways, but you would have to listen carefully and ask the right questions to discover that not one woman achieved what she came to therapy for.

Therapist Hilde Burton gives a third reason why positive client reports are the rule. "When people spend money and effort on something, they want to believe they got something out of it. They don't want to feel they were taken. So it's natural they won't bad-mouth it or that they tend to forget experiences that didn't work out." The technical name for such operations is the reduction of cognitive dissonance. On the one hand, the client knows he put forth much time, effort, and money in his therapy. On the other hand, he feels he got little in return. There is an obvious discrepancy. If he put out a lot, he should receive a lot, or at least something, in return, unless he is a fool, spending money on worthless

endeavors. Since he doesn't want to be thought a fool, he must resolve the discrepancy. One way is to forget the whole thing, and
another is to make the returns seem larger than they were. The need
for resolving dissonance regarding counseling is greater than for
many other activities because therapy usually involves a number
of sessions over a period of time. It is relatively easy to admit being
taken in a one-shot deal, of eating at a bad restaurant or being
fooled once by a used-car salesman. But that you went back to the
restaurant ten more times or bought three more cars from the same
dealer makes no sense. If you got little or nothing from therapy,
why did you keep going back? Somehow this question has to be
dealt with.

There is also the fact that many clients believe therapeutic failure
is their fault and they are therefore not exactly enthusiastic about
admitting to unfavorable encounters. If they didn't get what they
wanted, it's because they didn't try hard enough. After all, the
therapist can't do it all: he can only help you help yourself. I don't
know the origins of this idea, but it certainly is encouraged by the
therapeutic ideology that puts all or most of the responsibility for
success or failure on the client's shoulders. Most therapists in one
way or another let clients know that they are the only ones who can
help themselves and, when things are not going well, that they are
undermining or subverting the treatment. And most clients gladly
accept the responsibility.

While interviewing one woman, I had the feeling she was hiding
something and I asked her about this. With many apologies and
much embarrassment, she told me she had had sexual relations
with a therapist she had seen many years ago. From what she said,
the therapist had seduced her and their liaison had caused many
personal and marital problems. Yet she feared telling the story because "I was afraid you would think poorly of me, that I had seduced him. Sometimes even I think it was all my fault." Even in
such a clear-cut case, where the therapist had acted unethically and
unprofessionally (and this is true even if the client had acted se-
ductively), she did not feel free to complain. That this is not an
isolated example is suggested by similar stories I heard from other
women who had sex with their therapists and from men and women

who had been abused and exploited in other ways by their counselors. Few of them could come straight out and blame the therapy
or therapist. They were all to some extent, usually a large extent,
apologetic and guilty, feeling that it was at least partly their fault.

Several of these reasons played a part in the decision of one
woman to "fake it" when the therapist she had seen several years
before asked for her evaluation of the therapy. "I made his work
sound more successful than it had been and I even implied continued improvement since termination." She gave this answer when
I asked why she had felt it necessary to give distorted information:
"First, I didn't want to admit to a man I liked and respected that I
still had the problems I saw him about and that even the small gains
I made had vanished. Not having done better made me feel small
and unworthy, and also guilty for not having worked harder. Second,
he was always nice to me and I knew he did his best. I didn't want
to repay him with something that might make him feel bad. Given
all this, the last thing I wanted was a long discussion about my
therapy and my life. My experience is that positive comments are
usually accepted as given, while negative ones encourage further
questions and discussion. Giving cheerful reports is a good way of
ending discussion, which is exactly what I wanted to do."

From what was presented in the last chapter, it should be clear
that counselors engage in a lot of positive thinking about their work
and are hardly unbiased reporters. Like clients, therapists tend to
forget unsuccessful cases or pretend they weren't failures (as in the
example of the preorgasmic group). If the fact of failure is accepted, the client is often blamed: he was unanalyzable, untreatable,
too resistant. Accepting one's failures and limitations is difficult
for counselors because they are exposed to the same therapeutic
claims as is everyone else. It's not easy to admit only 50 percent
success when one reads that colleagues are getting 80 percent. One
fears the claims are true and the reason he is not doing as well is a
lack of competence. So it seems best to talk only about successes
and not mention the many failures, at least until someone else has
blown the whistle. After Michael Evans and I published a critique
of Masters and Johnson's sex therapy research, suggesting it was

full of errors and the success rate perhaps exaggerated, a number of therapists told us they couldn't come close to the results claimed in St. Louis. Although all of them were bothered by the discrepancy and most had started to doubt their own abilities, very few had discussed the issue with anyone else and none presented it at a professional meeting. A few suspected that Masters and Johnson's claims were inflated, but since they had no way of proving this, they kept quiet. Only after Evans and I questioned those claims did these therapists feel free to speak about their work.

There is also something else: therapists rarely have systematically collected and controlled information about their own cases from which to draw reliable conclusions about effectiveness. What they do have are their own general impressions, often based on unrepresentative data. The issue of change maintenance, what happens after termination to changes made in counseling, offers a good illustration. Therapists generally believe that such changes are long-lasting. Most of the counselors I've talked to responded positively to questions about change maintenance and all have a few examples to present. Several talked of cards and letters they received from former clients telling of continued progress. A number mentioned hearing similar things from ex-clients they saw at parties, in stores, or on the street. Although I declined several invitations to look at some of the success letters, I do not doubt their existence. I have received such letters myself and have also run into clients who have wonderful things to say. The point is not that such stories are false (although there is that possibility) but rather that they are almost certainly unrepresentative.

Clients who take the time to send letters to former therapists, or who talk to them at parties and elsewhere, are obviously the satisfied ones. Those who are dissatisfied, either because they didn't make much progress or because their gains were soon lost, are with very few exceptions unlikely to communicate with the therapist. In the years I have done counseling, I know there have been a number of people I didn't help or whose changes were short-lived, yet I have received only one letter reporting relapse and discontent with my work. I would love to believe that this couple is the only one unhappy with me, but to do so would be a grievous error.

Clients who don't maintain their changes usually blame themselves. They are no longer seeing the therapist, so how can he be responsible? Some patients do return to that counselor for further work, but many do not, at least partly because they are ashamed of what they see as their own shortcomings. A couple came to me to deal with serious marital problems. Several years before, they had gone to another therapist for the same problems. Therapy had been quickly and dramatically successful. Their marriage seemed new and exciting and satisfying when they ended treatment. The changes lasted only about a month, but they did not inform the therapist. When I asked why not, they replied that it was their fault, that the therapist had done a good job but they had somehow "blown it." For all I know, that counselor may refer to this case in his talks and writings as an example of great success. Because he did not contact the couple for a follow-up and they did not tell him what happened, he had no way of knowing that treatment was of very limited value.

This kind of thing happens all the time. Very few therapists do any follow-up evaluations and apparently many clients who suffer relapses do not inform the therapists they worked with. There are problems even when follow-ups are done because some proportion of clients give distorted information. Bernard Apfelbaum is one of the few therapists in private practice I have ever met who routinely collects follow-up information. At the end of treatment his clients are given three questionnaires to mail back at specified intervals. Since Apfelbaum sends a check for each completed questionnaire sent in, the return rate is high. How valid the answers are is something else. When I interviewed him, Apfelbaum said this: "If you just looked at the questionnaires, you would think I was the greatest therapist in the world. Not only is the problem we worked on in wonderful shape but many report making important changes in other areas. They tell me everything I want to hear, how effective therapy was and how important it was to them. But when I've had a chance to check this out, it's amazing how little correspondence there is between the written reports and reality. The report says everything is fine but when you see the clients you realize there's been a total relapse or things are significantly worse than at termination."

A follow-up study of a stop-smoking program found discrepancies between clients' reports of tobacco abstinence and blood tests. When confronted with the results of the blood tests, clients who had denied smoking admitted to "occasional" lapses. The falsifications were detected only because a reliable physiological measure was used. Since neither physiological nor behavioral measures are used in the vast majority of follow-ups, which typically rely only on self-report, usually by means of mail-in questionnaires, we have no idea how valid is the information collected.

If we can't take the word of clients and counselors, how can we determine the effects of therapy? I believe that systematic and con-trolled research holds the key. The whole purpose of such research, often called by the name of science, is to minimize the probability of arriving at erroneous conclusions. It has to be admitted that such investigation is not perfect — it cannot control for everything, it cannot guarantee valid answers, and it certainly can be done sloppily and misused — but it seems to be the best method available for finding out what is going on. Or, to put it differently, applying the words Winston Churchill once used to describe democracy, science is the worst form of inquiry except for all the others that have been tried. Since we will be reviewing the results of therapy research in later chapters, it is worthwhile to take a closer look at what it tries to do and why it causes so much difficulty among therapists.

To help in our discussion, let's use a hypothetical example. A few years ago you were a mess. Your husband walked out on you and you were more broken up, confused, and depressed than ever be-fore. Things started to go badly at work and there was no place where you felt secure and comfortable. After moping around for several weeks, half afraid you might kill yourself, you decided to get professional help. Just making the first appointment made you feel better and things improved considerably in the year and a half you were in treatment. You felt more like your old self and happier. Things picked up at work and you made new friends. You are grateful to the therapist, giving him much of the credit for pulling you out of the mire. Week in and week out he was there for you, listening, understanding, accepting, and supporting. He enabled you to heal and go back into the fray. On the basis of this experience you have concluded that counseling is enormously beneficial. You recommend it to others and would have no hesitation returning for more if your life started going downhill again.

Although many people form conclusions about counseling on the basis of this kind of information, it leaves a lot to be desired. A number of questions remain unanswered and we need to answer them if we want accurate information about counseling. We can start by asking about the cause of change. You say the therapy is what made you feel better. But a year and a half is a long time and therapy wasn't the only thing that happened during it. Could the mere passage of time, rather than therapy, be responsible for your changed feelings? We know that grieving for a lost love is a painful and depressing process, but we also know the loss gets easier to bear as time goes on, and the same is also true for many other things. While I don't mean to imply that everything gets better after a few weeks or months, it is true that many problems and feelings are self-limiting and improve after a while. This fact makes it easy to exaggerate the power of medical and psychological interventions. A very well done study comparing behavior therapy and psycho-analytically oriented psychotherapy, both conducted by highly experienced therapists, with a group of clients who received no formal counseling, found that 93 percent of the behavior therapy clients and 77 percent of the psychotherapy clients improved on a measure of overall adjustment. This looks incredibly impressive until you know that 77 percent of the control group also improved on this measure.

If therapy doesn't produce any different or greater change than what can be expected from time itself, it cannot be said to be effective no matter what the improvement rate is. You could save yourself a lot of effort and money by simply waiting it out. Getting back to our example of depression, it's important to remember that the passing of time wasn't the only thing that happened in the year and a half you were in counseling. You got a promotion at work, made new friends, and started playing tennis again. Is it possible that these things deserve some or all of the credit for your increased well-being? Promotions, new friends, and resuming old hobbies tend to make people feel better, and on the basis of just one case there is no way of determining whether these things or therapy is responsible for the changes.

For now we'll let these questions go and assume that therapy really was the important change agent. But other questions remain. Even though counseling worked for you, we don't know anything about either its general or relative effectiveness. Almost every conceivable method will work for someone. On the basis of case studies alone, it is possible to conclude that all interventions — including bleeding, castration and clitoridectomy, lobotomy, eating camel dung, and narcotics — are marvelously helpful. An important question concerns the general utility of a particular method. For every hundred people like you who receive a certain treatment, how many benefit? And, since benefit is always relative, how does this figure compare to those helped by other methods? Is your therapy as effective in terms of time, effort, and expense as talking to friends, taking a vacation, going on a shopping spree, antidepressive medication, or undertaking a different kind of therapy? These questions can't be answered in a meaningful way because all we have is an uncontrolled case study, from which it is almost impossible to draw valid conclusions. Adding more uncontrolled case reports doesn't help matters much, although a large number of cases always looks more impressive.

To answer our questions, we have to resort to different tactics. In order to determine whether the treatment had effects other than those produced by the passage of time, something has to be done to control for — to take account of and therefore be able to partial out — the effects of time. One way of doing this is to have what is called a control group, people who don't get treatment but who are similar to those who do and who have the same problems. If the people who are in therapy improve more than those who aren't, we will probably conclude that counseling produces greater benefits than does just the passing of time, especially if this result is found consistently over a number of studies. But this is only the beginning. We also want to know if the treatment has effects beyond providing the expectation of change (the placebo effect) and a forum for the regular discussion of problems. To take account of the effects of these two variables, we might set up a control group that looked like a treatment group: it would have a fancy name, such as cognitive-emotional reinforcement counseling; it would meet as often as the therapy group and its members would be encouraged to discuss their problems; and every effort would be made to instill the same expectations for change that exist in the clients receiving therapy. The therapy and control group would be similar in all respects but one: the presumed active ingredients of the therapy, the things that are thought to be crucial in causing change — be they therapist interpretations or advice, hypnotic inductions, relaxation training, or whatever — would not be given to the control group. If the therapy group showed greater change than the control group, we would conclude that the active ingredients are responsible.

Every therapy has at least one characteristic that is assumed to be the main agent of change. This characteristic can be as specific as certain types of clearly defined exercises or advice, or as broad as "a helping relationship" or "a therapeutic relationship," but each therapy has something that its proponents believe differentiates it from other forms of counseling and from what people do by themselves. The claims for the relative effectiveness of every therapeutic approach are based on the presumed power of these special attributes. No matter how specific or broad the therapeutic ingredients, they can be tested. Even if a counselor claimed that the active agent in his method consisted of the whole method, which had to be delivered as a package over a two-year period, we could test its relative effectiveness and tease out the change-producing ingredients by doing a series of studies in which his package was compared with other two-year treatments, each varying in a systematic way from the original package. I'm not saying it would be easy to do, only that it could be done.

The question of exactly what produces change is extremely important (though perhaps not for clients, who may care only whether they have achieved the results they wanted, regardless of how they came about). We are being grossly inefficient if we don't know what aspects of counseling actually cause change. Imagine what it would be like if we didn't know what parts of automobiles made them go. Some people would think the trunks were the essential element and therefore design cars with very large and elaborate trunks; others might do the same for steering wheels, rearview mirrors, or rear seats. Some of these cars wouldn't run at all, because in order to conserve space some designers, not realizing their importance, would leave out the engine or gas tank, and other cars would run poorly because very small engines would be hauling around very huge back seats and trunks. Since we actually do know what makes a car move, we can design very efficient ones, we can build different kinds of cars for different uses, and we can even do away with nonessential parts such as trunks and rear seats and build motorcycles and mopeds. When it comes to what is therapeutic about therapy, it seems that some people are still focusing on trunks and rear seats. At the very least, there is vast disagreement on what are the essential elements.

Most therapists, following Freud, believe in the curative power of insight. When you understand, have insight into, the causes of your suffering, you will change your behavior and feel better. Such therapists would say that you now feel better because, having understood the childhood origins of your fear of abandonment and being alone, you are able to keep things in perspective and not be so distraught about the breakup of your marriage. Other therapists believe in a different kind of insight. Some of them, for instance, would say you feel better because you now understand that while losing a husband is disappointing and frustrating, it isn't the end of the world. You're still a good and worthwhile person, and there's no reason you can't have a good life even though you don't have a husband. There is also a large group of therapists who don't put much stock in any kind of insight. Behavior therapists believe that changing behavior rather than gaining understanding is what's important. You were depressed because you weren't getting any goodies. After your husband left, you withdrew and moped. What's needed is to get you doing interesting things again: going out with friends, making new friends, playing tennis, and so forth. You're feeling better now precisely because you did these things. To come to some conclusions about what does lead to changed behavior, we could do a number of things — e.g., ask clients what about their therapy is responsible for their improvement or compare clients who changed a lot with those who didn't in terms of amount of insight gained, the number of interesting activities engaged in, and so on.

One question science can't precisely answer is how well a method will work for a particular individual. Although our main interest is of course in ourselves, science doesn't deal well with individuals. Something that works very well for one person may not work at all for anyone else and something that doesn't work for one may be beneficial for many others. The most that science can do is to find what produces the best results on the average for a particular problem, and such knowledge cannot be generated when dealing only with uncontrolled case reports. The obvious objection here is that we don't care how well the method works in general, we only want to know if it will help us. Unfortunately, there is no way of knowing before the fact except to depend on information gathered on groups of people who are somewhat like ourselves. Since no one is exactly like us, we can't gather the information necessary to make perfect predictions about our response. You may have encountered this issue with a physician when discussing surgery. The doctor says he has achieved 75 percent success with this operation, but that doesn't satisfy: you want to know your chances. Maybe the doctor can say more: since you are young, relatively healthy, and have responded well to two previous operations, he would guess your chances for a successful outcome are 85 to 90 percent. But he can go no further, and you are stuck with the possibility that you may be the one out of ten who, although young and healthy, does not improve.

There is another issue that needs attention: the definition and assessment of improvement. Here you may feel on very safe ground. You *know* you feel better — less depressed, more joyful — so what's to discuss? You may be surprised to learn that there are different ways of defining constructive change. Although almost all therapists would agree that changed feelings are important, many would not see them as sufficient evidence of real change. Analytically trained counselors would want to know if there have been what they consider to be deeper changes: have you, for instance, worked through childhood problems such as fear of abandonment that caused your great upset when your husband left? They might also want to know if you've resolved other problems that cause you always to find men who treat you badly and then leave. If these and similar questions can't be answered affirmatively, they might question what you've achieved. Other therapists might wonder about something else. They note that you seem to have a different attitude toward men since your therapy. You go out a lot but never get involved with anyone for more than a month and you constantly criticize the man you are dating at the moment and men in general. You appear to be very angry at all men and fearful of long-term involvement with them. As long as this pattern persists, the counselors might not consider the therapy a success.

Therapists and clients alike define improvement and change in many ways. Some look at behavior, some at feelings, some at understanding, some at whether consciousness is raised, and so on. When a therapist or client talks of improvement, it's often not clear exactly what is meant, and a lot of false conclusions are reached by those who listen. Science cannot help us decide on the best criteria of change since these are a matter of values and preference. What rigorous research can do is make us spell out exactly what our standards and measures are so we can be sure of what results are obtained. Since people are multilayered beings and since there is so much disagreement about which criteria are appropriate, good researchers take care to use a number of them.

But the assessment of therapeutic outcome is still a complex and difficult matter, as illustrated by the following. Suppose we could agree that in the case of a very simple problem, a fear of snakes, a good indicator of effectiveness is a decrease in anxiety when dealing with snakes. Despite the agreement, our troubles have only begun, for we need to determine how to measure changes in anxiety and what is meant by "dealing with snakes." Consider a few of the possibilities:

1. Ask the client how anxious he feels when fantasizing taking a hike in an area where there are snakes or touching a snake.
2. Put a caged snake in the room and determine how close the client will get to it when encouraged to approach it. We might hypothesize that the closer he gets, the less the anxiety.
3. Place a snake in the client's hands and then (if the client is still there) ask how anxious he feels.

4. To accommodate those who believe clients are too biased to give objective reports, ask the therapist to rate his client's anxiety.
5. For those who think therapists and clients are both biased, ask persons close to the client — spouse, friends, parents — to rate his anxiety. Or employ an expert judge (a therapist not involved in the research) to make assessments after interviewing the client before and after therapy.
6. To please those who don't trust anyone's judgment, use physiological measures of anxiety. There are several of these and we would have to decide which to employ.

Even with a very simple problem, things get complicated very fast. How do we decide which measures to use? We can pick the one that is easiest to use or the one that makes most sense to the researcher. But then we will be criticized by others for using the wrong measures. To avoid controversy, we can use all of them, assuming we have the time and resources. Unfortunately, we haven't quite solved the problem because various measures of outcome do not always correlate very highly. Suppose, as does happen, the client is now able to touch and pick up snakes but says he is just as scared as before and the physiological indicator registers only a slight decrease in anxiety. Should we say this case is a success, a failure, or what?

Remember that the snake phobia was chosen because of its simplicity. You can imagine what happens when we are dealing with more complex problems such as nonspecific anxiety, depression, general unhappiness, or inability to maintain relationships.

You may well feel at this point that if figuring out how well and why therapy works is so difficult, why not just forget the whole thing? Even given their biases, therapists and clients are convinced therapy is generally beneficial, and they can't be totally mistaken in this. Why not leave it at that? Only one reason: a lot of things known to be true have turned out on closer examination to be false. Paul Meehl, who is both therapist and researcher, comments:

The history of the healing arts furnishes ample grounds for skepticism as to our nonsystematic "clinical" observations. Most of my older relatives had all their teeth extracted because it was "known" in the 1920s that the clearing up of occult focal infections improved arthritis and other disorders. No doubt the physicians who treated our ancestors by [bleeding] had "observed" many "cures." . . . Like all therapists, I personally experience an utter inability not to believe I effect results in individual cases: but as a psychologist I know it is foolish to take this conviction at face value.

The history of medicine reveals an incredible number of known-to-be-effective interventions that turned out to be useless or worse. Not very long ago, everyone knew that children should have their tonsils removed at an early age. What everyone knew was wrong except in a small number of cases. More recently, everyone knew that radical mastectomies were the most effective method of dealing with breast cancer in women. Now that proper comparative research has been done, it is clear that such surgery is no more effective in general than less drastic and less disfiguring methods.

Let's look at one study that demonstrates the necessity of taking the trouble to be careful in our observations. The goal of this project was the prevention of delinquency in underprivileged children. Over 600 high-risk boys between age six and ten were chosen and grouped into pairs matched on a number of variables such as age, IQ, background, and behavior profile. The result was two groups of 325 boys whose chances of delinquency were equal or very similar. By a random method, one of each pair was chosen as a control and the other as a member of the treatment group. The counseling program consisted of individual therapy, either psychoanalytic or rogerian, academic tutoring, summer camp, and contact with organizations such as the Boy Scouts and YMCA. The boys and their families were urged to attend church, where priests and ministers were alerted to their problems. In short, both counseling and community social services were engaged in the attempt to prevent the treated boys from becoming delinquent. The average time in treatment was five years. No services of any kind were provided by the project to the boys in the control group.

Both counselors and counselees evaluated the program as helpful. Two-thirds of the boys said they benefited. Questionnaires filled out by former clients contained statements such as: "Helped keep me out of trouble"; "I was put on the right track"; and "gave me better insight on life in general." Counselors rated about two-thirds of the boys as having "substantially benefited" from their participation.

It seems impressive. Given the testimonials of both clients and therapists, we would have to conclude the project was of great value. This is where most studies and clinical reports end, with everyone feeling quite pleased with themselves. Fortunately in this case, the researchers demanded more.

Recall that half of the boys did not participate in treatment; they constituted the control group. For the program to be deemed successful in its goal of preventing delinquency, the boys who received counseling would have to come out better than those who didn't on measures of criminal behavior. When the two groups are compared on things such as number and severity of crimes committed, the results show little difference, with one exception: the treated boys were *more* likely to have committed more than one serious crime. Several follow-up studies show the same pattern. A thirty-year follow-up study revealed that on a number of other measures — including alcoholism, mental illness, stress-related diseases, and job satisfaction — the treated group was *worse* off than the control group. Joan McCord, who did the follow-up, concludes:

> The objective evidence presents a disturbing picture. The program seems not only to have failed to prevent its clients from committing crimes — thus corroborating studies of other projects — but also to have produced negative side effects.

Without the control group the program would have been judged a great success when it was actually a failure. If my readers are anything like the therapists who read early drafts of this section, they will immediately look for methodological flaws in this study in an attempt to invalidate its conclusions. This is a good habit to develop, because there are flaws in the research, which was called the Cambridge-Somerville Youth Study, just as there are flaws in every piece of research. But the fact is that this one remains, forty years after its inception, a sophisticated and well-executed study of the outcome of therapy.

The control group in this study did exactly what it was supposed to do, prevent the researchers from drawing erroneous conclusions about the effects of their treatment. But although the benefits of controlled research have been demonstrated in many ways and although therapists never cease to proclaim a scientific attitude, the vast majority find a lot of reasons why such research on their own work is unnecessary or impossible. And when research is done but doesn't come up with findings they like, therapists find many ways of discrediting the research or the researchers. The analytic counselors in the above study, for example, claimed the results would have been better had all the therapists done analytic therapy. And of course the rogerian counselors said that universal use of their methods would have produced more definite success. This despite the fact that there was no evidence that type of counseling made any difference. When the results of the thirty-year follow-up were published, one critic said the research hadn't looked in the right places (and here is a good example of the differences between those who focus on behavioral changes and those who look for subjective alterations):

> McCord's view is literal and simplistic. It lacks an appreciation of the intrapsychic processes that are affected by treatment. One wonders what her preconceived notions regarding this research may have been. . . . The consistently positive subjective reports of the treatment groups about their experiences must have some pervading impact on their lives today.

In other words, since clients report benefit, benefit there must be: the researchers just didn't know where to find it.

There are several reasons for the primitive state of our knowledge about counseling and for therapists' claim to wear the mantle of science while being unwilling to meet its requirements. Counseling, considered both an applied science and an art, is heavily dependent on the knowledge of other fields. Just as medicine leans on biology and chemistry, therapy derives from the study of human behavior, the specialties of psychology. But biology and chemistry are advanced and mature sciences, while psychology is a very young field, really at an infantile stage of development. The main characteristic of fields at this stage, called pre-paradigm by philosopher of science Thomas Kuhn, is disagreement on fundamentals. What Kuhn says of electrical research in the first half of the eighteenth century — "there were almost as many views about the nature of electricity as there were important electrical experimenters" — is true today in psychology. Disagreement, fragmentation, and confusion are the rule.

An important reason for the lack of agreement is the subject matter itself. Psychology is about people and therefore inherently a more difficult field than physics or chemistry, something given willing assent by almost all the scientists I've talked to. People are extremely complex and multilayered (they may know smoking is bad and think it's a nasty habit, yet continue to puff away); they don't always tell the truth (they may claim to be worse off than they are to ensure they will be accepted for treatment, and after it's over say they are better off than they are to please the therapist); they react in a variety of ways to being observed and studied; and their behavior is hard to isolate and define (e.g., how much assertiveness is sufficient and when does it become aggressiveness?). Unlike neutrons and microbes, people have varying goals and expectations. Two depressed women, for instance, may have entirely different reasons for being in therapy: one may want a cure, while the other only wants a place to talk regardless of the long-term results. Different goals and expectations make evaluation of outcome complex and difficult. There is also the matter of values. Most of us couldn't care less if the universe began with a big bang or a little whimper, if the moon really is made of green cheese, or even if the earth is flat. We'd have to adjust our thinking a bit and that would be it. But when it comes to the nature of human nature, the nature of change, how to deal with people in distress, and even how to define distress — the subject matters of psychology and therapy — most of us, including therapists and researchers, care deeply and have definite opinions. These are often based on fundamental values about the nature of life and are therefore difficult to change and to reach agreement about. Many insight-oriented counselors, for instance, at least theoretically place a high value on dealing with clients as whole human beings, on inner processes and especially feelings, and on not pushing change but allowing clients to decide whether and how much to move. They view behavior therapies, sex therapies, est, and many other approaches as violating all these values. So even when a behavior therapist claims impressive results, they are not impressed. They cannot agree with how behavior therapists look at human beings and treat them. What is evidence of success to one group of counselors is evidence of manipulativeness and dehumanization to another.

Because of the lack of agreement on fundamental issues, there are a large number of therapeutic approaches, several recent estimates running to over two hundred. Each has its own theory of personality and change; its own ideas about relevant phenomena and rules of evidence; its own books and journals (behavior therapy has over twenty journals of its own), usually read only by its adherents; its own jargon, much of which is not understood by outsiders; and on and on . . . even though the clients they serve and the problems they treat are quite similar.

Given this diversity and its attendant disagreements, it should be no surprise that there is little consensus on what research should be done and how it should be carried out. What may be surprising is that not everyone even agrees it should be done at all.

Two important ideas in science are peer verification and the null hypothesis. Taken together, they state that unless one can demonstrate otherwise to one's colleagues, one is considered guilty of having nothing useful to offer. Someone who claims to know something or to have an effective way of doing something is supposed to prove it to the satisfaction of his peers. The burden of proof is always on the one who claims knowledge or effectiveness. The skeptic need do nothing except state, "Show me." These ideas are hardly new. They form the basis of science as we know it and have been widely accepted for hundreds of years, at least in the mature sciences. In the therapy business, however, there are many who don't believe in them. Or, to put it more accurately, they say they believe but their actions belie their words.

There is a long tradition in therapy, going back to Freud, of refusing to conform to accepted scientific practice and research. Freud never offered any evidence of any kind for the effectiveness of his methods. When the Berlin Psychoanalytic Institute published a report of its results for the first ten years of its existence, Freud was not pleased. The statistics were not impressive, but Freud claimed statistics were generally uninstructive because "the material worked upon is so heterogeneous that only very large numbers would show anything. It is wiser to examine one's individual experience." In a later publication Freud indicated that he meant "one's individual experience" to be taken literally. He said that no one who had not been in psychoanalysis, either as patient or therapist, was in a position to evaluate it. This position effectively rules out the possibility of external verification and takes the burden of providing convincing proof off therapists. Anyone doing or receiving analysis, or any other therapy, can claim the method is wonderful, extremely effective, or best, without having to offer any evidence.

That this attitude is alive and well is demonstrated by the following quotation from the chapter on psychoanalysis in the *American Handbook of Psychiatry:*

> The heart has reasons of which the head knows nothing. . . . For the patient, his immediate knowledge of the effect of analysis is sufficient evidence of its worth, however skeptical the outside observer may be and however lacking the statistics to "prove" its usefulness.
>
> Perhaps its effectiveness can never be shown by scientific methods and possibly, because of the complexity and nature of the analytic process, it is a mistake even to attempt such a demonstration. Perhaps the experience of analysis is like that of beauty, of mysticism, of love — self-evident and world-shaking to him who knows it, but quite incommunicable to another who does not.

It is a bit disquieting to have a representative of establishment psychiatry sound like a member of the counterculture, but therapy makes for strange bedfellows. Can't we at least take a count of how many analytic patients had world-shaking experiences?

The vast majority of counselors, analytic or not, have taken their lead from Freud. They see no need to justify their claims or their work. Clinical experience and clinical observation, meaning unsystematic and uncontrolled observation, are sufficient for them. More serious types of research are anathema: they don't do any and don't read what is done by others. Information about therapy methods and results is usually transmitted by presentation of case studies.

Simple defensiveness is yet another reason for the relative paucity of careful research on the effects of therapy. It may be difficult to believe, but the same counselors who speak out so confidently on personal and social issues and make all sorts of claims about the efficacy of their methods are struck with fear at the idea of serious investigation. They know the research that has been done has not given much support to the usual therapeutic claims. No one wants to come out on the short end of another Cambridge-Somerville Study and no one wants to learn, and to have the public learn, that his favorite techniques are not as powerful as he thought and that the most cherished beliefs don't hold water. As far back as Freud and his circle, there has been a siege mentality among counselors, a sense that there are lots of internal and external enemies who want to discredit them. Those who raise questions and criticize, whether insiders or outsiders, have never been welcome and many have been dealt with harshly. The bitter ending of the relationships between Freud and many of his early followers over matters of doctrine and method is just one example of how disagreement is viewed as betrayal and the traitors are cast aside. In order to protect themselves from outside critics, therapists have often tried to keep the details of their work secret. For many years they refused to publish transcripts of their sessions or allow anyone to sit in or view through a one-way mirror. It was not until 1941, more than thirty years after the beginning of formal psychotherapy in America, that a complete transcript of a case was published (by Carl Rogers). And I have seen more than one prominent therapist in public appearances refuse to answer questions about the basis of their claims, although they were more than happy to go on and on making those claims. Some progress has been made. More transcripts have been made available, as have audio and video recordings, there has been more viewing through one-way screens, and more research has been done, but we are a long way from where we ought to be.

That more good research has been done in recent years is to a large extent the result of a challenge by one man, British psychologist Hans Eysenck, who enjoys almost universal disdain among therapists. In 1952 Eysenck, who is not a therapist, published a short article titled "The Effects of Psychotherapy." He compared the scanty data available on the outcome of counseling with the equally scanty data on improvement in those who hadn't received therapy. The improvement rates were essentially the same and Eysenck concluded that the data "fail to prove that psychotherapy, Freudian or otherwise, facilitates the recovery of neurotic patients." There were many things wrong with Eysenck's article. The treated and untreated groups he compared were very different and so were the standards of recovery. But this is mainly of historic interest now. An avalanche of papers quickly appeared, attacking Eysenck's methods, motives, and conclusions. Some even denied he had said anything of importance. But the powers of denial, formidable though they were among therapy advocates, were insufficient to withstand Eysenck's attack. He had raised the questions that required answers: namely, how do we know counseling is effective? and just how useful is it? It was clear to all but the most obtuse that despite the deficiencies of Eysenck's data, the burden of proof was on those who claimed therapy was helpful.

Research began in earnest. Carl Rogers and his colleagues were already engaged in this endeavor and turned out a number of important studies. The advent of modern behavior therapy in 1958 added considerably to the research. Strongly committed to the scientific advancement of knowledge and desirous of demonstrating their methods superior to traditional approaches, the behaviorists were soon publishing studies almost faster than anyone could read them. The cause of research was encouraged by the desire of the federal government and insurance companies, who were paying more and more of the cost of therapy, to know if they were getting their money's worth. Literally hundreds of controlled studies have now been done evaluating the effects of counseling. They all suffer from one or more defects, but nevertheless we have something that Eysenck did not have in 1952 — a substantial data base from which conclusions can be drawn.

As we review the evidence of therapy's effectiveness and when hearing claims for some wonderful old or new treatment, we should keep the main points of this chapter in mind. Psychology and therapy are far from being precise sciences. They are very young fields of study beset with vast disagreements and enormous difficulties. Uncontrolled observation and personal opinion rather than controlled investigation are the source of most of the claims made, and those making the claims have good reason to accentuate the positive. When someone talks of benefit gained, it is important to get a clear understanding of exactly what is meant, how it was measured and by whom, and if appropriate methods were used to control for the passage of time and other factors that might have influenced the outcome. Last, since benefit is always relative to something, you should ask how the results compare to those of alternative approaches. And be wary of those who refuse to answer these questions.

The Outcomes of
Therapy: Myths and Realities

"Sometimes the magic works, and sometimes it doesn't."

— THOMAS BERGER

"Psychotherapy is not a panacea. It never was, and I do not believe it ever will be. Psychotherapy comprises a specialized set of techniques, applicable to specific circumstances and conditions, and no more."

— HANS STRUPP

THE QUESTION OFTEN ASKED about counseling — Does it work? — can be answered affirmatively, at least at the most general level. In research studies, it is commonly found that 60 to 80 percent of therapy clients derive some benefit from treatment. When therapy clients are compared with some kind of control group, the treated ones usually improve more than the untreated ones. In some studies both groups improve to the same extent, but it is rare for a control group to do better than a therapy group. Putting all this together, it seems that in general your chances for feeling better and doing better are greater if you get some kind of counseling than if you do nothing.

The problem with this conclusion is that it is too general to be of much use to clients or therapists. It doesn't say anything about what kinds of results can be expected in what kinds of therapy for what problems; it doesn't offer any guides for thinking or action. Such guidelines are needed because a whole mythology has grown up about the effects of therapy. We believe all sorts of things about counseling, things that therapists, and many former clients as well, want us to believe. Some of our beliefs are partly true, some are based on conflicting evidence, and some are held despite abundant evidence to the contrary. In this chapter I consider some of the common myths about the effects of therapy, contrasting them with the best evidence, from research studies and case reports, now available.

Myth 1
There Is One Best Therapy

Therapists tend to believe their approach is the best for just about everything and tend to present it in that light. Not all of them go as far as Arthur Janov, who says his Primal Therapy is the only cure for neurosis; most have more subtle ways of getting the same message across regarding their own methods. So we have therapists, clients, and laypersons who swear by psychoanalysis, Transactional Analysis, family therapy, or something else as the only true therapy or certainly the very best.

With a few exceptions, to which I will turn shortly, the evidence does not support the idea of a best treatment. Most of the well-known methods usually produce similar results for most problems. Among the clients I interviewed, there seemed to be no important differences regarding type and extent of changes made that could be attributed to specific therapeutic approaches. The same holds true for different formats. By and large, similar changes are re-ported by those in individual, group, and couples therapy. The un-avoidable conclusion at this time is that if you're suffering from any of the common ailments that people take to psychotherapy — confusion, depression, low self-esteem, distressed relationships or inability to form a relationship, difficulties in decision-making, and so on — you can expect about the same results regardless of which therapy you choose.

There are a few exceptions to this rule. Enough evidence has accumulated to conclude that behavior therapy is significantly more effective for some problems: phobias, sexual problems such as lack of erection or orgasm, and some compulsions. Behavioral approaches have sometimes been equaled by other methods for these problems, but to my knowledge they have never been surpassed and often are considerably more successful. While behavioral methods are more beneficial than other methods for dealing with certain problems, they are less well suited for handling issues such as self-exploration and a search for meaning. An illustration is Arnold Lazarus's dis-covery that over twenty behavior therapists were themselves undergoing some form of nonbehavioral therapy. Lazarus's explanation seems reasonable: these clinicians were all "relatively assertive individuals without debilitating phobias, compulsions, or sexual aberrations," who wished to be in better touch with their feelings and to have greater understanding of their behavior. Behavior therapy is not designed to accomplish such ends. For those desiring understanding, exploration, and meaning, a nonbehavioral approach is indicated.

There is also an important exception regarding counseling formats. For marital difficulties, couples therapy is superior to individual therapy. As long as the goal is to improve the relationship, it makes sense that both partners should be seen together, though this does not rule out separate sessions some of the time. Too often when only one spouse goes for therapy, or when each goes to a different counselor (a not uncommon pattern), the goal of improving the relationship is lost sight of and replaced by that of individual fulfillment; these two goals are not always compatible and the marriage may suffer as a result.

With these few exceptions, there is precious little evidence to suggest that one therapeutic approach or format is better than others. Since some readers will undoubtedly object at this point, it is necessary briefly to discuss psychoanalysis, which many consider the ultimate therapy. Starting with Freud, analysts have claimed that while other methods achieved only "superficial symptomatic cures," analysis alone gets to the sources of a person's suffering by giving access to the repressed experiences of childhood, resulting in "thoroughgoing personality changes." Such claims have been made so frequently and for so long that it isn't surprising many people believe them. Whenever another therapy fails, it is tempting to think that the presumably deeper and more exhaustive probing of analysis could have produced a different outcome. The fact that analysis is based on a comprehensive and extremely rich theory of human behavior tends to give support to such thoughts, as does the fact that analysis is the longest — and therefore most expensive — therapy.

But there is little to back up the claims of analytic superiority. Analysts have long confused assertions of effectiveness with evidence of effectiveness, the most striking example of which is provided by Freud himself. Although he never ceased to proclaim the superiority of his method, he offered no supporting evidence at all. The cases he wrote about had mainly unsuccessful results. It is a tribute to his persuasive powers that he was able to gain support for his treatment without demonstrating its usefulness. To be fair to Freud, however, I should note that toward the end of his life he became less sanguine about the efficacy of analysis and said so:

> One ought not to be surprised if it should turn out . . . that the difference between a person who has not been analysed and the behaviour of a person after he has been analysed is not so thorough-going as we aim at making it and as we expect and maintain it to be . . . the power of the instruments with which analysis operates is not unlimited but restricted, and the final upshot always depends on the relative strength of the psychical agencies which are struggling with one another.

Despite such statements, his followers continued to boast of the power of analysis.

What they have not done, and what Freud could not do, is to present evidence that would persuade anyone not already a true believer. After an exhaustive review of the literature, two investigators sympathetic to psychoanalysis, Seymour Fisher and Roger Greenberg, come to this conclusion: "There is virtually no evidence that psychoanalysis generally results in more long-lasting or profound changes than other therapies," the same conclusion reached by a number of others. This is even more remarkable than it seems when one considers that analysts are far more selective than other therapists in whom they accept for treatment (sometimes taking as clients fewer than 15 percent of those who apply) and that analysis usually lasts far longer than other methods. Despite these ways of stacking the deck in favor of analysis, its results are no better. There is also something peculiar about the way in which analytic outcomes are assessed. A report published by the American Psychoanalytic Association concludes that 97 percent of those who "complete" analysis are cured or improved. This figure looks somewhat less impressive when one realizes that (1) about as many patients terminate therapy as complete it, and those who quit are not counted in the final tabulations, even though many of them had been in therapy for years; and (2) of the 97 percent who were said to be cured or improved, "symptom cure" took place in only 27 percent. This means that 70 percent of the improved group had not resolved the problems that brought them to analysis in the first place.

What analysis does provide more of than most other approaches, simply because of its duration and the great number of sessions, is the opportunity for leisurely self-exploration and the comfort of a long relationship with a professional healer. But this is not necessarily the same as changing one's behavior. One woman's experience is a case in point. Feeling generally dissatisfied with her life, especially with her relationships with men and with her lack of productivity at work, she began at the age of thirty what turned out to be an eight-year treatment with a well-regarded psychoanalyst. She spent many thousands of dollars on the three sessions per week of therapy and felt, as so many analytic clients do, that she learned a lot about herself. At the end, however, her relationships with men were about the same as before, as was her work, and she was still generally dissatisfied. Of self-exploration and insights there were a lot; of behavioral change very little.

For those who are willing to look at evidence, there is little room for any conclusion other than that psychoanalysis and the methods based on it — usually called dynamic or analytically oriented therapies — are no worse than most other therapeutic approaches and certainly no better.

Myth 2
Counseling Is Equally
Effective for All Problems

It has become routine to recommend counseling for almost everything that ails people. The implied assumption is that therapy can help no matter what the problem, from which it is easy to conclude that therapy is about equally effective for all problems. But this is far from being the case. Counseling's effective range of applicability is far narrower than many people think. Despite the best efforts of thousands of therapists over many years to make a panacea of therapy, its effectiveness has been established with only some problems. In general, the charge sometimes leveled against counseling is true: it works best for the less serious, less persistent difficulties.

The following problems fare best in psychotherapy:

Fears, anxieties, and phobias. The reduction of fear is a common outcome of counseling although, as already noted, behavioral methods are usually superior to others in this respect. Regardless of type of counseling, simple phobias such as fear of small animals and fear of flying respond much better than complex ones. The results of therapy with the most complex phobia, agoraphobia, the main feature of which is marked fear of being alone or being in public places from which escape might be difficult, are not impressive. For most complex phobias, including agoraphobia, antidepressant medication alone or in combination with psychotherapy yields better results than therapy alone. Don't ask why antidepressant medication: no one knows for sure why it helps in these cases.

Common anxieties are also treated with drugs and there is little doubt that antianxiety products like Librium, Dalmane, and Valium, the most widely prescribed drug in America, are effective for many people, allowing them to feel sufficiently relaxed to do things like public speaking that otherwise would be quite difficult or impossible for them. However, there are dangers, addiction to the medication being one of the worst. Antianxiety medications are highly addictive for some people, as easy to get hooked on and as hard to withdraw from as heroin. Anyone who doubts the devastating effects of withdrawing from these drugs might want to look at two popular books, Barbara Gordon's *I'm Dancing as Fast as I Can* and Mary Ann Cronshaw's *End of the Rainbow*. Many factors — including the intensity of the anxiety, the frequency with which it occurs, and the potential for drug dependency and addiction — need to be considered in deciding whether drugs or psychotherapy, or a combination of the two, should be used for a case of anxiety or "nerves."

Low self-esteem. If your main problem is not feeling very good about yourself, counseling may indeed be helpful. Many clients feel better about themselves and view themselves in a more positive way after therapy. In fact, as I shall shortly discuss in greater detail, this may be counseling's most important outcome, regardless of what kind of problems clients bring to it.

Some sex problems. Brief sex therapy is very helpful in teaching men to delay ejaculation and previously anorgasmic women to have orgasms under certain conditions (e.g., by masturbation or with partner hand or mouth stimulation). Success rates are lower for erection problems and inconsistency of orgasm, though still higher than with other methods. We do not have sufficient information about the outcome for cases of low sexual desire and different levels of desire between partners, but the results so far are less than encouraging.

Some kinds of marital and family distress. Couples and families often find improvement in how they communicate, address problems, and deal with other family members. This does not mean, however, that all relationship problems improve in therapy or that the changes that do take place are always large enough to make a significant difference in family relations.

Lack of assertiveness. Being better able to speak up and stand up for oneself is frequently reported to be a result of counseling.

There are also a number of problems for which current therapy methods are not particularly effective or for which other approaches seem better. I have already indicated that counseling seems not terribly effective for some complex phobias and some sexual complaints. There are also these other problems:

Depression. This is the most common psychological complaint for which therapy is sought and one of the most confusing because it really isn't one problem. There are many forms of depression with little agreement on what they are and what to call them. Therefore, it's often difficult to compare the results of different treatments. The depressed clients in one study may have little in common with those in another. Despite this, it is clear that nonpsychological methods have an edge except perhaps in the mildest cases. Electroconvulsive therapy (ECT) is highly effective, especially with psychotic depression. For manic-depression (periods of great excitement alternating with periods of severe depression) lithium carbonate is far more beneficial than anything else, and other antidepressant medication (tricyclics and monoamine oxidase inhibitors) has proved its worth with most types of depression.

However, there are problems with these methods. The use of ECT has been restricted because of a general revulsion against shock treatment. Drugs have side effects and many patients can't or won't take them. In cases where these medical methods can't be used, psychotherapy may be the only alternative, even given its lesser effectiveness. Even when drugs are used, they usually have little effect on clients' social functioning and psychotherapy is often used as a supplement to help with this issue.

An encouraging note was recently sounded when two well-done studies found a form of behavior therapy (cognitive behavior therapy) to be more successful than medication for the treatment of nonpsychotic depression, the first time any psychological method proved superior to drugs for this ailment. However, two studies are not sufficient base from which to draw firm conclusions and we have to await further studies to see if these results can be duplicated.

Addictions to food, drugs, and tobacco. What Albert Stunkard, a leading authority on the treatment of obesity, concluded over twenty years ago is as true today and applies as well to smoking, drinking, and drug abuse: "Most obese persons will not remain in treatment. Of those that remain in treatment, most will not lose weight, and of those who do lose weight, most will regain it." Although it is not uncommon to hear of marvelous new approaches and breakthroughs, nothing much works very well. Alcoholics Anonymous seems to be about as useful as professional therapy for drinking problems, but when drop-outs and relapses are considered, it is clear that far less than 50 percent of people are helped by either. Of course there are many people who break their addictions, but it has yet to be demonstrated that any formal therapy is more effective than what people do on their own.

Schizophrenia. Almost every medical and psychological intervention imaginable has been employed in the treatment of this disorder (actually a group of disorders), which for most people is the essence of insanity. Improvement rates are highest for patients whose problems are of recent onset: chronic patients do worse regardless of type of treatment. Antipsychotic medication is highly effective in reducing such symptoms as hallucinations, and because of these drugs the snake-pit atmosphere of mental institutions has largely disappeared. As you might expect by now, however, there are debilitating side effects with long-term use of these medications. Community support systems such as halfway houses or supportive families seem essential for the effective outpatient care of chronic schizophrenics, most of whom, with or without drugs, are not able to live completely independently. It has not yet been demonstrated that any form of psychotherapy is of significant value in the treatment of this complex and frightening disorder.

The sad lot of some chronic schizophrenics is illustrated by a man I talked with. He is better off than most since he is able to support himself (he is a computer whiz and has an understanding employer) and live on his own, despite six hospitalizations in eleven years. The combination of drugs he's taking generally keeps things under control as long as there isn't too much stress on the job. But the medications aren't perfect. Though they are powerful enough to calm an elephant, they have not reduced the incredible anxiety he feels around people. He literally shakes with fear when in the presence of others, especially women and strangers, and has been unable to form any friendships or romantic relationships, though he says he would very much like to. Most of his leisure time is spent in his small apartment, watching television and reading newspapers. Occasionally he musters the courage to go out and try to make contact with others, but the anxiety always gets the best of him and he returns home in humiliation and despair. Years of several different therapies have not improved his social skills or decreased the anxiety.

Sexually deviant behavior. There are a number of case reports of the successful treatment of exhibitionism, child-molesting, and rape, but few controlled studies. It has not yet been demonstrated that psychological interventions are useful with such problems.

The changing of sexual orientation received much attention in 1979 when Masters and Johnson claimed unprecedented success with, in effect, changing homosexuals into heterosexuals. However, their work has been criticized by a number of people, including me, and is generally considered to be badly flawed and unreproducible. Most therapists agree that changing sexual orientation is extremely difficult and that psychotherapy has not proven its worth with this problem.

Rehabilitation of criminals and prevention of delinquency. Whether or not these are appropriate areas for therapeutic intervention is a debatable question, but many counselors think they are and have sold their ideas to legislators, prison officials, and others. Despite all the hype surrounding every new effort, the results are not impressive. Few programs have escaped the fate of the Cambridge-Somerville study discussed in the last chapter. The conclusion of Robert Martinson's 1974 review still stands: "With few and isolated exceptions, the rehabilitative efforts that have been reported so far have had no appreciable effect on recidivism."

Psychiatrist Anthony Storr sums up psychotherapy's range of applicability this way:

> Psychotherapists seem to me to be best at treating the inhibited, the frightened, the shy, the self-distrustful, the fragmentated, the over-dependent, and the over-controlled. They are far less successful with those who lack control over their impulses. . . . Patients who show disturbances like over- or under-eating; who drink too much, or who smoke compulsively; who steal, who drive dangerously, or who commit sexual offenses or other criminal acts, are poor bets for individual psychotherapy.

This is pretty much what Freud thought and subsequent developments have by and large proven him right. Despite what many therapists would have us believe, and despite attempts to use their methods with every human problem, counseling is not a universal cure-all.

Myth 3
Behavior Change Is
Therapy's Most Common Outcome

This idea is grounded in common sense: people come to therapy with problems, change their behavior, and therefore resolve the difficulties. An example of this is a shy and unassertive man who comes for help because he is isolated from other people and very lonely. As a result of his counseling, he is able to approach others and form relationships: he makes some friends and starts a romance. We would have no trouble agreeing that his behavior has changed. He would undoubtedly concur and feel quite good about the therapy. Changes like this often occur in counseling and are familiar to all of us because they are the ones therapists and clients talk most about.

Let's look at this case in another way. This time the man's behavior does not change, or at least not much. He still feels shy and doesn't approach people more frequently than before counseling: he makes no friendships and begins no romances. He still is lonely much of the time. Nonetheless, something is different. He looks forward to seeing his therapist and during the sessions — whether they go on for a few weeks, months, or many years — he feels anything but lonely: he feels listened to, understood, valued, and cared for. He feels very good about therapist and therapy and wants to rush to their defense when he reads in a magazine that therapy doesn't work.

In the first version of this case there was a change in behavior which enabled the client to do things differently outside of counseling. In the second version this did not occur but the therapy itself provided valued comforts to him. Strictly speaking, there was a kind of behavior change in the second version: the client *felt* differently during his sessions. But this is not what is usually meant by therapy resolving problems and changing behavior. In the second case the outcome of therapy was provided by the fact of being in therapy and there was little generalization except for a sense of well-being the client may have carried with him for a short while after his sessions. Relief from isolation and loneliness were dependent upon remaining in therapy; he couldn't, or at least didn't, do anything differently outside of therapy.

It therefore seems appropriate to speak about two types of therapy outcome: people-changing and people-providing. This distinction is made by three researchers seeking to explain why a much larger proportion of encounter group members liked and felt moved by their group experiences than were actually changed by them.

> Perhaps the import of encounter groups lies not in how many people leave them with new ways of thinking about and responding to themselves and the world they live in and new strategies for coping with life [the traditional goals of therapy]. Perhaps there is a much simpler need that encounter groups are engineered to provide efficiently and effectively — that of momentary relief from alienation. . . .

I would go even further and suggest that the most common products of most therapies are not behavior change but caring, comforting, and structuring. Some people come to therapy looking specifically for these things rather than behavior change, and some come to solve a problem and then find, whether or not that is accomplished, they like other aspects of the program. Caring, comforting, and structuring are highly valued by most clients and those clients give therapy good reviews, whether or not any problems are solved or any behavior is changed.

Since my argument is controversial — especially among therapists, who like to think of themselves as practitioners of the difficult art of changing behavior — I offer a number of examples from my own work and that of others.

In a society where many people feel that no one listens to, understands, or cares about them, a high value will be attached to activities where these needs are met. Therapist Hilde Burton says that even if little or no change is made, clients "often feel very good about therapy if the relationship was positive and they could really talk there." A large number of the people I talked to made positive assessments of counseling even when their problems did not change because "I could really be myself" or "she listened nonjudgmentally and understood me." This is not surprising. We all know the power of having our feelings listened to. Even when nothing changes, we say it's good to talk, to clear the air, to get things off our chests, to share our thoughts. By talking we create community, even if temporarily, a bond based on what is expressed and on support, empathy, and sympathy.

Counseling is one of the few places where it is perfectly acceptable to think only about yourself. It is the perfect place, as Tom Wolfe would have it, to talk about me. As such, it is a haven for some people. One former client says, "I stayed in therapy because the weekly meetings gave me an opportunity to get away from the world and into myself, a time to take stock of where I was and where I was going. . . . I don't think it results in any great things but it was comforting at the time."

For many, therapy offers friendship, family, and community, areas in which many Americans feel deprived. In his study of why so many young men and women are turning to Eastern religions, Harvey Cox concluded "they are looking for warmth, affection, and close ties of feeling." What some find in religious communities, others find in counseling. A therapist in an urban community health center notes: "People come to the psychiatrist in the hope of getting their tenderness tanks topped off. Person after person comes in asking for love and understanding. . . ." A thirty-three-year-old woman, looking back over several years of participation in a number of groups, some labeled encounter and some labeled therapeutic, offered this comment: "I guess I was looking for a surrogate family without any of the hassles of a real family. In the groups I was free to do pretty much what I wanted. I could speak up or not, get involved with other people's problems or not, hang out with other members after the meetings or not. I kept my freedom but always had a feeling of belonging to and being cared for by the group I was in." And one participant said that what est's graduate seminars and special events have in common "is a wonderful sense of camaraderie and of being part of a community of people who are transforming their consciousness."

The strength of the bonds between client and therapist or client and group should not be underestimated. They often become the center of the client's life. A woman, now a therapist, gives this example: "When I was a student I had to take a course on small group behavior, and one of the requirements was participation in a sensitivity group. I didn't particularly want to take the group but I had no choice. I don't know how it happened, but by the third or fourth meeting I was completely involved. Everything that happened in the group was very important to me; my life centered on and was consumed by it. Were the leaders right in saying we weren't taking responsibility for running the group? Was Jack really attracted to me? Was I too fearful of expressing my real feelings? Silly questions like those became the most important items in my life. I often found myself thinking about them when I was studying or in class. I thought the group was marvelous and rushed out to join another one as soon as it was over."

For a few people, therapy seems to overshadow the rest of life. The following story was told to me by a colleague. His neighbor had steadily increased his involvement in therapy and was now going four times a week. He spent a great deal of time preparing for his sessions and going over what happened in them, but his wife and children felt left out and frequently interrupted his preparations and cogitations to get more of his attention. He grew less and less tolerant of their interruptions and of them in general. One day he told my friend: "I wish my wife and kids would just go away. They're interfering with my analysis."

That the caring-comforting-structuring aspects of therapy are more important than its problem-solving aspects for some people is well illustrated by two women, both who have been in counseling for years. The first expressed concern about her therapist's hints that she should consider ending treatment: "It's embarrassing. I know I don't have a legitimate reason for staying but I don't want to give it up. My therapist has become my best friend. I would be very lonely without her, there would be a void in my life. I don't know what I'd do without her and I'm going to hang on as long as she'll let me." The other woman mentioned some problems she was working on in therapy, but when prodded admitted they weren't the main reason she was going. "I like the regular contact. It helps structure my life. Now that the kids are gone and my husband travels so much, I have more contact with Dr. ———— than with anyone else. The problems aren't the main thing because we don't even talk about them most of the time. I just bring up whatever I want. I have no idea if it's going anywhere but I like the process."

As mentioned in an earlier chapter, therapy also serves as an antidote to loneliness. For a person seeking new friendships, new romances, new sexual relationships, or just to be in the company of others, many therapeutic events, especially groups and weekend encounters, are made to order. Not only do these therapies offer a host of people to meet but they include many activities that facilitate finding out about others and getting introduced to them. A real estate entrepreneur found his experience at Esalen rewarding. "For a weekend we really got into feeling. There were about eighteen people there and we really got close. Also I met a nice girl from Florida and took her home for a day and that was really nice."

Many other functions are provided by counseling. It's a way of learning the intimate details of other people's lives and, not surprisingly in an age when some therapists have attained the status of superstars, it's a form of entertainment. A young man who went to Actualizations rated it as moderately helpful but his rating seemed to be based as much on its entertainment value as on its usefulness in helping him deal with a personal problem. "It was the most exciting show I've seen in a long time. Here are all these people talking about their problems, hangups, and weaknesses, dealing with each other and the leaders in all sorts of ways, a real-life soap opera. It was a voyeur's delight." A couple I interviewed said personal growth was the reason they attended many weekend and other brief therapy programs, and then they added this: "You meet lots of interesting people, you hear how others are living their lives, and you get to see some very sensitive and powerful people [the leaders] in action. It's a great way to spend time, more informative and more enjoyable than going to the movies."

Therapy also provides new experiences for some participants, new ways of looking at themselves, others, and the world. Many people value these experiences — sensory awareness exercises, giving and getting massages, telling and hearing secrets, exploring different forms of relating and communicating — whether or not any lasting change results. Some didn't even seem to care about change: having the experience was the point. They frequently used phrases such as "interesting," "opened up new vistas," "saw new possibilities," and "added a new perspective."

Two other important and common outcomes of counseling require mention. One is the development of self-understanding. Most of the people I've talked to note this as a consequence of treatment and are pleased by it. They say things such as "I know more about what makes me tick," "I understand where my buttons are and how they get pushed," "I have greater insight into how I became the person I am." People value self-understanding as an inherent good, even when they are unable to change what they now have greater understanding about.

A large number of clients also mention an increased ability to cope. When people come to therapy, they are often overwhelmed, demoralized, and stuck. They don't know what to do about what's troubling them or even how to think about it. These feelings often change during counseling. Clients no longer feel so helpless or hopeless. They believe they have some control, that in one way or another they can handle their problems and get on with their lives. One man put it this way: "I have experienced a feeling of self-confidence and also an ability to cope with my problems to a greater extent." A woman said this: "Therapy made me question self-imposed limitations and see new possibilities. I know I can survive and feel good about myself even without a relationship." Another person said that one effect of therapy was a "greater ability to take care of myself, to be in touch with thoughts and feelings even though it's hard to express them." Because counseling has boosted their morale and confidence and given them some sense of control, they feel better and rate therapy highly.

There is no doubt that therapy does make a lot of people feel better. Whether because they believe they are cared for and understood, because they feel they have more strength to cope, because they are comforted and supported, because they share in an emotionally charged experience, or because of any number of other reasons, clients tend to feel good about their therapy experiences.

Although there is nothing wrong with making people feel better, or increasing their confidence or understanding, it is important to keep in mind that there is no necessary relationship between such things and changing behavior. The person who feels better able to cope will not necessarily cope better. The person with greater understanding will not necessarily be able to do anything constructive with this understanding. Therapy is apparently much more successful at making people feel better, at least for the moment, than it is at changing how they behave. Here are two of a number of examples from my interviews:

At the end of the client-centered treatment he had undertaken several years earlier for severe depression, this young man thought it had been very helpful. Some of the reasons for his assessment were: "Therapy helped me think about what was going on. . . . I felt that I was doing something about my problems and in that sense felt less stuck. . . . The fact that my therapist didn't dislike or reject me made me feel kind of good." In retrospect, however, he realized that except for getting out of bed to keep his therapy appointments, "there was no specific way that I was doing better."

A woman who has been in counseling for over seven years, several times a week, claims to have derived greater insight, mastery, and comfort. She likes her therapy and feels better for being in it. But there has been no improvement in the problem she went in with — unsatisfactory relationships with men — and in some ways it is worse. Though she has accumulated greater understanding of her relationship with her father and how that affects current relationships with men, and though she has explored her entire childhood and all her encounters with men over and over again, she has been unable to use her knowledge to any positive end.

In some ways therapy is similar to prayer. Both can be comforting and useful even when one does not get what one asks for. Both can keep hope alive; combat boredom and demoralization; decrease loneliness and alienation; help us get things off our chests and clear our minds; and make us feel more in control and more confident.

But that is not the same as resolving problems or changing behavior, and we are left confused as to what therapy actually does. Neither therapists nor clients make the necessary distinctions between different outcomes of counseling or between means and ends. The result is that the behavior-changing and problem-resolving effects of therapy are greatly exaggerated, while the extent to which it provides comfort and makes people feel better is ignored or understated. If we want to keep our thinking clear, it will help to remember that although counseling can and does result in changed behavior for some people, this is not its most common product.

The Outcomes
of Therapy, Continued

"If you hear that a mountain has moved, believe; but if you hear that a man has changed his character, believe it not."

— MOHAMMEDAN PROVERB

"I believe we are entering an era in which the claims and aspirations of psychotherapy will become more circumscribed and more focused. It may also spell a return to greater modesty, from which we should never have departed."

— HANS STRUPP

I NOW TURN TO COMMON BELIEFS about the extent and persistence of changes made in therapy, the benefits of long-term counseling, and the question of therapy-induced harm.

Myth 4
Great Changes Are the Rule

Therapy success stories usually involve dramatic changes. The client becomes, as Primal Scream's creator Arthur Janov puts it, "a new kind of human being." People go from sadness to gladness, from staleness to creativity, from powerlessness to pulling their own strings. Therapy can, we are led to believe, really change your life.

Whether a change is dramatic, modest, or insignificant depends on one's expectations and perspective and is therefore a highly personal matter. Nonetheless, changes made in counseling rarely live up to what is claimed by many therapists and believed by many clients. The dramatic kind of conversion undergone by Malcolm X, from dope pusher, pimp, and criminal to clean-living, disciplined political revolutionary, is uncommon in or out of therapy. Most therapy-induced changes are far more modest.

All the therapists I interviewed agreed that truly radical modifications were unusual. It is close to impossible, for example, to turn a chronically depressed person into a happy-go-lucky type. When asked about the possibility of doing so, psychoanalyst Kurt Schlesinger replied: "Theoretically yes, given unlimited time and resources, which means a full-time therapist for years and years. Since no one has such resources, it's utopian. Practically, the most you can hope for is limited change in their construal systems so that depressions are less frequent, less deep, and easier to shake." After thirty years of doing therapy based on the teachings of Freud and Jung, Anthony Storr concludes that there is no "convincing evidence that even years of analysis, in the most expert hands, radically alters a person's fundamental 'psychopathology.' "

The word *cure* embodies much of what is meant by dramatic change. To be cured means to be freed from something objectionable or harmful, or to be restored to health or soundness. But cures in therapy are not common. One psychiatry textbook notes that the use of the term *cure* in psychiatry "is not appropriate"; no matter how successful the treatment, patients do not lose "all their anxieties" or "their most general style of experiencing and approach." Some years ago, before he became a popular guru, Carl Rogers reviewed the research on his client-centered therapy and said it indicated "a sobering fact." The effects were "modest, even in the more successful cases. . . . Perhaps the changes due to therapeutic learning are always relatively small, though important."

Many clients improve in therapy, but not in the absolute way we think. Symptoms or presenting complaints rarely disappear. Rather, they become less intense and pervasive, and clients can cope with them somewhat more effectively. You may "overcome" your fear of snakes to the point of being able to go hiking in the woods, but that doesn't necessarily mean you won't be afraid if you see a small snake on the path or that you'll be able to touch your neighbor's pet boa constrictor. Your self-esteem may improve, but that doesn't mean you'll always, or even usually, like yourself and that there won't be days when you can't stand yourself. And liking yourself more doesn't necessarily mean that others will like you more or that you'll do anything different from what you were doing before.

Weight reduction is useful for getting a numerical sense of the extent of therapeutic changes. Hundreds of thousands of people flock to therapists of various persuasions to shed excess weight, and many claim to be successful. The question is, how many pounds are lost? The results of behavioral treatment for obesity, usually considered the most effective method for the problem, are consistent: average weight loss is less than fifteen pounds. This may be good news for those concerned with an extra five or ten pounds, but most of the people who go to weight control programs would barely notice the loss of a dozen pounds, even assuming the weight could be kept off.

As I was trying to decide which of a number of cases to use to illustrate the point about modest gains being the rule, I came across Janet Malcolm's remarkable articles in *The New Yorker* about a psychoanalyst she calls Aaron Green, dealing with his experiences both as an analytic patient and a therapist. This case has several advantages. First, since it has now been published as a book, *Psychoanalysis: The Impossible Profession*, it is easily accessible and interested readers can read the whole account themselves. Second, it is impossible to argue that the treatment wasn't sufficiently intensive or long. And third, there is little question that Green passionately believes in therapy and that it helped him. So herewith the case of Aaron Green, as much as possible in his own words.

Dr. Green has spent fifteen of his forty-six years as an analytic patient. His first analysis began when he was a medical student and lasted six years. The second was a training analysis, required of all psychoanalytic residents, and lasted nine years. Although no mention is made of the number of sessions per week, psychoanalysis requires at least three and usually four or five. We are talking about a lot of therapy hours. Although Green considers both analyses helpful, it was the second one "that opened my eyes and gradually changed me."

The most important change was that "I'm not so belligerent and abrasive anymore, so touchy and angry." He is certain that without therapy, his life would be "extremely constricted, full of bitterness and depression." There was also the removal of a symptom. "I used to have social anxiety before going to parties. . . . The symptom fell away during my analysis, and now I go to parties. . . ." Last, Green notes a lessening of neurotic inhibitions about pushing to get what he wants. These are the positive changes he mentions.

He acknowledges, "I haven't changed all that radically." His life is still somewhat constricted, and bitterness and depression are no strangers to him. He comments: "I don't think basic character structure ever changes. We're not that malleable."

Ironically, one thing that convinced him of the effectiveness of his analysis was the appearance of new symptoms.

> As I grew less nasty and pugnacious and argumentative — as I began more and more to say to myself, "Hell, you don't have to do that anymore" — I grew more and more anxious about things that I had never been anxious about before. Like being in crowds and sitting in the balcony at the theatre. I also developed a speaking anxiety, which I still have, and which really troubles me. It gets in the way of my teaching and prevents me from speaking at congresses. I was invited to speak at a meeting of the American Psychoanalytic Association . . . and I had to refuse. I just couldn't do it. The mere thought of being on that stage at the Waldorf terrified me. I feel flawed and humiliated by this symptom.

Green has always felt an outsider and his analyses have not changed that. "I've never felt 'in' anywhere — not in school, not in college, not in medical school, not in psychiatric training — and now I'm playing it out in relation to the analytic community." Although the wish is not without ambivalence, he would like to rise in the hierarchy of the analytic institute and become a training analyst. But the inhibitions against pushing himself were not completely removed by treatment. "The Oedipal rivalries, fears, guilts are still operative. They're not anywhere near as strong as they were before my second analysis, but they're still there, and they take their toll."

Although Green does not particularly like the company of other analysts and is disillusioned by the bickering and power politics at his institute, he remains a firm believer in the treatment and, in fact, is considering a third analysis for himself. His comments about the power of analysis, based on what he has been able to accomplish with his patients and what he accomplished for himself, seem applicable to all therapies:

> the changes achieved are very small. We live our lives according to the repetition compulsion, and analysis can go only so far in freeing us from them. Analysis leaves the patient with more freedom of choice than he had before — but how much more? This much: instead of going straight down the meridian, he will go five degrees, ten degrees — maybe fifteen degrees if you push very hard — to the left or to the right, but no more than that.

And that may be quite worthwhile to you and those around you. But it is not the same as becoming a new kind of human being or of achieving everything you hoped for.

More evidence for the modest effects of therapy, and even of absolute failure, comes from an examination of the lives of other therapists. If counseling does indeed produce great changes, the results should be easy to observe in therapists, for they have received more therapy than any other group of people and they have also had extensive training in methods of personal change, methods they could presumably use on themselves if they wished to.

The material that can be brought to bear on this issue is not as extensive or as rigorous as I would like, but it seems fair to say there is no evidence that counselors do better, feel better, or overcome more problems than anyone else. Freud continued smoking cigars even though he knew the dangers, even though he had a heart condition, and even after he developed cancer of the jaw, which necessitated a number of painful operations and the placement of a metal prosthesis in his mouth. He stopped smoking several times, but never for long. Fritz Perls was another therapist who continued smoking to the end. Perls was incapable of close, enduring relationships, his therapy work was often at odds with what he said it should be like, and the arrogant, browbeating way he dealt with many of his clients was poles apart from what he and other therapists recommend to people. Freud was, by his own admission, a neurotic, a diagnosis agreed with by his friend and biographer Ernest Jones.

Many of Freud's early followers were themselves seriously disturbed individuals and a surprising number of them committed suicide, despite the experience of analysis and the easy availability of more. The relationship of Freud to many of his disciples was disastrous, ending with great bitterness and rancor, hardly the kind of communion therapists preach about. There are numerous examples in the therapy movement, some quite recent, of counselors handling ideological disputes and differences regarding clinical practice about as well, or as poorly, as the rest of us handle serious differences: that is, with name-calling; refusing to speak to or even appear at the same meeting as the other; attempting to denigrate the accomplishments of the one who gets branded as heretic or, on the other hand, of the one who is branded as the rigid old fogy who won't change; and, as Freud did, drumming the ones who differ out of the movement.

Though largely forgotten now, Harry Stack Sullivan was one of the most important psychiatrists in America from the 1920s through World War II, famous for his work with young schizophrenics and for his optimistic brand of therapy called interpersonal relations. But his own life was not a therapeutic success story. He had psychotic episodes throughout his life, was an alcoholic, irresponsible in his handling of money, cruel toward his students, extremely secretive about the details of his life, and unable fully to accept his homosexual inclinations or to change them. He often despaired of his inability to achieve a "relationship of love."

The suicide rate of psychiatrists is one of the highest of any professional group, and the rate among female psychologists is also high. Drug and alcohol abuse are high among all health professionals, including therapists. And counselors seem to have at least as many problems in their relationships as do others. Their divorce rate is about the same, and the amount of marital dissatisfaction may be even greater. A survey of seven medical specialties by *Medical Economics* found that psychiatrists came out on top in more categories of marital problems, including sexual problems, than any other specialty. Anyone who keeps company with counselors knows that, no matter what they may be like with their clients, their personal lives are no freer than the lives of others from pettiness, depression, poor communication, power struggles, anxiety, bad habits, and other difficulties.

Since therapists now offer advice to institutions on how they should be run, it is of interest that Janet Malcolm, a sympathetic observer, concluded that psychoanalytic institutes were run in a "demented manner" and that my experience in organizations run by therapists and those run by people with little or no therapeutic experience reveals absolutely no difference. For all their knowledge of human behavior and ways of changing it, counselors have been unable to make their clinics, departments, and other organizations more productive, more efficient, less tension-filled, less frustrating, or less productive of job burnout than organizations run by people without such knowledge.

Myth 5
The Longer the Therapy,
the Better the Results

It seems almost logical to think that better results are obtained in long-term counseling and that some problems are so deep and complex that only treatment of great duration can help. After all, Rome wasn't built in a day and you shouldn't expect ingrained habits and long-standing difficulties to change overnight. This is one of the reasons that psychoanalysis — four to five sessions a week for three to seven years — is thought by many to be the most effective therapy.

The fact is that no relationship between results and duration of counseling has been demonstrated. A number of reviews of the relevant research conclude, to use the words of Lester Luborsky and his colleagues, that duration "seemed to make no significant difference in treatment results." My interviews indicated no consistent differences for longer and shorter therapies. Some people who had been in therapy for years said the changes they made could not have been effected in a shorter time, but others reported similar gains in much briefer treatment.

One of the most dramatic changes was reported by a man who, ten years before, had had five sessions of therapy. His presenting complaints included serious bouts of depression for several years and a "bitter and hostile" attitude toward "everyone." In therapy, "I learned why I was reacting with so much anger and I was able to change the behavior." The depressions lifted. A decade later he says, "I don't have those deep depressions anymore or angry outbursts. . . . I have continued to feel better and better about myself. . . . I think I would be a very bitter person if I hadn't had the therapy." Interestingly, this man says that an important element in his improvement was the therapist's telling him, during their fifth session, that he didn't need more counseling. "His telling me this reassured me. He let me know I was okay, that I wasn't a nut."

The results of brief treatment (twenty-five sessions or less) seem to be no less positive than those of therapies lasting two, three, ten, or even twenty times as long. A study done at the Mental Research Institute in Palo Alto, where therapy is limited to ten sessions and where almost no one, no matter how crazy, is turned away, revealed an improvement rate of 75 percent, which is similar to or higher than that reported for longer therapies. Of course some will argue that MRI's criteria of improvement are less stringent than those of analytically oriented therapists, the ones who usually do long therapy. But even the analytic literature offers little comfort for those who believe longer is better. A number of analysts — such as Alexander, Malan, Sifneos, Mann, and Davenloo — have presented evidence that the kinds of changes they are interested in can be made in counseling of less than six months' duration. And it should be remembered that Freud himself rarely saw patients for more than a year.

Why, despite the lack of evidence for the idea that longer is better, do most therapists continue to believe differently and indeed to pressure clients into believing the same thing? (That they do pressure clients to stay in treatment is beyond question; a large proportion of my respondents quit therapy despite the advice of their therapists that they needed more.) One reason is simply a matter of training. For a long time it was believed by almost everyone in the therapy business that long-term treatment was essential, and this idea was drummed into therapy students. They learned that real therapy takes a long time and acted accordingly, often spending countless sessions establishing rapport, making a diagnosis, and talking about things that have no relation to the problem the client wants help with. Once the idea of lengthy therapy is accepted, it is easy to find interesting things to fill the time, all of which are then used to rationalize the necessity for taking a long time.

Long counseling is also fostered by a desire for effectiveness. If what has already been done has not worked, there is a tendency to believe that more of the same or more of something else will help. Thus, if the insights have not resulted in the desired changes, it is tempting to think that the understanding was only intellectual and greater expression of emotion is required; or that the insights were not the important ones and it is necessary to discover earlier causes of the problems; or that the insights have to be "worked through." Whatever the idea, the result is to extend treatment.

Another important reason for lengthy therapy is that it is good for therapists. The longer the counseling they do, the more secure are their finances and the less need there is for new referrals. Private practitioners who do brief therapy are a less secure lot. Since they are always finishing with clients, they require a tremendous number of referrals to survive. A conversation I had with a friend who sees most of her clients for years nicely illustrates the point. Although I have kept my practice small, since I do only short-term therapy I need about two referrals a week to keep a full load. She was shocked by this. Although her practice is more than twice as large as mine, she needs only about four new referrals *a year* to stay full. There is also something comforting about seeing the same clients over a period of years and really getting to know them and what can be expected from them. Short-term therapists rarely experience this. By the time they have gotten to know the client, he or she is ready to leave therapy, to be replaced by a new person with a new problem.

Long-term therapies have a built-in feature that makes the therapy even longer. They go on for so long and the client becomes so dependent on the therapist that a special period of time — sometimes extending to six months or more — is required to get the client ready to leave.

Myth 6
Therapy Changes Are Permanent
or at Least Long-lasting

If you become more assertive, less depressed, better able to express yourself, or make any other changes in counseling, it is an article of faith among therapists and clients that these changes will persist over time. This belief is one of the main reasons therapists have not done many follow-up studies to determine how former clients are doing. When you assume "once cured, always cured," there is no need for such studies. And there is some evidence to support this belief. It is not hard to find people whose therapy-induced changes have persisted for many years. Recall the man mentioned on page 165 who has had no recurrence of his deep depressions or angry outbursts in the ten years since his therapy, and who continues to feel better and better about himself.

Because good follow-up studies are few and far between, we do not know as much about the long-term effects of therapy as we should, but what evidence we do have only partially supports the idea that changes persist for long periods. Counselors hear a lot of contrary evidence, as I did in my interviews: clients report they derived benefits from previous therapy but they "didn't last very long" or "it worked only for a while." For a time there is a change of language, mood, or action, then a gradual sliding back toward the pretherapy situation.

The experience of former political activist Jerry Rubin is not unusual.

> I've attended scores of "personal growth" workshops and learned all about losing my ego and dropping my attachments. I agree, feel good, am enlightened! Then the minute a crisis appears, the insights disappear and the devil in me takes over. I become that six-year-old Jerry who screams, cries, complains, and manipulates when he does not get his way.

Some clients do not admit this outright. They say their changes have been maintained or even expanded, but then, in discussing why they went to another therapy, they indicate the presenting problem was the same one that supposedly was already resolved.

Behavior therapist Arnold Lazarus sent follow-up questionnaires to over a hundred former clients and found that 36 percent had lost the gains made in treatment. Masters and Johnson claim a 7 percent relapse rate over five years for their sex therapy clients, but no one else has come up with anything close. Two other studies of sex therapy, for example, found relapse rates of 54 percent and 37 percent, the latter in only three months after the end of therapy. But these figures pale in comparison to the backsliding found after treatment for addictions. It is easy to stop smoking or drinking or overeating or taking drugs — many people have done it scores of times — but just as easy to begin again. Relapse rates for these problems are often over 90 percent. Backsliding is also common in the treatment of psychotics and criminals. For a while it looks as if a patient has his violent or psychotic tendencies under control and is capable of living independently, and therefore is released into the community. Too frequently, the stay is very short.

Three researchers who reviewed relevant clinical and research reports come to this pessimistic conclusion: "In the large majority of psychotherapeutic endeavors — be they psychodynamic, behavioral, existential, or otherwise — patient improvement neither persists nor generalizes to new settings." And therapist Richard Farson has chided his colleagues for the way they deal with this problem: "In an attempt to overcome our impotence we have made our therapeutic experiences increasingly emotional, exhausting, and excruciating, hoping that our clients will emerge from these experiences with such an exit velocity that they seemingly could not avoid going into permanent orbit."

Some clients pay heavily for believing in the permanence of therapy-made changes. When problems recur, they often feel confused and guilty. They wonder how this could happen and what they have done wrong.

While, as several recent books aimed at therapists have suggested, a lot more could be done to maximize the maintenance of change, therapists and clients would also benefit from more realistic thinking about the issue. Speaking of the myth of once cured, always cured, psychologists Nicholas Cummings and Gary Vandenbos note that "no other field of health care holds this conceptualization of treatment outcome." Dentists and their patients understand that the same tooth that was filled today may require further work in the future. Similarly, physicians and their patients know that the condition successfully treated this week may recur next month or next year. Why should psychotherapy be expected to produce more long-lasting results than medicine or dentistry?

This is not a defense of sloppy therapy. Relapses have to be taken into account in determining the uses and effectiveness of treatment, and ways of minimizing relapses should be used to best advantage. But expecting the impossible from therapy does not help matters.

Myth 7
At Worst, Counseling Is Harmless

Given the reckless abandon with which therapy is recommended to everyone with every possible problem, it is clear people believe it can only be for the good. At worst, counseling can only fail to help you change. This idea has long been held by therapists. The possibility that therapy might make clients worse was not taken seriously until recently, and only then thanks to the efforts of a few pioneers such as Allen Bergin and Hans Strupp.

A moment's thought should be sufficient to indicate that a method powerful enough to produce positive change is also capable of producing negative change. Any kind of power can be for better or worse, a conclusion supported by a number of research reports. Thus a review of studies of marital and family therapy states that, "On the whole . . . it appears that 5 to 10 percent of patients or of marital or family relationships worsen as the result of treatment." A large study of encounter groups found that 16 percent of the participants were worse off after the groups than before, and that their deterioration seemed a direct result of being in the groups.

We have already seen an example of harm caused by therapy. By his own account, Aaron Green, the psychoanalyst whose personal therapy was discussed on pages 161–163, was both helped and hurt by treatment. His abrasiveness was diminished, a positive result, but he developed a debilitating speaking anxiety that has stayed with him and gotten in the way of his professional advancement. Although Green believes that on balance therapy was beneficial, there is no doubt that it was also harmful to him.

A number of clients I interviewed said, usually reluctantly, that therapy had been harmful. One of them, a thirty-year-old woman, depressed and desperate after her husband left her, went to a weekend workshop for those dealing with the end of relationships. An encounter group atmosphere prevailed and, according to her, the therapist encouraged her physically to fight a younger woman whom she didn't like. "I got carried away, I bit her all over and drew blood. I was completely out of control. I wish someone had stopped it." She got scared "about all the anger in me" and felt "horrible guilt" about what she had done. She left the workshop feeling much worse than when she started. She judged the experience to be very harmful and says it took months to get over her guilt and her feeling of being out of control.

The following example involves an issue, therapist-client sexual relations, that unfortunately is more common than most people think. Although sex between therapist and client is condemned by all professional organizations, it occurs with some frequency and the results are almost always harmful to the client. A woman entered therapy because of problems in her marriage and depression. She had sex with her analyst throughout the year of treatment and for a year afterward. Although she enjoyed the affair at the time, she was left with a strong residue of guilt and shame. Ten years later, she still feels bad about it. She does not forgive herself for "cheating on my husband" and for "being so naive as to think that by screwing my shrink I was working to resolve my problems." In addition, she developed what she calls "fantasies of grandiosity," the sense that she was very beautiful and special, which she says have made her life more difficult. She is now in counseling with a different therapist, one of her purposes being to deal with the aftermath of the first therapy. It is no longer uncommon to meet people who are looking for, or starting out with, a therapist to resolve problems caused in a previous therapy.

These are only a few of the kinds of negative effects sometimes produced in counseling. Some clients with no history of severe disturbance become psychotic during counseling, some commit suicide, and some do other things that clearly indicate a worsening of their condition. Professional therapists frequently claim that negative effects are caused mainly by untrained counselors. While there is no way of testing this proposition at present, the fact is that the bulk of evidence we have regarding therapy-induced deterioration implicates professionals.

There are many technical questions about the incidence of therapy-induced harm that I have tried to spare the reader. Just because someone becomes psychotic or commits suicide during counseling does not necessarily mean counseling is to blame; the person may have gotten worse without therapy. After all, people have suffered serious emotional problems after plane trips, eating lunch, and going to birthday parties. Establishing reliable cause-and-effect relationships is more complex than determining what a person was doing just before he went berserk.

Nonetheless, it is now abundantly clear that therapy of any kind can harm as well as help. Clients and prospective clients should keep this in mind, as should therapists. Just as there are risks to undergoing surgery and other kinds of medical interventions, there are also risks to going to therapy. Unfortunately, we do not yet have precise information about the extent of the risks, what kinds of clients are most vulnerable, and what practices are most likely to harm, with one exception: if you have sex with your therapist, you can be fairly certain that harmed is what you are going to get.

Myth 8
One Course of Therapy
Is the Rule for Most Clients

In the past, before going to therapy was as acceptable as it now is, most clients attended only one therapy in their lives. Some returned if they experienced a recurrence of problems or if new and serious difficulties arose, but they were a minority. Because of this pattern, it is still widely believed that most people go to therapy only once.

But this is now a myth. One of the most consistent and important effects of counseling is a desire for more counseling. These days several courses of treatment are the rule. Some examples:

- One study found that 81 percent of growth center users and 56 percent of women in consciousness-raising groups had been or were currently in formal psychotherapy.
- In a study of over one hundred phobic patients, 59 percent had prior therapy, for an average duration of almost two and a half years.
- In another sample of therapy clients, consisting primarily of people in their early twenties, 64 percent had previous counseling.
- Psychoanalyst Allen Wheelis notes that the days are long gone when a second analysis was considered unusual. Recall that Aaron Green, whose two analyses took fifteen years, is considering a third one.
- The overwhelming majority of clients interviewed for this book had participated in more than one therapy, and a majority had been to three or more.
- More than 80 percent of the clients I have worked with in the last few years have had prior counseling for the same or different problems.

Whether the results of therapy are positive or not, many participants want and get more, something two observers call the "salted peanut effect."

It makes sense that those who fail to get relief in one therapy would seek another. The professional literature is full of examples. Thus one therapist writes of a thirty-two-year-old client:

By the time he was referred to me, he had received — in addition to [6 years of] psychoanalysis and his brief bout with behavior therapy — drug therapy, electroconvulsive therapy, primal therapy, transactional analysis, transcendental meditation, and existential therapy. He still suffered from agoraphobia and numerous other phobias, bathroom rituals, and other obsessive-compulsive problems.

Every therapist is familiar with cases like this. Some clients have had so much therapy that it takes a significant portion of the first visit(s) to list and briefly discuss it all. Not all clients go immediately to another program. Some give up for a while but then, months or years later, learn of another therapist or approach and decide to try again. Others wait until they feel they have sufficient time, money, and motivation for another attempt.

However, it is not only the failures who go on for more counseling. One study of patients who had just completed a course of therapy found that only 18 percent said they had "no need at all" for further treatment even though 80 percent said they were moderately to extremely satisfied with the counseling they just had. Those with the time and money are free to live out their therapy-going fantasies. In a period spanning about five years, Jerry Rubin attended over a score of New Wave therapies and far more than a score of therapeutic workshops. Exactly what he was looking for and what he achieved are not entirely clear, but his experience, though not typical, is no longer unusual. Many of the people I interviewed, though professing great benefit from and great satisfaction with Therapy A, soon thereafter went to Therapy B, and some to C, D, and E as well.

There are several reasons for this. One is to do more work on the same problems or issues, to integrate and extend changes already made. This shades into another reason, dealing with related issues. One example is a woman who became generally more assertive as a result of being in a women's group and then went to another program to work on being more assertive with her family. Another example comes from a couple who took Actualizations a few months after finishing the est training. They said they wanted the balance provided by the two programs: "est works mainly on the head, Actualizations on the heart." Dealing with relapses is another reason for seeking additional help. Clients may return to the original therapist or program or, for a variety of reasons, choose a new one.

People also go for more counseling when new problems come up, when a desire for further growth is felt, or when they experience any one of a number of dissatisfactions. The meta-message conveyed in therapy and in the culture at large is that if you experience almost any form of discontent, you should get expert assistance. This serves to bring new customers to therapy and to keep old ones coming back for more.

So far I have presented additional therapy as a serial matter, going to one program after another. But it happens simultaneously as well. It is no longer unusual for a person to be in more than one therapy at a time. Sometimes it is a matter of formats. A client goes for individual counseling and the therapist recommends simultaneous participation in a group. A couple goes to marital counseling and the therapist recommends that in addition to the joint sessions, each should also be in individual therapy with him. At other times it is a matter of a different kind of treatment. Couples in marital or sex therapy, for instance, might be told or decide on their own that a communications course or fair-fight training or Parent Effectiveness Training should be taken at the same time. Or, as has happened many times, a person in long-term individual therapy may decide to take est, sex therapy, or something else to supplement the treatment.

There is yet another way that therapy begets more therapy: continuing interminably with the treatment one started with. Although technically not the same as going from one program to another, it amounts to much the same thing, often involving more time and more sessions. Instead of seeking new healers and new approaches, or terminating at some point, the client stays on and on, finding new problems to deal with or doing more work on the old ones. Colleague Bernard Apfelbaum was consulted by a client who had been in psychoanalysis for thirty-one years, four times a week, without a break, and I recently read of a woman who had been seeing a psychiatrist for twenty-seven years. I have also heard therapists talk of clients who had been with them for fifteen, twenty, and more years. Such "lifers," as some therapists call them, are not as uncommon as many people think.

One way or another, therapy leads to more therapy for a large and apparently increasing number of people.

The main conclusions of our discussion of the outcomes of psychotherapy can be summed up as follows:

- For most problems, all the well-known methods achieve similar results.
- Some problems, those usually called neurotic, fare better in psychotherapy than do others. For a number of common complaints, including depression and most addictions, therapy is not especially effective or not as effective as other approaches.
- The large majority of clients report benefits from participation in therapy, benefits in the form of comfort, support, validation, increased knowledge and understanding, feeling better, and greater ability to cope. These clients feel good about their therapy experiences, seek more of them for themselves, and recommend counseling to friends.
- Behavior change is less often achieved than is commonly believed and the extent of change made is usually modest.
- Therapeutic changes, whatever their nature, are often short-lived.
- Counseling can harm as well as help.

What psychotherapy at its best can do is well captured by an old French maxim: "To cure sometimes, to help often, to comfort and console always." Therapy in our time can do no more — we will be lucky if it can do this much — and in the long run neither clients nor therapists benefit by pretending otherwise.

In order to develop a realistic perspective on the benefits and uses of therapy, there is one more myth that requires exploration. It is one of the most important of all, for it is both cause and consequence of our belief that there really are secret and powerful methods available for altering our lives and making us happier. That myth is the subject of the next chapter.

The Mystique
of Professional Therapy

"The soul that is sick cannot rightly prescribe for itself, except by following the instruction of wise men."

— CICERO

Myth 9
Only Specially Trained
Professionals Can Help People Change

WHAT CICERO SAID almost two thousand years ago is now received truth in America. More and more aspects of life are seen as symptoms and conditions that cannot be handled on one's own, requiring instead consultation and instruction from experts. It is understandable that professional therapists should believe there is something special, even unique, about what they offer and that they should belittle the attempts of others to comfort and aid people in distress, including the sufferers themselves. It is understandable for the simple reason that the less competent you seem to be and the more competent the experts are thought to be, the greater is this stature, power, and wealth. It is also understandable that those of us who aren't experts, given our respect for what therapists have to say and given our desire to believe there really is some magic out there to make thngs better, are buying the ideas therapists sell.

There are two main views as to what the specialness of therapy consists of. The first focuses on the relationship between therapist and client, a relationship said to be characterized by qualities such as objectivity, trust warmth, empathy, positive regard, caring, and confidentiality. Such relationships are often called helping relationships and are thought to be rare or nonexistent outside of therapists' offices, and participation in one is considered sufficient to allow clients to change and feel better. These special relationships are not limited to the traditional one therapist–one client format. In recent years, with the proliferation of various group therapies, much has been made of their specialness. In his fine textbook of social psychology, *The Social Animal*, Elliot Aronson describes a fruitful experience between Sam and Harry in an encounter group. He then says: "But who needs a group? Couldn't Sam and Harry have done just as well by themselves? No. They almost certainly would have ended by calling each other names, hurting each other's feelings, and making each other angry. . . . It is not easy to talk straight." Aronson seems to be denying the possibility of honesty and real communication outside of a group with a trained leader. He seems to be saying that therapy is the only place, or the main place, that people can feel secure, express and explore themselves, develop understanding, and make desired changes. His point of view is not unusual.

At times the therapeutic relationship seems almost a mystical entity, beyond understanding but nonetheless capable of great things. As a student, one of my first clients was a man awaiting trial for assault with a deadly weapon. Violence was almost a way of life for him and I had no idea how to be helpful. When I asked my supervisors for advice, which I frequently did, the answer was that I was already doing what was necessary, supplying a "unique relationship" or a "corrective emotional experience" that would somehow allow him to change. Although I saw this man for almost a year and the only changes I observed were in me — I became more and more frustrated and upset by my inability to help him — my supervisors insisted to the very end that I was doing something important merely by meeting with my client every week and therefore providing a therapeutic relationship.

The second view of therapeutic specialness involves superior knowledge and technology. Therapists know things that others do not: they can assess and diagnose problems and determine their origins, and they have special skills with which to change them. Behavior therapists and sex therapists are probably the best-known exemplars of this position, although many psychiatrists make the case that their medical training gives them special expertise in diagnosing problems and especially in separating physical and emotional components.

Three questions can be raised about the idea of therapeutic uniqueness, two concerning means, the other ends. Are professional therapists better than other people at providing so-called helping relationships? Do they have knowledge and skills that others lack? And, most important, do professionals achieve better results than those with little or no formal training?

Regarding helping relationships, there is fairly consistent evidence that professionals are no better at providing them than are lay people. One study found that laypersons with less than a hundred hours of training communicated to clients approximately the same levels of empathy and warmth as a group of highly experienced professionals, including Carl Rogers and Rollo May. The goal toward which the helping relationship aims, patient self-exploration, was about the same for clients seeing the professionals and the nonprofessionals. In another report, one dealing with simulated therapy interviews, interviewees rated untrained college student interviewers to be as warm, genuine, and empathic as experienced counselors; further, they felt more accepted and less anxious with the nonprofessionals. Similar findings have been reported in many studies.

If you think about it, there is nothing surprising about these results. No one has a monopoly on caring relationships. Some people are very good at such things and others are not, but since therapists are selected on the basis of academic performance and not because of relationship qualities, there is little reason to think they would excel in this area. And there is some evidence that professional training decreases the level of relationship skills.

There is little about helping relationships that most people can't get outside of therapy. With a spouse, parent, friend, teacher, cleric, and sometimes even a stranger you may be able to get respectful listening, sympathy and empathy, caring, and so forth. Here is a common example:

Let's use the hypothetical case from chapter 7 of the woman — call her Sue — whose husband left her. Recall that she was confused, depressed, not doing well at work, generally at loose ends, and she finally went into therapy. But now assume that instead of going to a counselor she decides to confide in Martha, a woman she has known for several years. Martha listens attentively as Sue describes what has been happening to her, and Sue feels better just getting the words and the feelings out. Then Sue listens as Martha recounts what she went through during her divorce, which was very similar to what Sue is now experiencing. It was difficult for a long time — lots of loneliness, sadness, and a sense of failure — but Martha managed to get through it and now, looking back, she is certain it was all for the best. She invites Sue to have lunch with her in a few days and says she will be available whenever Sue wants to talk or needs a shoulder to cry on. Sue leaves the discussion feeling much better and with a strong feeling that she too will manage. The idea of spending another night alone hurts, but as a result of her talk with Martha, she realizes that nights with her husband weren't exactly wonderful. She'll miss the company and the body contact, but it's a relief not to have the arguments and the withdrawals and, come to think about it, his snoring. She knows she'll cope and survive.

Most of us have had experiences something like this. Someone was there for us, listened and understood, conveyed a sense of confidence in our ability to muddle through, and perhaps shared similar experiences. We usually felt better after such exchanges and had more faith in ourselves — exactly what many people feel after going to therapy. Helping and comforting relationships are not special to professional therapy.

Some experts, however, have made much of the fact that a professional therapist is a socially sanctioned healer while most of the other people you might talk to are not, and that this may make a difference; that there may be more healing power in a professional relationship, even if there isn't more warmth, caring, and so forth, just because it is socially sanctioned. There may be something to this. Certainly some of us feel more confidence in what our physician tells us than in what Aunt Freida says, and we may be more willing to following the advice of the doctor than the aunt even though their messages are basically the same. But this is really a question of results and, as we shall soon see, there is not much support for the idea that socially sanctioned healers achieve better outcomes than others.

Regarding therapeutic knowledge: it is undoubtedly true that professionals know things that other people don't. Very few non-professionals have spent years studying the works of Freud, Jung, Rogers, Wolpe, Ellis, Berne, and other authorities. Very few non-therapists have tried to find their way through the labyrinth of the *Diagnostic and Statistical Manual of Mental Disorders* or know the difference between autism and anxiety neurosis. So it must be granted that therapists have knowledge few others do. But therapists would not want to leave it there. From their knowledge, they say, they have fashioned special skills, a technology of behavior change, and these skills are really what differentiate them from nonprofessionals. Who else but a trained professional would know how systematically to desensitize a phobia, to put someone in a deep hypnotic trance, when and how to interpret transference reactions, to train someone to safely become more assertive, or to teach a couple to fight fairly?

Certainly therapists have skills which are said to be useful for altering behavior, but I wonder just how special these skills are. Take the example of systematic desensitization, considered a high form of behavioral technology. More so than anything else, it is what made behavior therapy into the flourishing enterprise that it is today. Instead of merely talking with a client about his fears or, worse yet, spending years trying to determine where and when they developed, the therapist applies carefully trained skills. With the client's assistance, a list is compiled of all the fears in a given category, everything related to the fear of speaking in public, for example, in ascending order of fearfulness (e.g., from speaking out in a small gathering of friends to giving a formal speech before a large audience). Then the client is trained in a response, usually deep relaxation, that inhibits anxiety, and gradually the fearful items are presented to him in the presence of that inhibiting response. As soon as one item on the list no longer evokes anxiety, the next item is presented, until all items have been covered and none of them makes the client very fearful.

It sounds good and it often works. But is it uncommon knowledge, requiring a high degree of technical skill to administer? Joseph Wolpe, the developer of systematic desensitization, would like you to believe it is. In his only book for lay readers, *Our Useless Fears*, he repeatedly emphasizes the need for a trained therapist and gives the subtitle "Why Expert Help Is Necessary" to one of his chapters. Yet he is wrong. Systematic desensitization as he does it may be new and require special training, but the basic method has been common knowledge for a very long time. Wolpe himself gives several examples of the successful use of desensitization by people who had no knowledge of his work. And I saw it practiced frequently in my childhood, years before behavior therapy had been invented, on the beaches of New Jersey with children who were afraid of water. The child was given a trusted adult to hang on to and sometimes a favorite toy as well, which probably made him feel more secure and relaxed; a game was made of it by kicking and splashing, which is a nice distraction; very gradually "therapist" and "client" made their way into deeper water; and sometimes the child's competitive spirit was enlisted by pointing out that his brother or sister wasn't afraid. Most of the "treatments" I observed were successful in a short period of time. Were there failures? Certainly, but unsuccessful cases are not unknown in professional therapy either. And the same can be said about relapses. Ironically, Wolpe mentions a mother who desensitizes her child to the water and then he moves on as if this meant nothing at all. But it means a great deal.

What therapists overlook is that all of us to some extent are experts on doing therapy on ourselves and others. Almost every day of our lives each of us is involved in exploring, understanding, comforting, controlling, and changing ourselves and those around us. We are receiving and doing what would be called therapy if it was done by a professional. No doubt some of us are far more successful than others in our informal therapeutic attempts, but the same can be said of professionals. Here are some examples of self-therapy:

- "Whenever I find myself dwelling on the possibility of failure, I loudly tell myself to stop and then focus my attention on something more positive."
- "When I do something that's hard for me, like studying for three

straight hours, I reward myself with an hour of television or a special meal."

- "If I feel ready to explode, I either beat the shit out of my punching bag or drive on the freeway with my windows closed and just scream whatever obscenities come to mind."

- "If I'm uptight during sex, I fight off the negative feelings by focusing on how he's touching me and how good it feels, just getting into the sensations, and usually that makes me more relaxed and I get more turned on."

- "When I've had a stressful day at work, I come home, put on the headphones and turn on the stereo, lay on the couch and pretty soon there's nothing but me and the music, and sometimes me disappears and there's only sweet sound. Everything slows down and I emerge feeling calmer and stronger."

All of these devices, as well as countless others, have been taken over by therapists, given fancy labels, and made to sound esoteric. (The technical names for the examples given are, in order, thought stopping, positive reinforcement, catharsis, sensate focus, and either trance induction or deep relaxation.) But all these things, or something very much like them, have been common knowledge and in common use for a long, long time. Self-therapy becomes especially prominent when problems arise. People are by nature problem-solving creatures and we get very busy when confronted by difficulties. But our own efforts don't seem very impressive to us — often we are even oblivious to what we are doing. Nonetheless they are remarkably effective much of the time and not very different from the similar "treatments" we are willing to applaud when done by professionals.

We also help one another. In an age when some people seem uncertain what families are for, it is perhaps necessary to state that one of their main functions has been to support, comfort, control, and guide their members. What is called behavioral technology is one of the things that people, in and out of families, have to offer to each other. Sex therapy, like systematic desensitization, is considered by many to consist of uncommon skills; this is what makes it more effective than traditional talking therapy. But millions of people had these skills before professional therapists started dealing with sex problems. Here is an example I've heard countless times and which I am sure has been repeated since the first time men and women thought it might be interesting to get together.

> For years I thought sex was weird. Some guy would paw you a while, then get on top and hump away a few minutes, and that was it. I couldn't figure out what was so interesting about the whole thing. Until I met Frank. He said he wanted to make it good for me and asked what I liked, a question I couldn't even answer then. He caressed me all over nice and lovingly and, as it went on, I really started to feel good, and we didn't have intercourse until I was ready. About the third or fourth time we did this, I had an orgasm for the first time in my life and I've been having them ever since.

In their book, *Shared Intimacies,* based on interviews with over a hundred women, Lonnie Barbach and Linda Levine report that virtually all of the women had experienced sex problems at some time. "A few sought professional help, but they were by far in the minority. Most who succeeded in overcoming their problems did so on their own or with the aid of their partner." The high technology supposedly developed by and the exclusive property of professional counselors is actually not much more than common sense applied to a particular problem, and common sense is not as rare as we are beginning to think.

With very few exceptions, therapists have little verifiable understanding of what causes change, though this doesn't prevent them from talking as if they do. Stripped of jargon, their explanations usually come down to vague generalities or common sense; e.g., some kind of understanding of the problem (but what is meant by understanding and exactly what should it be of — the cause of the problem, what is maintaining it now, or something else?); some kind of relationship with a professional healer (but what kind of relationship and how does this differ from relationships with nonprofessionals?); communication or expressiveness (of what? to whom? in what ways?); feedback from others (of what? under what circumstances? which others?); and exposure to the things we fear (which is probably true but tells us little we already didn't know because it turns out that all kinds of exposure, including the exact opposite of desensitization, prolonged exposure to feared objects under conditions that elicit very high levels of anxiety — what therapists call implosion or flooding and what laypeople refer to as a "sink or swim" approach — work equally well). In addition, some cherished beliefs about change held by the experts are simply erroneous, or at least are not supported by research. An example is provided by the literature on encounter groups, which is full of strongly held beliefs about what is essential for change to take place. A well-done and large-scale study of encounter groups sought to determine the validity of these opinions. The investigators found that a number of the processes thought to be crucial failed to show any association with change. "The expression of anger, of rage, the experience of profound emotions, the receipt of feedback, self-disclosures in and of themselves, appeared not to differentiate markedly those who learned and those who remained unchanged." They also didn't differentiate between those who were harmed by the group experience and those who weren't.

That professional therapists should have so many, often contradictory, theories of change, each vigorously defended by its proponents and equally vigorously attacked by other experts, should alert us to two possibilities: that all these explanations are true of some people some of the time, and that our knowledge of what causes change, in or out of therapy, is not very profound.

But the question of therapeutic uniqueness and superiority cannot be decided by looking at the validity of therapeutic theories. The real test lies elsewhere: in whether or not professionals produce better results than those without special training. The answer, hard as it may be to accept, is that they don't.

That healers with little or no formal training are as good as professional therapists has been demonstrated in a number of studies. In what is probably the best of them, done at Vanderbilt University by Hans Strupp and his colleagues, young male clients were seen in individual therapy for no more than twenty-five sessions by either professional therapists or nonprofessionals. The professionals were chosen on the basis of their reputation for clinical expertise; average length of experience doing counseling was twenty-three years. These were highly competent and experienced counselors. The nonprofessionals "were college professors selected on the basis of their reputation for warmth, trustworthiness, and interest in students." None of them had any training or experience in therapy. The results were quite clear: "Patients undergoing psychotherapy with college professors showed, on the average, quantitatively as much improvement as patients treated by experienced professional therapists."

Although numerous attempts have been made to belittle or discredit these results, including by the Vanderbilt researchers themselves, it is very hard to do so on any reasonable basis. While it is true that severely disturbed and suicidal patients were screened out, the clients accepted for treatment were typical of those seen in most clinics and private practices: depression and anxiety reaction were the main diagnoses, but even borderline personalities and obsessional trends were present. While the clients were typical, the professional therapists were not: they were the best that could be found. Despite the evidence that the study was indeed a fair test and that the results mean exactly what they say, Strupp and others argue that professionals really are better. For example, Strupp writes that "some professors experienced difficulty in discharging their assignment (e.g., they seemed to run out of relevant material to discuss, they were unable to work toward specific goals and very few of them would have been willing or able to treat patients over more extended periods of time)." This is a curious point. Why should the professors find more things to discuss if the problem was already resolved or it was clear that no progress, or no more progress, could be made? Why should they see clients for longer? There is little doubt, given the long-term bias of most therapists, that the professionals could have extended treatment far beyond twenty-five sessions and that they could have found mountains of material to discuss. But to what end? There is no evidence that any of this would have changed the results. Immediately after the sentence quoted above, Strupp adds this: "Professional therapists, by virtue of their training and clinical experience, are clearly much better equipped to deal with the vagaries and vicissitudes encountered in the interactions with most patients." Yet this statement amounts to little more than wishful thinking and has nothing to do with the study Strupp conducted or any other studies I am aware of. The professional counselors in Strupp's research — despite their long experience and perceived competence, despite their ability to deal with "the vagaries and vicissitudes" of clinical practice, and despite their skill in finding relevant material to discuss and their willingness to extend the length of treatment — could not, or at least did not, get better results than the nonprofessional therapists, and that is really the only thing that matters.

A recent review comparing the effectiveness of professional therapists with paraprofessionals (those with little therapy training) in forty-two studies strongly suggests that the Vanderbilt results are not a fluke. In only one of these studies were professionals significantly more effective than paraprofessionals. The two groups were equally helpful in a majority of the investigations but paraprofessionals came out best in twelve reports. And the problems involved in these studies just about covered the board, including the treatment of hospitalized psychotics. The reviewer, psychologist Joseph Durlak, concludes:

> These data suggest that professionals do not necessarily possess demonstrably superior clinical skills, in terms of measurable outcome, when compared with paraprofessionals. Moreover, professional mental health education, training, and experience are not necessarily prerequisites for an effective helping person.

A striking illustration of nonprofessional or paraprofessional effectiveness come from two people widely and erroneously thought to be therapy professionals, Masters and Johnson. Although several critics, including me, have questioned their research and results, there are many who accept their claims, higher than almost anyone else's, as valid. Such acceptance creates an interesting situation because it indicates that those without professional therapy training do better than most professionals. Masters's medical training was in gynecology and Johnson has no college degree at all, not even a B.A. By no stretch of the imagination can either be considered a professional therapist and the same is true of Robert Kolodny, director of training at the Masters and Johnson Institute, whose medical specialty is endocrinology. Kolodny received his therapy training from two nonprofessionals, Masters and Johnson. Similar examples are found in psychoanalysis. When Freud was alive, becoming an analyst was more dependent upon being accepted by him than upon credentials and training. Two of the leading analysts of the last thirty years, Freud's daughter Anna and Erik Erikson, had only high school educations. I have no way of determining their therapeutic effectiveness, but I have never heard anyone say it was less than that of their presumably better trained colleagues.

Encounter groups provide another example of the ability of people to get what they need from each other or with minimal professional help. Some encounter groups do not have leaders but use tape-recordings for guidance. These recordings, prepared by therapists, offer material for discussion and exercises to do. Surprisingly, tape groups don't differ much in outcome from groups led by therapists and other trained leaders. Two tape groups were among the seventeen groups studied by Lieberman, Yalom, and Miles at Stanford University, the other fifteen of which were led by highly experienced leaders. One of the tape groups was the second most successful of all the groups and the other was average. It can be said that since professionals made the tapes, they should receive some credit for the results. Granted, but something is surely amiss if packaged tape instructions, prepared months ahead of time by someone who has no knowledge of the group participants and no feedback about what goes on in the group, lead to the same results as groups with trained leaders in attendance and in control throughout the sessions. Besides, there is evidence that at least one of these groups was more an example of self-help than of tape-help. The group that did so well was less than satisfied with the taped instructions and followed them only "when we felt like it." It is also of interest that the two tape groups produced fewer negative effects than many of the groups with trained leaders and that the percentage of group members suffering harm in the Stanford project was much higher than that in an encounter group study in Berkeley, where most of the leaders were nonprofessionals with very little training.

Self-help organizations offer more evidence for the efficacy of nonprofessional help, or at least for the lack of superiority of professional guidance. Although the results of treatment for addictions are nothing to brag about, self-help groups do no worse than professional therapists. I have already noted that AA is about as useful to alcoholics as is professional counseling. Another example comes from Albert Stunkard's study of Take Off Pounds Sensibly (TOPS), founded by a Milwaukee housewife and now claiming over 350,000 members. Stunkard compared twenty-two TOPS chapters with each other and with fourteen groups of obese patients treated by medical/psychological methods. His conclusion:

> The results achieved by the single most effective TOPS chapter were better than those of any of the reported medical studies. The five most effective TOPS chapters ranked with the best in the medical literature. The average for all TOPS chapters was similar to the average achieved by medical treatment. . . . These comparisons offer strong evidence of the effectiveness of TOPS, since the medical results with one exception are not those of the average practitioner but were obtained by physicians specializing in the treatment of obesity.

Here, as in the Vanderbilt study, nonprofessionals were the equal of not just average clinicians but of real experts. In the late 1960s Synanon claimed to be, and many believed that it was, more effective than professional programs in rehabilitating drug addicts. These claims have since been discredited, but it still appears that Synanon was about as effective as professionals.

Actually, when it comes to breaking addictions it seems that the greatest success is achieved when people don't get any sort of outside help. Most people who have given up smoking, drinking, and drugs, or who have lost weight have done so on their own. As far as has been determined to date, the success rates of these truly self-help efforts are far higher than those achieved by outside experts. It is not clear if the lower effectiveness of professional helpers is due to the fact of working with a more difficult population, those who have been unsuccessful at helping themselves, or because the helpers hamper rather than facilitate change.

There is one objection to what has been presented that I want to

discuss. While acknowledging that some laypersons and paraprofessionals are effective healers, this objection nevertheless concludes
that professionals are better. The reasoning goes like this. The good
laypeople are precisely the ones selected for research studies and
paraprofessional training, but there aren't many of them. The
chances that you can find one in your environment are not great.
Most of the laypeople you consult will not be effective. On the other
hand most professionals, because of their long training and because
they have survived several screening processes (admission to graduate or medical school, supervision and testing during school and
internships, and licensing examinations), are at least competent.
The chances of getting quality help are therefore higher with professionals than with nonprofessionals.

This argument has several fallacies. It fails to explain, for instance, why there is so much evidence, such as presented earlier,
indicating that laypeople are as effective or more effective than professionals, even when the latter are chosen because of great experience and skill. There is also reason to question the assumption that
most professionals are competent. Doubts have been expressed by
a number of therapist-researchers who have been exposed to the
work of large numbers of counselors and in many cases to their
clients as well. Hans Strupp shares Paul Meehl's estimate that only
one-fifth of therapists are competent, and Allen Bergin, without
giving a number, fully agreed "that many therapists are not very
competent." What makes these statements impossible to dismiss is
the fact that Strupp and Bergin are two of the most respected names
in psychotherapy research in America. After reviewing research on
how therapists relate to their clients, two leading researchers conclude that two out of three counselors "are ineffective or harmful."
Carl Rogers, long a critic of how therapists are selected and trained,
says "there are as many *certified* charlatans and exploiters of people
as there are uncertified." In his *Complete Guide to Therapy*, psychiatrist Joel Kovel states, "It is impossible to avoid the observation that ineptitude is more the rule than the exception in the world
of therapy." And in conversations with many counselors over more
than a decade, I have been struck by how many believe that most
of their colleagues aren't very good.

It is not certain exactly what should be made of the foregoing. Some of the negative judgments are probably due to the lack of basic knowledge and consensus about therapy. Since counselors often do not agree about means and ends, many believe that those whose practice differs from their own are ipso facto incompetent. We also shouldn't forget about petty jealousy and other feelings that make people demean the work of others. Whatever explanations are given, however, it seems foolhardy at this point to ignore the fact that many therapists, including some of the leading figures in the field, do not agree that therapeutic competence is the rule. So far professional counselors have not demonstrated either that they are more effective than nonprofessionals or even that most of them are competent.

This is not to say, of course, that most laypeople are effective healers. Some are generally good, some are better with certain problems and issues than others, some probably aren't helpful at all, and undoubtedly some are harmful more often than not. But it appears that the same is probably true of professionals. There simply is no evidence that you will accomplish more with a carefully chosen professional than with a carefully chosen nonprofessional or, to do it another way, with a randomly selected professional or randomly selected nonprofessional.

Therapists and the public alike have been seduced by jargon and written material without end into thinking that something of great importance must be going on. But the evidence simply will not support either the idea of therapeutic uniqueness or professional supremacy. As two therapy researchers say, "For too long we have viewed psychotherapy as an isolated, highly unique situation. Clearly, it is not." It is difficult to avoid the conclusion that the special knowledge therapists do possess — what they learn in school and spout back in their licensing examinations — is mainly a formality and a distraction. Though perhaps interesting in its own right, this knowledge has little to do with making people feel good and helping them to change.

Psychotherapy — the consoling, supporting, and influencing of people — is ubiquitous. It goes on every day of our lives, and we are the ones who are doing and receiving it. In general, professionals don't know more about it than laypeople do and aren't more successful in its application. But that is a hard conclusion to accept in a society deeply imbued with the conviction that somewhere out there is someone who has a secret method that will heal whatever ails us.

Some Consequences
of Chasing Rainbows

"With the aid of therapeutic ideas and notions, we are able to cultivate our problems with a refinement perhaps unknown to any other nation in history. We have become connoiseurs of grievance — one nation problematical, with anxiety and aggravation for all."

— JOSEPH EPSTEIN

"We must grudgingly admit that even as we were trying to devise, with scientific determinism, a therapy for the few, we were led to promote an ethical disease among the many."

— ERIK ERIKSON

"The 'cure' . . . consists precisely in the individual's reconciliation to that modest extent to which he or she can grow. To pretend that there are no boundaries to that space invites disaster."

—R. D. ROSEN

I HAVE JUST GIVEN a talk about love and sex. I am tired and want to go to my hotel and sleep, but there is a long line of people who want a few minutes of my time, to express appreciation, to disagree, and, more often than not, to tell me their troubles and ask for advice. So I stay and listen. Although it happens all the time, I am still surprised by the concern and anxiety I hear. Most of the questions have to do with relationships and sex, but lots of other things also come up. People ask how to avoid developing problems with their partners; how to make better use of their time and abilities; how to be more loving; how to know if they really understand what their spouses are thinking and feeling; how to know if their partner has an orgasm, is sexually satisfied, or is having an affair; what to do in situations where they don't know what they want; how to have a more positive attitude toward life; what to do now that they didn't get all they wanted from therapy. Mixed in with these questions are the many dealing with their children: how to prevent them from taking drugs and from developing destructive ways of dealing with each other; how to prevent homosexuality, promiscuity, and sexual irresponsibility; how to help them find, be, and develop themselves to the limit; how to make them take more responsibility. The constant themes are confusion, regret, guilt, and fear. Similar themes are sounded by my own clients and by people who call for information about therapy. They are apologetic about everything: their inhibitions and passivity, not communicating better, not having done better in past therapies, not having sought help sooner. In some bizarre Kafkaesque way, they have tried themselves in the court of life and found themselves guilty, even though they often aren't sure of what. All they seem to know for certain is that they aren't as good or as skillful or as competent as they could and should be.

What I hear is not unusual; others who give talks hear much the same things. You can hear it too. Listen to the voices of callers and members of the audience as they ask the experts on radio and television if they have done and are doing right by themselves, their spouses, lovers, friends, and others.

How can this be? How is it that we hear so much self-reproach, fear, and discontent among those who have been therapized and presumably liberated? How is it that those who have lived by therapeutic suggestion, as most in my audiences and most of my clients have, still seem so insecure and so unsure of themselves? The answer, in a nutshell, is that therapeutic ideology and practice carry messages and encourage expectations that lead to such feelings. Without denying that counseling is beneficial to many people, I am saying that it also leads to anxiety, guilt, and unhappiness. There are prices to be paid for the pursuit of the therapeutic dream, and these prices are steeper than is generally assumed.

I realize that these statements may sound strange to many readers. Except for the kinds of negative effects discussed in chapter 9, harm done because of misdiagnosis or wrongfully applied treatment, and for the financial cost of being in therapy, we are not used to thinking that counseling exacts a toll. At worst, it's just a waste of time and money. I suggest there's a lot more to it than this.

Let's start at the most general level, with therapy's implied statement about you. We have come to believe that therapy is unlike other institutions. Religions, families, schools, and other societal agencies all have long lists of dos and don'ts, all have lots of reasons why you're bad or wrong (mainly because you don't live up to their standards), and all want to change the way you are. Therapy, on the other hand, is believed to be a unique haven of unconditional acceptance where you can be yourself. A woman can be aggressive and a man tender, you can talk about homosexual or sadistic fantasies, and you can scream, cry, laugh, or do anything you want. No shoulds, no oughts, no rules, and no limiting definitions. Or so the story goes.

But therapy carries the same message as other institutions and belief systems: there is something wrong with the way you are and you ought to do something about it. Richard Farson's comment about his brand of therapy is relevant to all therapeutic thinking: "Instead of accepting and honoring human beings, humanistic psychology now seems bent on reforming them." When it comes down to it, therapy isn't any more accepting of people than are other institutions. It looks more accepting, but looks in this case are deceptive. You are encouraged to be open and say whatever you want because that is considered a prerequisite for finding out what the matter is with you and how to change it. You can say and do things that wouldn't go elsewhere not because therapy doesn't have rules and standards but rather because therapy has somewhat different rules. If you want to determine for yourself how accepting therapy is, try one of the following: refuse to share your feelings in an encounter group or to role-play when your counselor suggests it; don't follow the now common therapeutic rule of using "I language" but instead say things like "*we* enjoyed the trip" or "*you* make me angry"; don't do homework assigned by the therapist; disagree with his interpretation of what your problem is and how it developed; disobey est's rules regarding eating and going to the bathroom; or tell your therapist that although you haven't worked on or resolved all the issues he thinks you should, you feel ready to leave counseling.

It is a basic tenet of therapeutic ideology that people are not okay as they are; that's why they need therapy. In the therapeutic view, people are not regarded as evil nor as having done anything they should feel guilty about, but there is certainly something wrong with them. Specifically, they are too guilty, too inhibited, not confident and assertive enough, not able to express and fulfill themselves properly, and without a doubt not as joyful and as free from stress as they ought to be. The cardinal sin of our time, which therapy both serves and exploits, seems to be not making the most of ourselves, allowing ourselves to be held back by unnecessary constraints, not getting all we can from life. Therapeutic thinking finds us doing at least as many things wrong as churches, parents, and others find, and has at least as many rules for being different. Just as some religions emphasize sinfulness and threaten eternal damnation in order to sell salvation, therapy emphasizes incompetence and threatens lack of fulfillment in order to sell itself. As therapeutic thinking spreads to more and more areas of life, it calls attention to more and more things you aren't doing right. Even if you don't have a full-blown psychosis or neurosis, you're not off the hook. You'll soon hear, if you haven't already, that your communication skills, work patterns, use of time, child-rearing, or something else is not as it should be.

Disdain for people as they are, regardless of the source of the feeling, has predictable results. It produces concern, fear, guilt, and anxiety. Therapists often lament the low esteem in which people hold themselves and blame religion and parents. But counselors themselves are also responsible. Through their continual pointing out of places where people are not living up to their potential and are not doing things in the approved therapeutic manner they help produce the problems they inveigh against. Therapists encourage us to look at and take seriously things which we might otherwise overlook or at least not get worked up about, encourage us to become aware of every nook and cranny of our lives and to make problems out of annoyances and difficulties. We can no longer brush aside the fact that we're not very assertive or don't usually express what's on our minds. These things are not trivial, they are very important. It becomes harder to overlook anything and we become increasingly dissatisfied with ourselves. Whatever the shape of our lives, it pales in comparison with what we hear about peak experiences, total communication, ecstatic sex, ever-growing and joyful relationships, and so on. Good feelings, good relationships, good sex always seem somewhere out there, things we have yet to attain, while our own lives look impoverished and our own efforts incompetent. Vast dissatisfaction with oneself is one of therapeutic thinking's most important products.

I don't wish to give therapy more credit or blame than it deserves. It is not the only institution in this society that generates disdain for us and what we have. As we know, whole industries are involved in the attempt to make us discontented with how we look and smell, what we eat, and what we own, from clothes to cars to furniture and homes. Therapy continues an old American tradition consisting of two ideas: whatever you are doing right now is not quite enough, and true happiness is possible if only you change your ways (get a different mouthwash, make more money, buy a different car, get involved in a new therapy). Tocqueville observed the effects of this tradition a hundred and fifty years ago. Noting that Americans "are forever brooding over advantages they do not possess," he went on:

> Besides the good things that he possesses, he every instant fancies a thousand others that death will prevent him from trying if he does not try them soon. This thought fills him with anxiety, fear, and regret and keeps his mind in ceaseless trepidation, which leads him perpetually to change his plans and his abode. . . . Death at length overtakes him, but it is before he is weary of this bootless chase of that complete felicity which forever escapes him.

The phenomenon lives on. Not long ago we called it "keeping up with the Joneses," the attempt to acquire as many material goods as our neighbors; this would relieve our anxiety by proving we were as good as others and it might even make us happy. Although material wealth is still important, greater attention is now focused on psychological aspects of life: how open, how free, how expressive, and how fulfilled we are. I don't think Tocqueville would have been surprised by the anxiety and concern so many of us feel about how we are doing in these areas. Nor would he have been surprised by what I saw several years ago when I visited a friend on the final day of his advanced Arica training. The scene in his hotel room was straight out of Fellini. There were fifteen to twenty Arica students in various stages of undress and states of unconsciousness, most of them babbling incoherently about being blissed out and enlightened. At one point, someone started talking about what he was going to do next, which brought most of the group into a semi-conscious state. Despite the fact that all of them had participated in the Arica program for over a year, almost all were on their way to other growth programs, where they hoped to elevate themselves still further. When my friend announced that I had attended est, where many of them were going next, I became the center of attention. What had est done for me? Would it be useful to people as enlightened as they thought themselves to be? Was it best to go directly to est or should they do something else first? If they did go to est, where should they go afterward? Even in my confused state, which was probably appropriate for an unenlightened clod like me, I remember being struck by the anxiety I heard and thinking that this was a group on a quest, always searching for more and never being satisfied with what they found.

Most forms of human discontent are the result of a disparity between what we have and are and what we feel we should have and be. Therapeutic thinking serves to widen the discrepancy both by finding more things wrong with how we are and by holding out increasingly utopian notions of what we should be, thereby producing a permanent state of discontent. Let's look at some examples.

Mental health experts have helped create an expectation that one should feel good most of the time. A book by psychiatrist David Burns, appropriately titled *Feeling Good*, informs us that "depression is *not* a precious, genuine, or important human experience. It is a phony, synthetic counterfeit." So we don't have to feel depressed. What about moodiness? That's not necessary either. Arthur Janov says that after Primal Therapy clients are "never moody." Well, what about anxiety? We can live without that as well. A prominent theme in therapeutic thinking over the years has been, as Rollo May puts it, that "mental health is living without anxiety." Psychoanalysts even thought it was possible to teach parents how to raise children who felt no anxiety. Wayne Dyer tells us that guilt and worry are "useless emotions" and that you can say farewell to anger.

So we got the idea that we didn't have to put up with negative affect, obviously a notion with tremendous appeal. Even if we experienced some of the unnecessary feelings, it wouldn't have to be for long. They could be expressed and dealt with simply and directly, leaving us with mainly good feelings. But somehow it didn't work. Despite the reading, the courses, and the therapy we still were anxious, depressed, guilty, and angry. Some people keep trying, figuring they just need a better therapy or to try harder. Others have found a better way: chemical additives that make them feel better. Some of these people become addicted or suffer in other ways from their chemical cures and then go or are sent to therapists, who themselves had a part in causing the problem. It is hard to disagree with what Nicholas Cummings said in his Presidential Address to the American Psychological Association:

It may be that the mental health movement has promised the American people a freedom from anxiety that is neither possible nor realistic, resulting in an expectation that we have a right to feel good. We may never know to what extent we ourselves have contributed to the steep rise in alcohol consumption and the almost universal reliance by physicians on the tranquilizer.

Therapeutic ideology has also had considerable impact on our intimate relationships. A national survey published by the Family Services Association reports that the main reasons for divorce are no longer desertion, finances, religious differences, brutality, and adultery. Rather, the three leading complaints are failures in communication, difficulties in child-rearing, and sexual dissatisfaction. Richard Farson comments:

If we were to ask where married couples got the idea that they should be able to communicate openly, raise children effectively, and enjoy fulfilled sex lives, the answer would be that, at least to some degree, they have gotten these expectations from [therapists]. In our effort to improve those aspects of life we may have so emphasized them that they have become problems, enormous problems, problems that simply did not exist before our applications of technology provided new definitions of what relationships were supposed to be.

While therapists gleefully attack old myths about relationships — e.g., love conquers all and people in love don't fight — they posit new standards that cause as much trouble. They glorify both individuality (independence and self-assertiveness) and closeness (intimacy and connectedness), without being willing to confront the tension and even contradiction between the two. They paint rosy pictures of loving, cooperative, nonsexist, and growing relationships in which partners treat each other with respect and understanding, share intimate details of psychic goings-on, and help one another become whoever they want to be. Our soul doctors do allow that conflicts and bad feelings are part of close unions but these, they assure us, are easily resolved just as they are in therapy by communication in accord with certain rules and by simple techniques such as fair fighting.

Instead of realizing that loving relationships are incredibly difficult and that inherent in them are a lot of stress and a lot of problems, we assume that something like perfection is possible. We have been so innundated with what a relationship should be like that we are almost forced to dwell on the ways that the relationship we have falls short. Since all relationships have areas of great disagreement and difficulty, some of which cannot be changed no matter what is done, there is always something to worry and feel bad about. The doubts and worries increase when we try more communication and fair fighting and they don't help, when the conflicts and bad feelings remain. We wonder what is wrong with us, if we're really in love, if we need therapy or more therapy, or if we could do better with someone else. Such is hardly the route to contentment.

Relationships are difficult enough as it is. Our overblown expectations only make them worse. Accepting that strife and bad feelings — not the kind of prissy fights and expression of feeling therapists advocate, but cold-as-ice withdrawal; feelings of absolute oppression and the urge to kill; and dish-throwing, obscenity-screaming, totally unfair fights — are integral parts of intimate relationships, as are unresolvable differences, is extremely difficult these days, to a great extent because of what we have learned from therapists.

Sex is another area that has been significantly influenced by therapeutic notions. While there is no doubt that past and present sex experts have achieved some good, they have also created many problems, one of which concerns female orgasms. The trouble started with Freud's pronouncement that there was a right way for women to have orgasms, namely through the thrusting of the penis in the vagina. Anything else was "immature" and a sign of "frigidity." Here we have the usual therapeutic polarity: what you are now doing is wrong and there is a better, healthier way. A lot of women who had been happily orgasmic via clitoral stimulation realized there was something wrong with them and felt bad. Some of them went into psychoanalysis for their "problem," but continued to feel bad because analysis was not very successful in helping them have vaginal orgasms. In the 1960s and '70s, with the advent of the feminist movement and sex therapy, there was a rebellion against vaginal orgasms and the clitoris became enshrined as *the* site of female sexual response. Books and articles appeared in great number arguing that most of the vagina had few nerve endings and was therefore relatively insensitive to penile thrusting. The clitoris was where the nerves and the action were; far from being atypical or neurotic, clitoral orgasms were said to be the norm. The tables were turned. Women who regularly felt sensation in their vaginas during intercourse and had orgasms with penile thrusting wondered if they were put together properly. And, contrary to what the new sex experts said, there were a great many women in this group. One of them, a woman in her fifties, said this: "My orgasms have always come from intercourse. I was thirty-eight before I even heard of a clitoral orgasm, and then I felt like a freak." Since the clitoris was now everything, something had to be done about women who, although orgasmic in intercourse, could not climax with clitoral stimulation. Why should these women, just because they had vaginal orgasms, think they were functioning well? A new official problem was created just for them, what Masters and Johnson call "masturbatory orgasmic inadequacy."

Since the clitoris is easily stimulated by the woman herself, as the vagina is not, masturbation came to be seen by therapists as the main tool for teaching women to have orgasms, and therapeutic dogma became: you ought to masturbate, it's good for you. This represented a total about-face in medical and therapeutic thinking. The same group that gave us masturbation-leads-to-insanity-and-a-host-of-other-problems was now saying masturbation-is-normal-and-healthy-and-a-great-way-to-learn-about-yourself. Obviously today's physicians and therapists cannot be held responsible for the errors of their predecessors, but you might want to keep this about-face in mind the next time you hear an expert state with absolute certainty that so-and-so is what's right. Many of the women who come to me with sex problems and who don't masturbate feel guilty. They have accepted prevailing therapeutic notions about the subject — they believe masturbation isn't harmful and that they should do it. They neither well understand nor can make a case for their reluctance or, as they often call it, their "resistance." They apologize profusely for their inhibitions and hang-ups. They are also concerned that I'm going to try to persuade them. So in addition to the problem they bring in, they also have all this to worry and feel bad about.

As if this wasn't enough, recently some sex experts decided to reclaim the vagina. They said there is a place in the vagina (called the G spot in honor of its discoverer, gynecologist Ernest Grafenberg) whose stimulation results in orgasm for many women and even in ejaculation for quite a few. There is nothing exceptional about these ideas — clearly many women have exquisitely sensitive areas in their vaginas and apparently a small number of women expel some kind of fluid through their urethras during orgasm — and they are worthy of study. But before any of the hypotheses were tested and any of the basic facts were known — before, for instance, it was determined if the G spot is a true anatomical structure found in all women or what exactly is meant by female ejaculation and how widespread a phenomenon it was — several sex experts rushed to make the news public in a flurry of articles, interviews, and then a book, and they were soon followed by others in the field. The results were predictable. Therapists began to get letters and visits from women and their partners concerned about their inability to find the G spot, their inability to have orgasms when it was stimulated, and their inability to ejaculate. One woman wrote that her husband's question of "Did you come? did you come?" had been replaced with "Did you spurt? did you spurt?" She continued: "It was bad enough being watched over about having a climax. Now I'm supposed to ejaculate." Another woman had this to say: "Now my husband insists that every woman has a G spot, and last night he spent an hour trying to get me to find mine." Before he learned about G spots, she says, her husband was "perfectly content" with their sex life. "Now he's so eager to explore new ways that we're always fighting."

Even putting aside proper types of orgasm, masturbation, and female ejaculation, sex experts have issued a lot of proclamations about what sex should be like. I guess I shouldn't complain about these things because they have brought me many clients. People with no particular problems come in because sex doesn't match something they've read about: it's not as passionate, not as explosive, not as spontaneous, not as fulfilling. Men have fully accepted the idea that they should give their partners orgasms and satisfaction, and sometimes worry themselves into erection problems when their partners don't seem satisfied. Women have accepted the idea that they should have orgasms and sometimes prevent themselves from having them by trying so hard. Desire problems have become commonplace, partly because some people have felt so overwhelmed by all the requirements of sex that they've lost all interest; partly also because some other people have been persuaded that sex is terribly important and they're not going to tolerate one whit less than they think they need.

While affairs and open marriages were not invented by counselors, the experts have lent their prestige to extracurricular activities. Look at how one of the chief mischief-makers, Alex Comfort, stacks the deck against monogamy:

> Members of an open marriage are equals, support each other, divide what has to be done between them, discuss and resolve fairly the competing claims of their separate ambitions and wishes, avoid hurting or rejecting each other but don't rely on blackmail to keep property rights in one another. They are loving and committed but not jealous, and try to build security on adult instead of neurotic attitudes.

It might seem that jealousy would create an obstacle for advocates of open relationships, but the issue is quickly dismissed by calling it neurotic and by assurances such as the following from Comfort: "Secure and communicating couples who include each other in all their fantasies and pleasures aren't jealous."

Many people are encouraged by such statements to live out their fantasies. Some show no ill effects, but quite a few do. A distraught man called while I was on a radio talk show. He needed help but wasn't exactly sure what kind of help. About a year before he and his wife, after hearing a lot about open marriages, decided to give it a try. Things went reasonably well until the night he watched her have sex with another man. What he saw was very painful. She was in ecstasy; "she never moved or moaned like that when I was with her." The problem was compounded when his wife talked about how wonderful sex had been with this man. The caller felt wretched. He had lost confidence in himself as a man and a lover. Sex with his wife was no longer satisfying and the marriage was rapidly deteriorating. What could he do? When I asked if he and his wife had considered giving up sex with others, he replied they had stopped several months ago because of what was happening to their relationship. So what was the problem now? I asked. The problem, he said, was that "I can't forget what I saw and heard that night. It's with me all the time, in and out of bed."

I have talked to far too many people with similar stories to think this example is extreme. I have seen marriages destroyed by such goings-on and others that became much worse, and I am talking only about situations where it was agreed upon by both partners to have sex with other people. In *Thy Neighbor's Wife*, Gay Talese relates the pathetic story of John Bullaro who, along with his wife, experimented at Sandstone with sexual sharing. Bullaro does not end up well. He loses his wife, his job, and just about everything else. In Talese's words: "He saw whatever love and order that had been the stability of his life sacrificed to the whim of experimentation and change. . . . He was alone, jobless, without a sense of hope." Talese also tells us that John Williamson, founder of Sandstone and guru of sexual freedom, nonpossessiveness, and brave new vistas, brooded in his bedroom and barely spoke to anyone for almost two months after one of his favorite women ran off with another man.

Sexual possessiveness and jealousy may not be some of our more noble emotions but they are real and not as easy to deal with as therapists who write and conduct workshops about them would have us believe. Unfortunately, many have trusted counselors and others who preach liberation from everything and discovered only too late how wrong they were.

Parent-child relationships have received special attention from counselors and immeasurable havoc has resulted. Beginning with the work of Freud and the early behaviorists at the beginning of this century, the idea gained currency that parents could do irreparable harm to their children and, on the other hand, that correct training would lead to near-perfect or at least nonneurotic adults. Psychiatrist C. B. Chisholm told the World Health Organization that "the training of children is making a thousand neurotics for every one that psychiatrists can hope to cure." Parents were blamed for everything including schizophrenia, anxiety, homosexuality, alcoholism, and drug addiction. They were taught that "every action and every word of theirs had a lasting influence on the child's mind" and became incredibly vigilant and concerned, analyzing all possibilities, feelings, and behaviors, fearful they might make mistakes that would have momentous consequence. As Catherine Storr notes:

> When the child has night terrors, balks at going to school, is finicky about food, tells lies, is quarrelsome, jealous, rebellious — in short, shows any of the innumerable symptoms of normal childhood, the parents' confidence in their own judgment, even in their own feelings, is gravely undermined. They meant to do so well. They believed everything was going as it should, and now it appears that their good intentions have simply led them along the proverbial downward road, and, which increases their guilt still more, taking the child with them.

Parents became hyperalert and obsessed, lost confidence in themselves, and felt very guilty — the qualities I hear when people ask if they should do this or that regarding their children. Unless you equate confusion, concern, and guilt with effectiveness, it is doubtful they became better parents; it is far more likely that the opposite is true. But what about the children? — surely they benefited from their psychologically informed upbringing. Maybe they did, but you would have a hard time demonstrating it. Even as committed an advocate of such upbringing as Anna Freud notes that some of the tasks assigned to parents, such as ridding the child of anxiety, proved to be "impossible." Her conclusion:

> Psychoanalytic education did not succeed in becoming the preventive measure it had set out to be. It is true that the children who grew up under its influence were in some respects different from earlier generations, *but they were not freer from anxiety or from conflicts, and therefore not less exposed to neurotic or other mental illnesses.* [Emphasis added.]

Nonetheless, the heat goes on. Parents continue to be held responsible for all the usual things and new ones are continually added. A recent addition is sexism. If your son or daughter grows up believing in traditional ideas of what a man or woman is, guess who's at fault? Perhaps the most celebrated book on the subject is Letty Pogrebin's *Growing Up Free*, which comes complete with endorsements from a past president of the American Psychological Association, Dr. Benjamin Spock, and Phil Donahue. Ms. Pogrebin is not a psychologist, but her work is a good example of the therapeutic sensibility. She makes no bones about what she is doing: "My intention is to question everything we do with, to, for, and around children — our speaking habits, living styles, adult relationships, household chores, academic standards and our way of dealing with punishment, privilege, religion, television, sex, money, and love." Parents reading this book will find no end of things to be concerned and guilty about, things they are doing wrong, and better ways to handle just about everything. Rules, warnings, prohibitions, and commands are everywhere, hardly in keeping with the book's title. We are given "Ten Commandments for Nonhomophobic Parenthood," "Twelve Dos and Don'ts for Promoting Free-Flowing Gender-Blind Alliances," four ways of determining "whether any situation is growth-producing or not," four ways "to countermand sexist sex education," and so forth. There is even advice on colors for rooms, toys, and clothes. You should "ban pink and blue from babyland," and "insist on such gender-neutral infancy pastels as pale yellow, lime green, or white." You will want to follow the many suggestions in the book because, as Dr. Spock tells us on the cover, sex stereotyping is a "blight" and a "crippling disease." The effect that this book and others like it have on some people is illustrated by the experience of one reviewer. She began reading it feeling confident that it wouldn't teach her anything because she and her husband "had the model non-sexist household," but she was quickly disabused of this idea. "It took just two pages to tell me how wrong I was, and that the opportunities for improvement in my own backyard were multitudinous." The fear behind these thoughts is soon revealed: "As I became totally engrossed in *Growing Up Free*, I wondered if it was too late for our daughters (aged eight and five). Had I unconsciously done irreversible damage?" The reviewer finds nothing wrong with the book — in fact writes that she is "ever grateful" to its author — and has become even more determined to root out every vestige of sex-role behavior in her family, but it can be asked whether her feelings of concern, fear, and guilt, and the behavior now stemming from them, represent a step forward.

Because it tends to give people the idea that they are responsible for everything, therapeutic thinking is probably even more burdensome and guilt-producing than are other belief systems. No other system of thought holds that you and you alone are responsible for your life. Although religions produce plenty of guilt and bad feelings, they leave some space. There is room for fate, karma, the work of the devil, and the fact that God goes about His business in mysterious ways. The idea has always been that man was not responsible for everything and could not change everything. Some burdens and problems had to be understood as the work of forces beyond human comprehension and control. Not a great concession, perhaps, but enough to leave some breathing room.

The therapeutic sensibility tends not to concede as much. There is no God and no fate, we are told, no random events and no accidents. We and we alone are responsible for what we are and what we do. But wait, some readers will say, this isn't so. Aren't therapists the ones who say we are moved by unconscious forces for which we are not responsible, that the alcoholic, for instance, is sick and therefore unaccountable? And aren't therapists the ones who often work so hard to help patients see that the responsibility and guilt they feel for events beyond their control are irrational? It is true that some therapists, though by no means all of them, say and do such things. There is a contradiction or at least an ambivalence about the doctrine of responsibility that pervades the therapy field, and often both sides of the issue are manifested by the same counselor. Nonetheless, I suggest that the dominant side has been and remains the idea that people are or should be responsible.

The contradiction goes back at least to Freud. In Victorian times, willpower was everything: you could be the captain of your soul, the master of your fate, if only you tried hard enough. As a result, people felt terribly guilty for not being the way they ought to be. At times Freud seemed to believe that his discoveries about the influence of unconscious processes absolved people from the great burden of Victorian guilt. If your behavior was the consequence of forces beyond your comprehension and control, you would not be held accountable for it. Taken literally, this idea would absolve everyone of responsibility for everything. It is difficult to maintain such a position, and Freud was unable to do so. Though you might not understand why you did this or that, nonetheless it was you that did it and to that extent it was your responsibility. Everything in Freud's system was determined, caused, by someone or something, even what might at first look like accidents or trivial slips of the tongue or lapses of memory. One did not have to look far to find the responsible agent. In one of his books, Freud says, "When a member of my family complains to me of having bitten his tongue, pinched a finger, and the like, he does not get the sympathy he hoped for, but instead the question, 'Why did you do that?' " The clear implication is that you are the causal agent and have, or can have, knowledge as to why you did what you did.

And it goes much further than this, for Freud held that patients secretly desire to be sick. In his discussion of Dora, a young woman he treated for a few months, Freud wrote that an attempt must be made "to convince the patient herself of the existence in her of an intention to be ill." From here it is but a small step to blaming patients for not owning up to, not taking responsibility for, the desire to be neurotic, the desire not to get better, and not accepting therapeutic interpretation and advice. There is a practical matter, too. Counselors are often in a situation similar to what parents sometimes face with their children. They see what the client is doing wrong and know their suggestions would help, but the client refuses to carry them out. It is easy to believe the client really doesn't want to get better, that he relishes his problem, and it's just as easy to tell him this. The therapy literature is full of examples, the Dora case being just one of many, of the therapist badgering and blaming the client for what in essence is not taking responsibility for having the problem and for not getting better. But Freudians generally do not use the term *responsibility* and most would view my examples as illustrations of misguided clinical practice; to do otherwise would be to invalidate or compromise the importance of the unconscious, the backbone of analytic theory and therapy.

Some therapists have seen analytic emphasis on the unconscious as a way of dodging the issue of responsibility, as a cop-out that allows us to blame God, fate, our parents, anyone but ourselves, and they insist that we put ourselves back in the driver's seat and hold ourselves responsible . . . for everything. Whatever happens or does not happen is because we choose it to be that way. Will Schutz says, "I chose everything in my life from the beginning"; the founder of gestalt therapy tells us that "it is oneself who determines in most instances whether [the events in one's own life] shall or shall not continue to exist"; I have personally heard more than one respected counselor tell audiences that rape victims are responsible for the crimes committed against them; and Harold Greenwald gives us this formula:

See each problem not as something that just happened to you, or as just the way you are, but as: (1) something you decided to do, (2) some way you decided to be, or (3) some way you decided to see other people. In other words, see your problem as a decision you have made.

What has happened, in short, is that despite some efforts in the opposite directions, therapists have basically reinstated Victorian notions of responsibility and control and in some cases gone even beyond them. Everything has a cause, and that cause is you.

The doctrine of responsibility is seductive because it implies power. As Will Schutz says, "Once we accept responsibility for choosing our lives, everything is different. We have the power. We decide. We are in control." This feeds fantasies of omnipotence. We don't have to bear any burden or put up with anything we don't like. We've chosen it and therefore can change it. But once this train of thought takes hold, there's no end to its application. Every issue or hassle therapists point to, or we find on our own, becomes something we don't have to tolerate. We feel compelled to act, to change things to our satisfaction. We get busy trying to reform ourselves and those around us, and often discover that making the changes we want is not as easy as anticipated and sometimes simply impossible. Especially in the most important relationships, we have little ability to change things. The control we have is largely what Richard Farson calls "terminal control," the ability to end the relationship. We can quit our jobs, leave our spouses or children or parents, or run away, exactly what many are doing. Once expectations have been raised, it's not easy to leave things as they are. When our attempts at change fail, we look for professional help, leave, or make a new resolution to accept what we just tried to change, but that is now more difficult. Once we've had a glimpse of the promised land, it's difficult to settle for reality.

But the most damaging effects of the responsibility notion involve the guilt produced by it and can be most easily seen in cases of physical disease. I recall a man who tearfully asked if I agreed with another therapist who told him that he was responsible for his multiple sclerosis. He was greatly distressed because he more than half believed her and was now blaming himself for being ill. I was convinced that he had misunderstood the counselor: I couldn't believe she had told him this. But when I asked her, she not only admitted telling him but bragged about it. By getting him to accept full responsibility for the disease, she said, she was putting him on the road to recovery. The idea had worked for her, she continued, enabling her to see without glasses despite a congenital eye defect. At least then I was able to make sense of something: why she always seemed to be squinting and was continually bumping into tables and walls.

It was only because of my naiveté that I thought this situation was unusual. Blaming patients for what ails them — under the guise of getting them to be responsible — is common practice.

A man I'll call John found he had terminal cancer and went for treatment at a center that preaches the now widespread doctrine that you get cancer because of your behavior. You haven't been sufficiently expressive, assertive, and hopeful. If you accept your part in causing the disease and change your ways, you may overcome the cancer or at least slow its growth. John, though very successful in his work, was fairly passive and nonexpressive, and therefore a perfect candidate for the treatment. In one sense, therapy worked. John returned home a changed man. He was much more miserable, much more guilty, and much harder to get along with. He regretted all of his life, convinced that his lack of expressiveness caused the cancer. He could have been different, in which case he would not now be sick. And there was still a chance. If he could express himself more, he might make it. In desperation, he tried. Friends characterize his behavior after therapy as "truculent" and "aggressive," a last-ditch attempt to redo his personality and atone for his sins. The attempt failed: John died about the time the doctors said he would. Because of the hope that he really could conquer the disease, and because he was consumed by feelings of self-reproach and self-blame, he was unable to enjoy any of the time left to him and unable to accept the inevitable and make his peace with it.

Some therapists have not taken kindly to the last two examples, insisting there is a great difference between taking responsibility for oneself, which is what they claim to teach, and blaming oneself. My answer is that such distinctions sound nice but are extremely difficult to convey in practice. If clients are told and believe that their illnesses and other problems are the result of behaving one way rather than another, many are going to feel bad about the way they did behave, whether or not the therapist had such a result in mind. Like John, they will blame themselves for not doing the right thing, for not living properly.

That this happens is acknowledged by physician Carl Simonton, whose psychological methods for treating cancer have received widespread attention in the last decade. In an interview with Maggie Scarf, Simonton admitted that "most people do feel worse" at the beginning of his treatment. *"The patient may feel worse, die faster."* Obviously he also believes that his approach helps some patients, but the data he presents in support of this point are far from convincing and have not persuaded many cancer specialists. Even if these data are accepted, the chances of benefit would have to be weighed against the undisputed possibility of harm.

Another example of the damage done by the doctrine of responsibility, and also of how problems are created out of normal differences among people, concerns obesity. As the saying goes, you can't be too rich or too thin, and Americans, always overly concerned with wealth, have in recent years also become overly concerned with slenderness. Not only do we believe that fat is physically harmful (a belief with far less empirical support than most people think), but also that it is unattractive and indicates a weakness of character. Instead of acknowledging an undisputed fact — that people vary considerably in terms of bodyweight and fat — we have made a problem of it, and the message has gone out that fat people, especially women, are responsible for their "problem" and ought to do something about it. If only they would take charge of themselves, use their willpower, control their appetites, get off their duffs and exercise, and so forth, they could change. Those who are overweight by societal or their own standards generally accept the message and spend much of their time in self-criticism and self-hate, trying to hide their bodies, and desperately seeking new diets, new programs, and new therapists who will help them shed their "excess" weight. On and on it goes, in a never-ending obsession and a never-ending battle against themselves. Although therapists did not start and are not the only ones involved in perpetuating this nasty game, they have done at least their share by lending their prestige to the notion that fat is a problem, one that is resolvable if clients take responsibility for it and undertake the psychological work necessary to make alterations.

The evidence is somewhat different from what therapists and many others tell us about obesity. It is not even clear, except at the most extreme level, that overweight is a health hazard; there is a strong possibility that it's not the kind of problem we think it is, that maybe it's not a problem at all. Even if it really is a problem, the evidence clearly does not support the conclusion that it's a re-solvable one. Regardless of the diet or program, over ninety percent of those who lose weight regain it, and many of them put back on *more* than they lost. The evidence also suggests three other things. First, that bodyweight is more a genetic than a psychological matter (some people being physiologically programmed to be heavier than others); second, that repeated weight fluctuations, a result of the weight loss, weight gain merry-go-round many fat people get on, is almost certainly detrimental to health; and third, that successful weight loss itself causes unhappiness for some people. Instead of taking this information to indicate that someone is trying to tell us something, therapists and clients alike turn frantically to new diets and new methods, and everyone faults clients for insufficient moti-vation.

What is the point of making a serious problem of something that is better understood as normal human variation, especially when there is no effective way of dealing with it? What is gained by mak-ing obese people feel so ashamed, so guilty, so bad about them-selves? Why tell them to take responsibility for something they probably are not and cannot be responsible for? Unfortunately, the great preachers of responsibility rarely ask themselves such questions.

The notion of personal responsibility, though sometimes of value when used carefully and appropriately, puts people into a number of traps from which escape is extremely difficult. If they don't do anything about their situation — let's stick with obesity — it's their fault. They can no longer ignore or deny the problem (after all, fatness is a very serious and official problem), blame it on heredity or sluggish glands (that's a cop-out), or pretend that nothing can be done (changes can be made by those who really want them). If they try to lose weight and fail, it's not the fault of the diet or doctor; the clients are to blame. They were too ambivalent, too resistant, they didn't follow the rules, didn't give it their all. In a phrase increasingly popular among therapists and believed by many clients, they sabotaged the treatment. Now they can feel guilty about this as well as about being fat. Even if the attempt is successful, they are not off the hook. If clients regain the weight, which is the norm, or if they keep it off but aren't any happier, it's their doing, their responsibility. The responsibility doctrine, in short, makes a lot of people feel like hell. Psychologist Bernard Apfelbaum notes that "many clients I see nowadays feel like doomed creatures, corrupt and cancerous, toxic to themselves and others," because they blame themselves for being the way they are and not being able to change.

If the doctrine of total responsibility is wrong-headed and harmful, so too is the opposite notion, pushed by a minority of therapists, that some people aren't responsible for anything. The best place to see this idea in action is in courtrooms where therapists hired by the defense contend that although the accused did indeed commit the crime, usually murder, he is innocent by reason of insanity. Although the legal definition of insanity has to do with the culprit's knowledge of right and wrong at the time of the crime, the defense therapists' testimony often boils down to a modern version of "the Devil made him do it." And what interesting devils we now have. Dan White got away with murder because psychiatrists convinced the jury that at the time he killed San Francisco Mayor George Moscone and Supervisor Harvey Milk he suffered from diminished capacity, the result of manic depression aggravated by excessive sugar intake, mainly in the form of Cokes and Twinkies. Terms like manic depression and paranoid schizophrenia sound more scientific than being under the influence of the Devil, but they really aren't. Even the defense experts often disagree as to precisely what kind of mental illness the defendant presumably had.

There are costs to be paid for this kind of thinking. Although documentation is hard to come by, surely it does something to those who haven't committed crimes to see that some people can get away with atrocities even when there is overwhelming evidence of guilt. The citizens who rioted in the streets of San Francisco after the White verdict was announced were but a small number of those who felt that injustice had triumphed and that the social bond had been violated. One man involved in the rioting put it this way when I asked why: "I wasn't thinking much at the time, just acting out of a sense of outrage, but when I look back I see it this way: if he [White] doesn't have to follow the rules, then neither do I. If I get caught I'll say I've been eating Twinkies and my head's all messed up." There are also other prices. These supposedly insane people tend to get better rather fast, which is surprising when you consider how ineffective are the treatments for insanity. Dan White, for instance, was already cured when he entered prison (to serve seven and a half years for voluntary manslaughter). The tests he took there showed no signs of mental disorder. Undoubtedly a change of diet was responsible. Many such persons are quickly released into the community once their "insanity" is thought to be cured, and a number of them return to crime. Their new victims, and the widespread fear felt by many citizens aware that such once-insane-now-presumably-cured murderers and sex offenders are loose, are among the prices society pays.

Much of what we have been talking about has to do with the raising of expectations. Many counselors and others argue that making people aware of their deficiencies, showing them that things could be better, and getting them to take responsibility for where they are and for making desired changes lead to better, happier people. Only by making them aware of their potential for growth, raising their expectations, can they be led to fulfill themselves. Such assertions are often backed up by quotes all of us have heard; for example, "I didn't know what I was capable of until my therapist [or teacher, coach, parent, spouse] pushed me to see my potential and how I could develop it." I am not denying the validity of such statements, but only asking that the other side, of which little enough is heard these days, be taken into account.

For many people, as Charlie Brown's friend Linus says of himself, "there's no heavier burden than a great potential." Believing they are capable of more serves mainly to make them feel discontented with what they have, pressured to do more, fearful of not being as good as they now think they ought to be, and guilty about their shortcomings. We always hear of the athletes, writers, students, politicians, and others who fulfilled their great expectations despite great odds. Rarely is much said about the misery of those whose expectations turned out to be unrealistic or, realistic or not, couldn't be achieved, but such misery is not uncommon. It seems fair to say that John, the cancer patient discussed earlier, would have been far better off had he not been encouraged to raise his expectations and believe that he had the power to defeat his disease, and it is quite clear that the multiple sclerosis patient also mentioned earlier would have been much happier had he not been led to "take responsibility" for his illness. Many people, including parents, spouses, workers, and therapy clients as well, would be in better shape if they had not been pushed to have grandiose expectations of themselves and life itself. As psychologist George Bach observes,

> Today's patient aspires to be happy, successful, strong, self-sufficient, stress-free, capable of coping with every situation. It is an unrealistic picture bound to disappoint and to leave the client feeling more inadequate than ever. It is no wonder that people enter therapy with excessive demands, unreasonable expectations, and a hunger that can't be satisfied.

Another great cost of the therapeutic sensibility is a loss of confidence in ourselves. If we are basically flawed and not living as we should, we need to depend on experts to set us straight. We need their advice even to learn that we don't need it, that we are really okay, that we can take care of ourselves. We seem to be losing our faith in ourselves: in our ability to cope with the vicissitudes of life, to know our situation, to make the right decisions, to deal with ourselves and others in decent and satisfying ways. Without expert advice, we believe, we are doomed to error, incompetence, and lack of fulfillment. Therapists tell us we should trust our feelings but they, along with other professionals, have made us fearful of trusting anything not validated by experts. This loss of confidence is illustrated by the following from a mother of two: "There were times when I actually believed I was destroying my kids if I became angry over bad behavior. Sometimes I just didn't confront problems, rather than do the wrong thing."

What Lewis Thomas says about physical health is as true of emotional health:

> Nothing has changed so much in the health-care system over the past twenty-five years as the public's perception of its own health. The change amounts to a loss of confidence in the human form. The general belief these days seems to be that the body is fundamentally flawed, subject to disintegration at any moment, always on the verge of mortal disease, always in need of continual monitoring and support by health-care professionals. . . . Left alone, unadvised by professionals, the tendency of the human body is perceived as prone to steady failure. . . . We are in some danger of becoming a nation of healthy hypochondriacs.

We have developed what Thomas calls "an overwhelming demand for reassurance." Millions of people each year come to physicians and therapists just to make sure they aren't coming down with something serious. They don't really have anything wrong with them; they just want to know that nothing is about to be wrong. You never can tell. They want to be told that they are not going crazy and that they are managing their lives in healthy ways. They want to know that their feelings and perceptions are appropriate and accurate. This desire for validation, as counselors often call it, has reached gigantic proportions. It is often manifest in issues around decision-making. Clients ask if they are making the right decision to take up a certain course of study, or a certain career, or even a certain investment; to marry, to have children, to divorce; to change diets; to start or stop exercising; to hire or fire an employee. Thomas says he knows a pediatrician who has received visits from intelligent, well-educated parents who only want to know if their children should start Sunday school. Former clients sometimes call for an appointment so I can check their thinking before they make a decision, while those now in therapy interrupt what we are working on for the same reason. Have they covered all the important issues or have they left something out? Are they being influenced by unconscious or unhealthy considerations? Is their conclusion correct? They seem enormously relieved when I find nothing to say. Almost invariably they could have received the reassurance from a friend or relative, but they believe in experts and nothing less than expert consultation will do. We seem to be heading toward a society in which no one does anything without first getting professional consultation.

As pointed out in the first section of the book, there are good reasons for the confusion and insecurity, and for the desire for validation and reassurance. But going to experts, while offering temporary relief, only compounds the problems. The more we rely on professionals, the more we have to rely on them because we fail to develop our own resources. We forget that logical and critical thinking are not the special province of a particular group of experts and that we could just as well check our own thinking or get help from those around us. We usually feel comforted and relieved when we get expert advice, if for no other reason than we think we have done all that we could to get help, and that becomes another reason for seeking more of it. If our problem is resolved or if our decision turns out to be a good one, we tend to give credit to the experts, whether or not they really made a contribution, and this encourages us to continue the pattern of getting expert advice.

The results of this pattern are obvious in the whole health-care system. People have less confidence in themselves and in their ability to care for themselves. They flock to experts for matters trivial and irrelevant. Professionals are swamped; more tests are done, more prescriptions are written, and more treatments are taken; prices go up and waiting lists get longer; and the cry goes out for more preventive measures, more research, more training, more experts. We get all these things, but they make no difference. No medical or mental health system can be large enough to meet the demands of a population that sees itself as horribly flawed and with little ability to deal effectively with the difficulties and changes of ordinary living.

The paradox of the mental health movement is that by emphasizing problems, great possibilities, and self-responsibility, it has contributed to the frustration, anxiety, guilt, unhappiness, and lack of confidence for which it hoped to be the cure. A lot of us are paying high prices for our belief in the therapeutic sensibility. Unless we can gain a better understanding of this paradox and take steps to keep expectations under control, we may be doomed, as Richard Farson puts it, "to create an increasing number of human calamities."

Limits to Change
and the Myth of Malleability

"The more things change the more I am the same."

— HUGH PRATHER

"It is only in romances that people undergo a sudden metamorphosis. In real life, even after the most terrible experiences, the main character remains exactly the same."

— ISADORA DUNCAN

WE HAVE SEEN THAT AMERICAN ATTITUDES toward change and therapy are based on three assumptions: that people are easily changed; that there are few or no limits to the alterations they can make; and that they need to be changed. I hope to demonstrate that all three are wrong. I take up the first two assumptions in this chapter, leaving the third for the next chapter.

Human Malleability
and Resistance to Change

I suggest that people are not nearly as malleable as we assume in our therapeutic age. It is not easy to change people. Before presenting evidence in support of this assertion, a caveat is in order. Despite the epigraphs above, I do not mean to deny the fact of human change. Change is one of the polarities of life for individuals and groups. While some societies and organizations are relatively stable, there is no such thing as a changeless society or group. The same is true of individuals. The only people who aren't changing are those in cemeteries. None of us is exactly the same as he was as a child, as he was ten years ago, or even a month ago. People change all the time, but most change is not planned. Different ages, environments, and situations cause alterations of mood, thought, and behavior. We say that Sally has become more mature, assertive, or happier since her marriage, or since leaving her marriage. We believe the Marines made a man of John. Linda has been depressed since she lost her job and Bob has not quite been himself since his accident. These are just a few examples of changes we observe all the time.

While change cannot be denied, our interest is in change that is planned, where all, some, or at least one of the concerned parties decides that certain alterations should be effected. It is in this area that Americans have a penchant for exaggerating possibilities and minimizing limits. The evidence for the difficulty of such change is far from scarce but we try not to see it. We titillate ourselves with stories of brainwashing and mind control, as well as with therapy success stories. We think and apparently want to think there really are powerful methods for changing people. They are so powerful, in fact, that we have to be concerned lest someone use them to make zombies or conformists of all of us.

But this is the stuff of fantasy, of imagination run riot. There are some dangers, to be sure — therapy can harm, and the constant raising of expectations by therapists and others can cause greater unhappiness — but in general change methods currently available are weak and seriously limited. I have already presented some of the evidence: the fact, for instance, that changes made by the presumably sophisticated methods of therapy are usually modest and not much different from what people achieve on their own or with the help of their friends.

There is also plenty of supporting evidence from elsewhere. Even when one has total control of the environment — as in prisons and mental institutions — the results hardly support the conclusion of tremendous effect. With such control one can get most people, but never all of them, to follow certain rules. But the whole business doesn't work very well — consider what went on in mental institutions before the advent of antipsychotic medications, and the number of murders, suicides, and riots in prisons today — and whatever effects it does have are generally lost when people are released. It is difficult to prove that incarceration has any kind of positive result; it certainly doesn't prevent people from doing exactly what got them incarcerated in the first place.

The military deserves attention because it is supposed to accomplish a great alteration of behavior. It is supposed to take ordinary adolescents and in a short time make radical changes in their attitudes and behavior regarding the following of orders and the taking of human life. Obviously armies have some success in transforming people; otherwise there wouldn't be any wars. What is not widely known is that with all its power, the military fails far more often than it succeeds.

Fortunately there is a clear criterion of military success with its therapeutic endeavor, at least for the infantry, and that is the firing of weapons at the enemy. Everything else done by the military is merely preparation for this goal. And how often is it achieved? A large-scale study done in World War II by the distinguished military historian General S. L. A. Marshall provides the data. He found that less than one in five soldiers who were in combat and were supposed to fire their guns actually did so, and this includes everyone who fired even one shot. In his interviews with four hundred infantry companies, Marshall found that on the average, "not more than 15 percent of the men had actually fired at the enemy positions or personnel." Even this figure exaggerates the extent to which military training changes people. A significant proportion of the soldiers who did fire were what Marshall calls "bad actors" and "rough characters," men who were always unruly and aggressive and who had spent much of their time in the guardhouse. They were fighters to begin with and could perform well in battle, doing what they always did. Once the battle was over, they "almost invariably relapsed again. They could fight like hell but they couldn't soldier." The army failed to make most of these rough characters into respectable soldiers, just as it failed to make most of the other men into fighters. Marshall concedes that because the American soldier is the product of a society which, while hardly nonviolent, does not take lightly the snuffing out of human life, "the Army cannot unmake him." The prohibition against killing "stays his trigger finger even though he is hardly conscious that it is restraint upon him." Despite the indoctrination, despite the dangers of not firing, despite the fear of disapproval and failure, and despite the fact that World War II was a war supported by most Americans, the army failed to convert a large majority of its soldiers. Deeply ingrained patterns are not easily overturned.

Brainwashing as carried on in the Soviet Union, Korea, and China has been the basis of many of our hopes and fears about psychological power. My reading of the literature has left me impressed not with the potency of the methods but instead with their futility. Despite absolute control of the environment and absolute power, the results are not remarkable. Concern about thought reform surfaced after the Korean war when it was claimed that American prisoners of war had been brainwashed into collaboration with the Communists. But the truth is that fewer than one percent of the over thirty-five hundred POWs ever made pro-Communist statements and only twenty-five soldiers refused to be repatriated when the war was over. In other circumstances where brainwashing was used, some people confessed to crimes they didn't commit, some denounced friends, country, and principles, but only some people some of the time. Those who escaped or were set free soon went back to their former principles, ways, and friends. As far as I can tell, the psychological methods had little effect except for disorienting and frightening people. Usually it was the fear of physical punishment, not the brainwashing, that led to the changed behavior. Jerome Frank's comments about brainwashing seem apposite:

> The main lesson to be drawn from thought reform is not its success in generating false confessions but its failures to produce permament changes in attitude. . . . Adult [belief] systems . . . are very resistant to change, and changes such as those produced by extreme environmental pressures tend to snap back once these are removed.
>
> These findings raise some doubts about the claims of certain schools of psychotherapy to produce fundamental personality change. From this perspective, such changes may be analogous to false confessions. That is, the person has not changed fundamentally, but rather has learned to couch his problems and to report improvement in the therapist's terms.

In the last decade, new concerns about thought reform have been encouraged by reports that religious cults such as the Moonies are brainwashing the youth of America. Former cult members and deprogrammers have glutted the market with accounts of how young minds are twisted and snapped. But the facts are somewhat different from what the public now believes. Everything about the cults, including even their size, has been exaggerated. The careful research of David Bromley and Anson Shupe clearly indicates that the recruitment and so-called programming methods of the cults are incredibly ineffective. If anyone can be said to have been brainwashed, it is the American public, for its view of the power of brainwashing is totally at odds with the known facts.

But what about Jonestown? Didn't hundreds of men and women drink cyanide because they had been brainwashed by Jim Jones? While we will probably never know exactly what happened during the last day at Jonestown, two things should be kept in mind. First, killing oneself or allowing oneself to be killed for one's religious beliefs is not necessarily the result of brainwashing, unless we are willing to say that the early Christian martyrs and the Jews at Masada were also brainwashed. Second, it is clear that many who died at Jonestown did not go willingly: they were shot or forced to drink cyanide at gunpoint.

Perhaps the most powerful change mechanism is fear. You can get a lot of people to do what you want by holding a gun to their heads. But not everyone will comply and those who do will stop as soon as the gun is removed. The use of fear is hardly a modern invention and it doesn't seem to work any better or worse today than it did thousands of years ago. And even fear isn't as effective as we assume. Look at how many millions of people continue to smoke despite the news from the Surgeon General's office. Look at how many continue to overindulge in alcohol and other chemical substances despite what is known about the dangers. Even when fear of fines and imprisonment is added — as it was for alcohol during Prohibition and as it is today for many drugs — people continue to do what they want. Look at how many children continue doing what they're doing despite the admonition that "one more time and you're going to get it." And how many adults do the same despite the warning from their spouses that "one more time and I'm leaving."

But, you may say, that is because people delude themselves about the consequences of their behavior. They don't think about lung cancer when they smoke, they don't think about their livers when they drink, they don't consider they could get caught and be punished for their crimes. This is all true, for the simple reason that people are people. Delusion, denial, and isolation come easily to us — they are part of the way we are put together, part of our nature — and that is one of the reasons that even fear of terrible punishment doesn't work very well.

Let's take another example. Since the revolution in 1917, the Soviet Union has become the largest-scale experiment in history on the changing of people. There has been a deliberate attempt to create a new type of person, a new socialist or Communist citizen; and carrot, stick, and everything in between has been employed in the attempt. The result has been a miserable failure in almost every area. The new socialist farmer was supposed to believe in working collectively, but despite the killing of millions of peasants and the propaganda of several generations, the state has been unable to convince farmers to do much work on collective farms. This is the main reason the Soviet Union is unable to feed itself even though it contains some of the richest agricultural land in the world. Farmers seem unwilling to get with socialist ideas, and they put most of their effort into the small private plots the state was forced to cede to them; though these plots occupy only three percent of the total arable land, they provide one-fourth of total farm output. The new socialist citizen was supposed to be beyond needing such opiates as religion, but despite intense and persistent antireligious education and propaganda for over fifty years, many Russians cling to their old religious beliefs. The new socialist citizen was supposed to want to defend the revolution against all enemies, especially the reactionary Nazis. But when the Nazis invaded in 1941, Russians were generally unwilling to fight in defense of their socialist paradise: the invaders were welcomed in many places and whole Russian armies surrendered without much struggle. That the Russians finally did turn against the Nazis and drive them out stemmed more from the cruelty and stupidity of the Germans, and old-fashioned love of country, something contrary to the tenets of Communism, than from any socialist ideas. All in all, it cannot be said that the Soviet experiment to produce a new kind of person has been successful.

To be sure, most of the examples given so far are extreme, and that is precisely the point. Even when the rights of people don't have to be considered, even when they can be and are killed for disobedience, and even when the available power is so absolute that the average therapist can barely imagine it, the results are far less impressive than might be expected. People are not that easy to modify.

Of course it can be argued that this is because the customers are unwilling and are being coerced. Even with less powerful methods, the argument goes, people are easier to change when they freely choose to change. Let us turn to places where coercion is not a factor and see if this holds. There is no law against smoking and few people are coerced into stopping. Presumably most who try to quit do so of their own volition. Yet we have seen that while some have been successful, most have not, and similar things can be said regarding other addictions. In medicine, we find that adherence to medical regimens — keeping appointments, taking medications, sticking to prescribed diets and following exercise recommendations — is quite variable and often not high. There is no force involved in these cases and the presumption is that the patients do want to get and stay well, yet very often they do not do what they are supposed to do. What happens to New Year's resolutions is so common and well known it has become a national joke.

Another illustration of the difficulty of making desired changes is provided by the communes that sprang up across the country in the 1960s and '70s. The motivating force underlying the communes was the idea that they could develop a better way to live, and an important goal in many of them was equality — the suppression of power and status hierarchies, especially those based on sex-role distinctions. While some success was achieved by some communes, it was not great. A study of 120 communes found that although a number gave highest priority to abolishing sex-role distinctions, not one "has come anywhere close." Benjamin Zablocki, who did the research, writes that he "did not find a single example of a commune without a power hierarchy or of one in which the men did as much . . . 'women's work' as did the women." He concludes that human tendencies toward sex-role categorization and pecking orders "are not among the behavior patterns that can be easily willed away, even by men and women of the most sincere commitment."

Now back to therapy, where we find something curious. Most clients come of their own free will to make changes of their own choosing, and they often have to pay a pretty penny for the opportunity. And what happens? They frequently resist the treatment. They do not do what they are supposed to do to achieve their goals. Freud early on recognized the problem:

> The resistance accompanies the treatment step by step. Every single association, every act of the person under treatment must reckon with the resistance and represents a compromise between the forces that are striving towards recovery and the opposing ones.

Although different counselors have different ideas about resistance and what to do about it, the phenomenon is well nigh universal; it is found by all counselors and in all forms of counseling. Fritz Perls claimed that "roughly ninety percent don't go to a therapist to be cured." Perls often accused those who sat in his hot seat of not wanting help but desiring instead to put him down. Albert Ellis acknowledges "the individual's recalcitrance in getting and staying better" in his own rational-emotive therapy. In est, resistant students are said to be playing the right-wrong game, trying to make themselves right and the trainer wrong. There are many students of meditative therapies who do not meditate at home or who stop once the course is over. Resistance is such a widespread and difficult problem that it is generally acknowledged that one of the main characteristics of a good therapist is the ability to deal effectively with it. Milton Erickson's reputation is based largely on his talent for circumventing resistance and the same is true for a number of other famous counselors.

It needs to be said that some resistance is created by therapists themselves. They act in such ways or demand such things from clients that the most reasonable response is to resist. But much resistance is not created by therapists. Even the best and most experienced counselors, those who try their best to tailor treatment to the values, needs, and circumstances of their clients, often encounter it. I think there is no stronger argument for the proposition that people are not nearly as malleable as we like to think.

That people often seem reluctant to part with problems that cause them much grief is a difficult fact to entertain. It just doesn't make any sense. How should we think about a person who comes for therapy and then fights against resolving the problem he came for help with? And what are we to make of a person who makes a desired change and enjoys all the benefits — more efficient use of time, less depression, more satisfying communication or relationships, or whatever — and then slips back to the old ways as if pulled by a powerful magnet? All sorts of ideas have been generated to cover these phenomena, e.g., that the clients were ambivalent about change, that they were more comfortable with the original situation, that the problem is like an old friend and they feel lonely without it, that the problem is an important part of their identity and they don't feel like themselves without it, or that they are masochistic. The problem with all the explanations is that it is easy to get caught up in them and forget the point they seek to explain: namely, that people often display incredible tenacity in hanging on to the very things they say they want to modify.

It is not simply that therapy clients fight change. Resistance to change is widespread in all of life. There seems to be a strong conservative impulse in most of us. Those working for social or organizational change have written volumes about its strength. Despite all the celebration of growth, change, and newness in America, especially in recent years, people tend to cling to stability and continuity. This is adaptive because predictability and control, which all humans seem to desire, depend on internal and external things not changing too fast or too much. No matter how bad things are, at least the situation is familiar and one knows what to expect. Change may hold out the possibility of less suffering and greater satisfaction, but who knows how it will turn out and how much one will like the new order of things? Besides, change means doing things differently and that is often experienced as a bother. It requires awareness and effort, whereas doing what one is used to doing is automatic and effortless.

An illustration of resistance to change — to the acceptance of new ideas in this case — comes from the scientific community. It is especially relevant to our topic because receptivity to new ideas — about oneself, others, and the world — is usually essential for therapeutic progress. By inclination and training, scientists are committed to the search for truth, to discovering new facts and developing better theories to encompass important findings. Yet despite the commitment, their record of receptivity to new ideas is not impressive. Findings and ideas that challenged conventional understanding were generally vehemently resisted when first introduced. Copernicus's ideas were not accepted until almost a century after his death and Newton's work did not meet with general acceptance for more than half a century. The problem of converting scientists to new views has often been noted by scientists themselves. In his *Origin of Species*, Darwin wrote that he did not expect "to convince naturalists whose minds are stocked with a multitude of facts all viewed . . . from a point of view directly opposite to mine." Max Planck, whose quantum theory revolutionized physics, observed that "a new scientific truth does not triumph by convincing its opponents and making them see the light, but rather because its opponents eventually die, and a new generation grows up that is familiar with it."

In retrospect, it is tempting to accuse those scientists who rejected what were later seen as successful innovations of prejudice, stodginess, and even stupidity. Indeed, we tend to speak disparagingly of anyone who resists change: they are uptight, blind to their own best interests, and against progress. Therapists often talk this way about their resistant clients. But it is well to remember there is another side. The scientists who rejected successful innovations also rejected many new ideas that turned out to be worthless. If they had accepted every new idea that came along, scientific progress would have been seriously hindered. It would be nice, of course, if they accepted only useful innovations and rejected only the others, but that is asking a great deal from mere human beings.

That those committed to the search for new facts and ideas should themselves be resistant to change should tell us something important about people. Change is fine when viewed in retrospect and when it is trivial, such as trying a new restaurant, but present and important changes often are experienced as threatening in one way or another and lead to desperate battles against acceptance of the new. Resistance to change is widespread and an everyday event, meaning that people are not as malleable as we often assume.

Some Limits to Personal Change

The issue of limits to change is not a popular one among therapists and therapy apologists. They would rather pretend there are no limits and tell you things like the sky's the limit. Nonetheless, there are many limits to the kind and extent of changes each of us can make. I discuss what seem to be some of the more important ones. Although I have separated the limits for purposes of discussion, in actuality they often interact. Therapy remains my main example of how these things operate, but it should not be difficult to see how they limit change in other areas as well.

PHYSIOLOGY AND HEREDITY

We are made of flesh and blood, a fact which imposes rather severe limits on us. Flesh and blood must age and die and also must have food and rest. The particular constellation of human flesh and blood makes it incapable of certain things such as lifting mountains and flying without the aid of machines. All of this seems too obvious for attention, but things have gotten so far out of hand that some have claimed, and others have believed, that even these limits can be overcome. To give but one illustration, a few years ago, Maharishi Mahesh Yogi, the founder of Transcendental Meditation, claimed to be able to fly without an airplane. Other meditators have made similar claims. Yet so far no public demonstrations have been offered and no supporting evidence has been presented. This doesn't necessarily mean the meditators can't fly, but their unwillingness to supply evidence of any kind does make one wonder.

There are other physiological limits. A man who is five feet tall is not going to play in the National Basketball Association no matter how much he practices and how much positive thinking he does, and a man or woman who weighs 250 pounds is not going to be a champion jockey or runner. There are limits to what training, therapy, quick diets, and even plastic surgery can accomplish. The size, strength, coordination, stamina, health, and appearance of our bodies place some definite restrictions on what is possible for each of us.

And it goes much farther than this. We are not born equal; we come into the world with some things already determined. This point is not a popular one, particularly among therapists who, along with many others, tend to be staunch environmentalists. Yet, as John Passmore says, "it is a highly implausible view that it makes no difference whatsoever what kind of brain, or nervous system, or hormonal balance a man inherits." Environment and learning are surely important, but they are not everything. It may surprise some readers to learn that Freud repeatedly emphasized the role of constitutional factors in creating neuroses and in placing limits on what analysis could accomplish. He was not as much an environmentalist as he is often portrayed and as were most of his followers. After his first meeting with Ernest Jones, Freud called him a "fanatic" because "he denies all heredity." But Freud was in a bind. Although he recognized the importance of heredity and the limits to the effectiveness of psychoanalysis, he was also the leader and chief salesman of a new movement and therapy, and didn't want to say anything in public that might be damaging. The consequences of the conflict are clear in a letter to Jung:

> I should not even claim that every case of hysteria can be cured by [psychoanalysis], let alone all the states that go by that name. . . . It is not possible to explain everything to a hostile public; accordingly I have kept certain things that might be said concerning the limits of therapy and its mechanisms to myself. . . .

It is not surprising that Freud's words on constitutional factors, and generally on the limits of change, have been lost sight of. As Frank Sulloway notes, "Freud's theories have consistently been reinterpreted, especially by an optimistic America, in a more purely environmentalist, and hence more psychological, vein than Freud ever intended." The reasons for the reinterpretations, and for the general emphasis by therapists on environment or learning, are not hard to discern. Since what therapists offer is psychological treatment, they feel they need to posit psychological causes. If biological or constitutional factors are responsible, there may be no treatment or the treatment is likely to be medical or pharmacological, which doesn't leave much room for nonmedical therapists. If, on the other hand, problems are basically the result of learning (psychology), then psychotherapy has an important role to play.

The best conclusion I can draw from contemporary research is that a number of disorders — including autism, schizophrenia, some types of depression, and perhaps agoraphobia — are caused or strongly influenced by inheritance. It also seems possible that some forms of antisocial behavior are similarly influenced. Not that a person inherits a criminal mind or criminality, but he may inherit a disposition to impulsivity or a weakness in what later will become his social conscience and under certain circumstances get involved in criminal acts easier than other people. Although the research is hardly clear-cut, it may be that some addictions are biologically influenced.

We know that infants are markedly different from each other before the environment and learning have had a chance to exert much of an effect, and it doesn't seem to be stretching a point to think that they have different strengths, weaknesses, and susceptibilities, any of which could lead to trouble under some circumstances. For instance, some infants are very noisy and active; we often call them "strong, healthy babies." They may well be that, but if the tendency toward activity is terribly strong and is not brought under control, the child may have trouble with playmates and in school, and trouble there may set the stage for more trouble later on. The behavior that leads us to call the infant strong and healthy may later be called by different names, such as hyperactivity, impulsiveness, or aggressiveness. Some babies seem to be more frightened than others by new things. They do not react well to new people and situations; the world seems to scare them. In a benign environment, they will probably turn out fine, though perhaps more introverted and fearful than others. But a not so friendly environment can deepen their fears, resulting in their becoming anxious, unassertive, and lonely adults.

Congenital abnormalities, deficits, and susceptibilities are not necessarily unchangeable, but they do present serious problems, for in many cases they appear to set limits as to how much change is possible. For instance, although many manic-depressives and schizophrenics can be helped by shock treatment or medication, they are not usually cured. These treatments are often worthwhile — patients feel better and function better — but medication must be continued; relapses are common; drop-out rates for drug therapy are high, meaning that a significant number of patients receive little or no benefit; and even with continued treatment, many of the patients do not behave in normal or acceptable ways. Psychotherapy and education are not necessarily ruled out because a problem is genetically influenced, but again there are limits. Mentally retarded people can learn some things, but not as much or as fast as others, and there are many things they cannot learn and do. The alcoholic may learn to stop or control his drinking, but he will probably not be comfortable around alcohol. He will have to fight temptation frequently and the battle will be especially hard during times of stress. The woman who has been depressed as far back as she can remember is going to have an extremely difficult time becoming a happily disposed person no matter how many pills she takes and how much therapy she gets.

EARLY LEARNING AND TRAUMA

Although most of the therapists I interviewed thought that negative experiences in infancy and childhood — such as abuse and insufficient love — placed limits on what could later be changed, it should be noted that separating the effects of early learning from the effects of heredity is extremely difficult. Being environmentalists, therapists talk about early experiences, but what looks like the consequence of childhood events may in fact be the consequence of genetic factors. With this caveat in mind, we can say a few things about early events.

What comes first is important because around it are built the structures and assumptions through which later events will be observed and evaluated. I am not suggesting that everything necessarily gets set in concrete during the first month or year of life. If an infant's first experiences with feeding are not good but then things get smoothed out and continue being satisfactory, he will probably not carry away a negative lesson. But first experiences, if repeated often enough and with few contrary experiences, can set up expectations and assumptions which are very resistant to change. If a child does not develop what Erik Erikson calls a sense of basic trust — that is, if he does not learn that the world and others can be counted on to deal fairly and sensitively with him — his way of dealing with the world will differ from that of another child. Since he "knows" that others cannot be counted on to treat him well, he may not notice it when they do or he may construe their behavior in a way that reinforces rather than contradicts his expectation. In addition, he will probably act in ways that betray his discomfort, suspiciousness, and mistrust, which will lead others not to treat him well. Once the expectation is set that people are untrustworthy or bad, he will find many ingenious ways of confirming it. Such closed circles are difficult to break.

The child who learns early that he is not lovable may simply give up, believing that nothing will gain him the love and approval he desires, or may spend much of his life running from one project or person to another, valiantly trying to prove his worth and lovableness, but at the same time refusing to accept the appreciation and love he is given. Many therapists believe that some people just can't get enough love and approval to make up for the lack of these qualities in their early lives.

Therapy can help some of these people, but their early learning, reinforced thousands of times, limits how far they can go. The ones who did not develop basic trust can learn to drop some of their suspiciousness and distrust, but these feelings will usually not be far away and will be ready to assert themselves when stress or anger makes the person less able to control himself. People who did not feel approved of and loved may learn to see things more objectively, to notice when they do receive approval and affection and to understand that they are inherently lovable, no matter how their parents treated them. But the gnawing feeling that they are not worthy, that they are empty, is rarely far away and can cause trouble in many areas.

Greater understanding and better coping can often be had, but despite all the hype to the contrary, individual history cannot be made to disappear. The slate can be made cleaner, can in fact be made quite attractive, but it cannot be altogether wiped clean.

The relationship between childhood and adulthood behavior is not the same for everyone. Some people change greatly through the life cycle, while others change very little. Some who suffer greatly as children and should be basket cases go on to successful and satisfying lives, whereas some who get all the right things end up badly. So it is not fair to suggest that all with negative experiences in childhood, including abuse, are going to have psychological problems in adulthood and be unable to make much change. Nonetheless, it seems clear that early experiences do place powerful obstacles for some people to the amount of change they can make in or out of therapy. This is especially true when early negative experiences continue through adolescence and early adulthood.

The main problem for some is that their first experiences do get set in concrete and do not leave room for modification, a phenomenon nicely captured by the comment about the man who was said not to have thirteen years of experience, but rather one year of experience repeated thirteen times. Some people have social problems that go back to childhood. They didn't feel comfortable and secure in their families and almost every other experience with people has been difficult and less than satisfying. They often show up for social skills training, at shyness clinics and other therapy programs, where many are helped to develop some confidence and skills needed to deal with others. But they can go only so far. I have never seen a person in this group develop the kind of comfort, skill, and confidence that seems almost natural to many other people.

Another example is of men who don't express their feelings and whose lovers or wives complain because they can't find out what the men are thinking or feeling. In most cases I have dealt with, the problem seems to go way back and change is difficult. Some modification can usually be made — the man can learn to say something about his day when he walks in the door at night, or to tell his wife when he's angry with her, or to express positive feelings some of the time — but generally the change is small and forced. Whether the man has had years of psychoanalysis, courses of assertiveness training and communication work, or whatever, he remains somewhat reluctant to express himself and when he does you can almost hear the tumblers turn. "*Click*, what she said an hour ago was annoying. *Click*, according to Dr. X, I should say I'm annoyed. *Click*, how should I say it? *Click*, okay, I'll say I don't like it when she tells people I'm sloppy. *Click*, One, Two, Three, Say It!" The results are often far from the spontaneous sharing of feeling wanted by their partners, but are sometimes enough to make a difference. Clearly, there is a ceiling as to how far they can go.

GENERAL WELL-BEING AND THE SEVERITY AND COMPLEXITY OF PROBLEMS

The more severe, pervasive, and complex the presenting problem, the less the chance of resolution. Acute, isolated, and milder problems have a better prognosis. This is another way of saying that the general well-being of the client — often called ego-strength — is of tremendous importance. High ego-strength means the person is relatively well put together, that he has resources for coping with his difficulties, and that he can function despite them, or at least has a history of effective functioning.

As an example, consider two men with erection problems. John has a long history of gratifying sexual experiences, has always considered himself a good lover, knows how to have satisfying sex without an erection, and has a basically good relationship with his wife. Lately, however, he often doesn't get erections when they have sex. The couple continues to enjoy each other physically, but both are perplexed and at times upset that they can't have intercourse. Harry is also having erection difficulties but they are nothing new to him. Sex has been problematic for him as far back as he can remember, and lack of erection is commonplace. He considers himself something of a sexual flop — when he calls himself impotent, you believe it — and has little confidence in his sexual abilities. When sex doesn't work out, he pulls away from his partner in shame or anger. His relationship suffers from a number of serious problems, many of them exacerbated by the tension that envelops the bedroom. Harry is close to panic because he fears his lover will turn to other men who are better, sexually and otherwise. Obviously, John has a better chance of overcoming his erection problem than does Harry. John simply has a lot more going for him — confidence, an isolated problem of short duration, a good relationship, the ability to cope with the problem, and a sense of perspective even while being concerned. Harry has none of these things and change is therefore going to be much harder. It's not that Harry cannot be helped — he is a real client and was helped — but the chances are less, the treatment more difficult, and at the end Harry was still not anywhere near as good and confident a lover as John. His situation at the beginning of therapy put limits on how far he could go.

The view that healthier clients improve more has recently been challenged by several investigators. Their point is that less healthy clients often improve as much as healthier ones, but this is often lost sight of because they still look less well at the end of the treatment than clients who started at a higher level. I think the argument is valid, but it does not detract from the conclusion that severity of problem and condition of personality limit how much change can be made. John and Harry provide one illustration. Let's take another. On a test of depression, Ann rates as mildly and intermittently depressed whereas Joan scores as severely and chronically depressed. Therapy is beneficial for both. On the same test given a few months after the end of the treatment, each raises her score by ten points. The ten-point difference moves Ann into the low end of the normal range. Her depressions are less frequent than before, last a shorter time, and interfere with her work and family life less than previously. The ten-point difference moves Joan into the low end of the moderately depressed range. She is still depressed much of the time but the feelings are less deep, she thinks about suicide much less frequently, and she is able to hold a job, something that was impossible before. There is no doubt that both Ann and Joan improved. In fact, the change in Joan is probably more dramatic than that in Ann. Nonetheless, Ann is in far better shape. She feels better than

Joan, is better able to function, and is probably far more attractive to potential romantic partners and employers. The severity of Joan's problems, whatever the cause, puts a ceiling on how much change she can make. She can be helped by medication or therapy, but she can't catch up to Ann.

Because of our attachment to the idea of equality, many of us are rubbed the wrong way by examples like these and are tempted to think that Joan and Harry could get to the level of Ann and John by the simple expedient of getting more help. Why can't Joan stay in therapy or get into another one and move up another ten points, and then perhaps go into a third program and move up the scale again? I'm not sure I can give a satisfactory answer to the question, but I do know there is little in the literature or in the interviews I did to support the conclusion that such things can be done. Recall that there is no relationship between duration of treatment and improvement.

TIME AND ENERGY

Time and energy are powerful and largely neglected limiting factors. Both are required for change. In addition to attending sessions, most change processes need clients to spend time doing homework. Experience shows that for many people a few hours a week are more than they can spare: they don't set aside enough time for their therapy tasks or they are so tired when they get to them that what they do is ineffective. Such people are often called unmotivated, but the term doesn't always fit. Sometimes they are very motivated — they do want to make the change — but they also want to do everything else they are doing and can't find a way of cutting down on other activities. Time and energy are also necessary to maintain changes, and things get problematic after therapy is concluded. Without the necessity of reporting regularly to a counselor, required maintenance tasks are often soon forgotten or put aside.

Though we don't like to hear it, time and energy are limited. What is put into one area or activity cannot be put into another. Those who try to be good at all things with few exceptions end up not being good at any of them. Those who want to make and maintain changes in one area must often forgo doing the same in another area.

A couple comes to therapy because of dissatisfaction with their family life. Though they obviously care for each other and for their children, they aren't spending much quality time together. There is little intimacy and family outings have become rare. They would like to feel closer and spend more time together. But both are unshakably committed to excelling in their careers. They work at least ten hours a day at their offices and then bring work home. After eating supper and attending to emergencies, household chores, and the work they bring home, there is little time or energy to be with the children or with each other. Though they both say they would like to restore frequency and vigor to their sex life, by the time they finish all the other important things, they can barely think about sex, let alone do something about it. In short, excelling at work is their top priority and gets their best shot. The meager time and energy remaining has to be carefully rationed. The main problem is that their fantasies about marriage and family life are not being satisfied, but these fantasies did not include two people so single-mindedly devoted to their careers. Having a satisfying family life can take a great deal of time and energy, something many learn to their surprise and dismay. This couple was able to make a few small changes that give them a bit more time for each other and for the children, but I think the main contribution of therapy was to help them understand they couldn't have everything, that the fantasies of family life would have to remain fantasies as long as they were unwilling to reduce the effort given to work.

Learning Difficulties

Change requires learning. The client has to learn to pay attention to certain things, to make new connections, to think differently, to gain new perspectives, to act differently. If none of these things occur, there is no change. That's fine, you say — all one has to do is learn some new things; no problem there. Yet there is a problem because learning is not as easy as we often assume and there are vast individual differences in ability to learn.

There is abundant evidence about the difficulty of learning, yet it seems not to register. It is now quite clear that after years and years of education, many high school and even college graduates cannot use the English language in anything approaching an appropriate manner, cannot do simple arithmetic, and know very little about the history of their country or how its government works. It is not my intention to blame students, teachers, or anyone else; I merely want to point out that learning simple facts is very difficult for many people. Whatever the roles and responsibilities of parents, teachers, and schools, at least a fair portion of the variance is accounted for by individual abilities among students. Even in the worst schools in the worst areas with the worst teachers, some students do very well; and even in the best schools in the best areas with the best teachers, some students learn almost nothing.

A similar situation obtains in all of life. Some people learn very quickly, others more slowly, and some never or at best very little and very slowly. An example of learning difficulties familiar to those who saw the movie *Patton* concerns the general himself and is very similar to what often happens in therapy. Patton's main goal in life was to accomplish great things on the battlefield, and World War II gave him his chance. He had the talent — even his enemies acknowledged his greatness as a warrior — but he had a problem. He acted as impulsively off the battlefield as on — criticizing his superiors, peers, and our allies; hitting an enlisted man — with the result that he was always in hot water and saw less action than otherwise would have been the case. He knew the problem, shooting off his mouth, and was fully aware of the consequences. To achieve his goal of command, all he had to do was keep his mouth shut. It's difficult to think of a more clear-cut therapeutic task. Yet Patton, an intelligent man with motivation to spare, couldn't do it. He paid heavily for his impulsivity, but he seemed to learn nothing from his bad experiences, or at least nothing he could usefully apply.

Another example: A man comes to therapy to deal with his ulcer. One thing he needs to learn is to be aware of his level of stress — as indicated, for example, by the knot in his stomach — so he can take appropriate action when it gets too high. This seems very simple

— just pay attention to your stomach — and it is . . . for some people. For others, it is extremely difficult. No matter how many times therapist and client go over the point, and no matter in how many different ways, it doesn't register. The client pays attention when the therapist directs him in the office, but never on his own. On the outside, he notices his stomach only after it is too late.

Clients who don't learn — who don't get it — are immensely frustrating to therapists, equally as frustrating as clients who don't carry out therapeutic assignments, and are usually called resistant. Therapists believe they don't want to learn. The man secretly gets satisfaction from having his ulcer and Patton really liked his martyr role. There may be some truth in these explanations for some people, but we should also leave room for learning difficulties. Some people can't seem to learn some things or they can only with great difficulty.

Of course there are different learning styles. Some clients who are unable to learn in one type of therapy may do much better in another kind. Some prefer the intellectual exchange of psychoanalysis while others learn better in an experiential therapy. But again there are limits. Some people have gone through all or most types of counseling and the different styles and formats have not helped at all. They can't learn or change no matter what.

UNWILLINGNESS TO CARRY OUT
THERAPEUTIC AND MAINTENANCE PROCEDURES

Many people who come to counseling do not do what is necessary to make the changes they desire, which brings to mind what Edna St. Vincent Millay once wrote: "Please give me some good advice in your next letter. I promise not to follow it." The psychoanalytic patient who won't free-associate and establish a transference relationship with the analyst, the Jungian client who doesn't have any dreams or won't write them down, the gestalt client who won't role-play, the encounter group member who won't open up and won't participate in group exercises, and the behavior therapy client who won't do his homework are all examples of what we are discussing. Resistance is usually how such behaviors are described. Regardless of the reasons for noncompliance, the main point is that in most cases there will be no change if the procedures are not carried out.

A skillful therapist will be able to help many of his clients through or around their resistances one way or another and will be careful not to engender resistance by inappropriate or badly put suggestions, but there still remain many who can't or won't do what is necessary. Helping them change is extremely difficult. Whatever it is that won't allow them to do what is required places severe limits on their ability to change.

For change to be maintained, clients need to keep doing certain things — be aware of certain feelings, do exercises, meditate, keep a journal, and so on. We have noted that time and energy are obstacles, but they are not the only ones. Sometimes a client won't do what is necessary because it reminds him of the way he used to be and that is painful. Not doing the procedures helps erase the memories and avoids pain. It is also true that many no longer see a reason for doing their exercises. The change has been made, things are better, and they forget the past. The alcoholic forgets what it is like to be controlled by liquor and accepts the drink offered by his host. One drink never killed anyone. Soon one drink becomes several, but what the hell, it's a party and everyone is drinking. And soon he is on his way back to what he used to be.

Maintenance procedures are difficult because they make a person feel abnormal and require special effort. Everyone else here is drinking so why should I be different? Besides, I feel so stupid asking for ginger ale or standing here without a drink in my hand. The meditator begins to wonder why he has to wake up twenty minutes early to meditate. It's much easier to stay in bed or, if he does get up, to turn on the morning news. Couples who agree in therapy to keep an evening a week for themselves find it difficult to stick to the schedule. They have to turn down invitations and can't go to classes or meetings on that night. And they feel so stupid when someone asks why they can't go out on Wednesdays. The person who has learned special ways of communicating feels great relief when he doesn't use those ways but just does what comes naturally.

If the new ways can be maintained long enough, they become

integrated into one's life and seem natural and spontaneous. Everyone knows the Joneses don't go out Wednesday night and that's that. And the Joneses have been taking Wednesday evenings for themselves for so long now that it doesn't even occur to them there is another way. But it takes a very long time for habits to become so well established, usually years. Just think how long it took us to learn to brush our teeth, and with toothbrushing we had lots of help, namely the watchfulness of our parents and the immediate reward of a cleaner-feeling mouth. With most other things, there is no such help. Even with all the assistance we got with toothbrushing, dentists say many of us don't do it properly or long enough. And look at how many of us use the seat belts in our cars only sporadically or not at all, despite all the publicity about their benefits and despite the fact that their use is the essence of simplicity and requires almost no time.

A lovely example of difficulties in maintenance comes from Stephan Appelbaum, a psychonolyst who took training in many of the newer therapies, including Transcendental Meditation. While agreeing that TM is easy to learn and do, he says his meditating career lasted only as long as he was getting instruction. Appelbaum told his teacher he was too busy to meditate, to which the teacher replied, "If you are too busy to meditate, you are too busy."

> About that, he was right. When I consider how I waste forty minutes in the course of the day, frequently because I suffer from the tiredness that meditation would probably help me overcome, my excuse seems hollow indeed. Nonetheless, I like to think that the early morning is when I do my best work, and I cannot afford twenty of those golden minutes. In the evening I can't relax until I read the mail and deal with the day's emergencies. In high dudgeon I am liable to say to myself, if I spent all that time meditating, how the hell would this book get written? The fact is that if I meditated regularly it might well have been written faster, easier, and better.

Despite this, and despite Appelbaum's belief "that meditation is a great, relatively untapped source of various kinds of health," he did not persist in meditating.

Appelbaum's experience is a common one. Despite the knowledge that something would be helpful in many ways, we don't do it for long. My guess is that most of us could change with sufficient inducement. Perhaps one million dollars would get Appelbaum to meditate regularly for a year. But such incentive is hard to come by.

The point is that our lives have particular configurations which are not easily changed by therapeutic methods, though they can and do change for other reasons. One person is in the habit of sleeping as late as possible, another likes to spend a leisurely breakfast reading the paper, and a third just has to start the day with physical exercise. All of these people can probably change, substituting meditation, conversing with spouses, doing massage, or writing in a journal for their preferred activities, at least for a while. But as soon as the course is over or the pressure is off, there is a good chance they will suddenly or gradually go back to what they used to do.

LACK OF ENVIRONMENTAL SUPPORT FOR CHANGE

Humans are social beings. To a very great extent, the amount of change that can be made and maintained is dependent on how much it is supported or fought by important others. For many, there is little support and even outright hostility. A few examples follow.

A woman comes to counseling to become more assertive and independent. Her husband is not involved in the treatment but gives his blessing. The wife takes a few steps forward. She decides to go out with a woman friend on Thursday evenings, something she hasn't done since her marriage. She also does her assertiveness homework and tells her husband she doesn't appreciate his leaving his dirty clothes on the floor. Husband starts having second thoughts about therapy. He didn't realize she was going to get assertive with *him*, and he finds he doesn't like sitting alone on Thursday nights wondering where she is. If he meets her attempts at change with criticism and hostility, she is going to have great difficulty changing. She may decide to give up the attempt at change to forestall his criticism and the bad feelings that follow.

Consider people trying to break or control an addiction. Do their spouses serve a big chocolate cake for their birthdays or do they offer fruit salad instead? Do their friends go out of their way to serve soda or juice at dinner or do they have only wine? Do they constantly smoke in front of them and offer cigarettes? These things make a big difference.

A man learns to meditate and wants to do it every morning, but his wife and children (or roommates) interrupt with questions and conversation. They stop after repeated requests, but now they have the television on in the next room so loud that he focuses more on the news than on his mantra. Will he do something about this, and whatever they come up with next, or simply give up?

One can to a great extent fight environmental pressures. One can be assertive or expressive regardless of other people's reaction. One can refuse a drink even if everyone else is drinking. One can meditate elsewhere or get others to keep quiet. One can even change friends, homes, and marital partners. These things can be done, and there is no shortage of examples of them being done. But they are difficult to do and many times it is easier to yield to pressure and go back to the old ways.

LUCK

Although luck is a nebulous and unscientific word, and though we don't understand it well, it is real and important. Bad fortune can undermine the best laid plans of counselor and client, and good luck can undo serious therapeutic errors and make for contentment even against great odds.

A couple enters therapy to work on marital problems and some progress is made. Then their oldest son announces his plans to marry a woman they don't approve of. Two weeks later, the wife's mother finds she has terminal cancer. These two issues become part of the therapy, but because the wife is spending more time on the East Coast with her mother and because of medical and transportation costs, the couple decides to stop. A year later they return to counseling. They say they are over the worst of the grieving for the wife's mother and things are better with their son, who decided against marrying the woman. We work for several months and some change is made, but less than any of us believe would have been made a year before. None of us can say why, but it seems to all of us that something is missing. A year ago, they were "hot," as the husband puts it. They were raring to work on their problems and make a better marriage. Now they are still willing, but the edge is gone. Of course no one can be certain how things would have gone a year ago, but it does feel as if the right time or best time has passed.

I believe that some changes can only be made or can best be made at certain times, while other times are not as propitious. I realize how nebulous and mystical this sounds, but there are many parallels in the rest of life. For example, a number of times a book comes highly recommended but when I try to read it, I can't get into it or stay with it. The expression "I can't relate to it" captures my feeling exactly. But sometimes, months or years later, I pick up the same book and get a great deal from it. It works the other way as well. Sometimes I have gone back to a book that I once considered brilliant or moving, but now I find it superficial or boring; I can no longer relate to it. Coming back to therapy, I have been able to help some clients who failed in previous counseling very similar to mine. Of course no two therapies or therapists are exactly the same and it may be that the differences between the two programs or counselors, as small as they seem, were what made the difference. It may also be that the first program prepared the clients to do better in the second, just as people usually better their scores when they take a test the second time. I cannot rule out these possibilities, but I continue to believe that timing was important. Most of the clients I have discussed this with agree, saying things like "I wasn't ready to work on my marriage then" or "Somehow the time didn't seem right for making the change."

The problem is that it is extremely difficult to know when the right time is. Such things are obvious only in retrospect. But some people generally hit the right times and others generally the wrong ones, and I call that a matter of luck. The ones with bad luck have less chance of making desired changes.

Fortune also plays a crucial role in determining whether changes are maintained. When most people end therapy, their new behaviors are shaky and not well integrated into their lives. During at least the first year after termination, their new patterns are extremely vulnerable to disruption. If fortune smiles on them, they may be able to maintain the changes. With bad luck, the chances are not good. In a study of former clients who had relapsed, Arnold Lazarus found that most of them lost gains made in therapy after stressful situations that had not, and probably could not have, been predicted, things like disappointment in love or friendship, the disapproved marriage of a son or daughter, or new responsibilities at work. Relapses also often occur after traumas such as the death of a loved one, serious illness or bodily injury, and loss of job.

Many of us seem to have our share of both good and bad luck, but there are some on each extreme. There are those we call lucky: the gods always seem to favor them. There are also those on the other side: the gods seem to have it in for them. Tragedy and misfortune stalk them. As soon as they recover from their automobile accident, their daughter finds she is accidentally and unhappily pregnant or their son fails out of school or their home is burglarized, and it is predictable that in the weeks or months ahead someone close will lose a job and someone else will need a biopsy. Whether we believe that such people create their own misfortune or don't take responsibility or have bad karma, the point is that they are seriously limited in how much change they can make and maintain.

The obvious conclusion to what has been said so far is that there are limits to how much each of us can change. The limits of human malleability are much closer to the ground than they are to the sky. Even a person who is relatively well put together and has a wise and skillful teacher, therapist, or guru may not be able to change as much as or in the direction that he desires. And for some people and some problems — regardless of how much effort and skill are expended — there is going to be little change or none at all. There is nothing unusual about this conclusion — it also holds true in other human endeavors such as education, medicine, business, and sports — but may be harder to take because we have come to expect so much from therapy. We expect it to have magical powers to fix personal and interpersonal problems, and even huge and complex social difficulties as well. I suggest that nothing is that powerful; even magic, as we should have learned from Merlin, has its limits.

An important implication of this conclusion is that we may have to give up some of our ideas about what is possible for humans, individually and collectively, and may have to question the utopian notions put forth by therapists. We may need to supplant such notions with greater reliance on our own experiences. These experiences tell us that life is not a continuous series of peak experiences or a process of ever-expanding satisfaction, and that it is hard even under the best of circumstances. There are always disappointments, conflicts both within and without, frustrations, anxieties, plans that go awry, friends who betray or go away, and the sickness and death of loved ones. Murphy's Law, one of the most valid statements ever made about human endeavors, is not amenable to therapeutic manipulation. Somewhere deep down we also know that life is profoundly unfair and undemocratic. Aptitude, skill, attractiveness, and sensitivity are not equally distributed. Not everyone can make lots of money, be a leader or a celebrity, write great books or do well on the ballfield, have wonderful relationships and ecstatic sex. There are many who can't even cope with the events of everyday life. This is simply the way it is and not all the therapy, drugs, magic, or government programs in the world can alter it. Therapy is not a cure for the human condition.

Our experience teaches that suffering and evil are inherent parts of life, even though the therapeutic enterprise in America to a great extent denies them. We know there have always been drunks and idiots; those who couldn't get along with their children, parents, spouses, and neighbors; those who were too passive or too aggressive; those whose behavior upset others and who were in trouble with the powers that be; and some who committed homicide and suicide. But there is now a strong tendency to explain all problems and evil in psychological terms — illness, deprivation, insanity, diminished capacity — and therefore to explain them away. As long as we cling to notions of sickness and deprivation, which in theory are alterable, we don't have to confront insoluble problems and evil. When we have a society in which all wrongs have been righted and

all diseases cured — when everyone has lots of love and understanding, a good education and a fulfilling job that pays well, higher
than average self-esteem, satisfying relationships, no unresolved
traumas, regular sexual expression, and free access to medical and
psychological services — then, we are led to believe, there won't
be any personal conflicts and tragedies, or any murders, rapes, suicides, and Jonestowns.

We may have to face the possibility that such notions are fantasies, that not everything can be changed, that there are insoluble
problems and insufferable people, as well as some who, because of
genetic endowment or upbringing, are ill equipped to live normal
lives in a free society. We may also have to acknowledge that the
capacity for evil is at least as great as the capacity for good, and
that the former outweighs the latter in many people. There are some
in society for whom violence is a way of life: they kill and maim
with barely a regret, although they are good at acting remorseful
when they believe this will get them a shorter sentence or a parole.
The only choices for society may be to channel their violence in
acceptable directions, for example in military service, lock them up
for good, or kill them. It is clear that not a lot of them are going to
change their ways because of therapeutic interventions. Similarly,
some people are going to take their own lives and there is not much
that can be done about it. Suicide prevention centers do *not* lower
the suicide rates, and neither do cradle-to-grave welfare services.
The highest suicide rates in the world are found in those countries
— Finland, Austria, Denmark, and Switzerland — with the most
highly developed welfare systems. And plenty of people who kill
themselves are in therapy at the time. I'm not blaming the counselors, just pointing out they often can't help.

These conclusions can be depressing, especially for people who
believe that nothing is impossible, that sorrow and tragedy are unnecessary. But they can also be looked at in another way. In the
next chapter I suggest there may be a great deal of relief and a
kind of freedom in the realization that not everything needs to be
worked on and changed, that we are probably healthier and better
off than we believe. For now I will introduce another thought. To
change everything we think needs changing, especially problems

such as violence toward self and others, would require a technology of behavior change more powerful than anything that currently exists, even in countries ruled by totalitarian regimes, something on the order of what is portrayed by George Orwell in *1984* or Aldous Huxley in *Brave New World*. Should such a technology ever exist, we would soon discover what a real problem is, for there is no way of assuring that those who possess it would use it in ways the rest of us find acceptable. Given what we know about the use to which powerful methods are put, it is almost certain it would become a tool of oppression. Not having such a technology is one of the surest guarantees of our freedom, just as having it would represent the greatest threat to freedom. If we had a choice, we might well decide that living with our current problems and accepting our limits to make changes are by far the best alternatives.

Change
in Perspective

"The essence of being human is that one does not seek perfection."

— GEORGE ORWELL

"I have examined myself thoroughly and come to the conclusion that I don't need to change much."

— SIGMUND FREUD

"I'm not OK — you're not OK, and that's OK."

— WILLIAM SLOANE COFFIN

THE LIMITS OF PERSONAL CHANGE discussed so far become less depressing and easier to accept with the realization that there is far less reason for changing ourselves then we have been led to believe, and that there are advantages to not trying to improve ourselves. The third American assumption about malleability, that people need to change, is largely a myth. We are not nearly as bad off and in need of fixing as therapists tell us. Much of what we now think of as problems — things that ought to be altered and for which there are solutions — are not so much problems as inescapable limits and predicaments of life. We see them as problems only because we have developed peculiar notions about what life can and should be. Putting these things in perspective, seeing them as inherent in the structure of life rather than as problems we can solve, will not make them go away but may allow us to avoid the dangers of pursuing unrealistic expectations and the self-criticism that so often accompanies failure to change.

One of the main reasons for wanting to improve ourselves is the belief that we are worse off than previous generations. Somehow — because of the often cited "stresses of modern living," capitalism, technology, or some other bogeyman — everything has gone to the dogs and we think we are less healthy, less loving, less expressive, more stressed, more violent, and suffer from more symptoms and problems. Despite widespread acceptance of this belief, there is precious little to support it. There is not a shred of evidence that we are under more psychological stress than were our ancestors. Until recently the masses of people suffered the daily stress of not knowing if there was going to be enough food to eat and they also had to deal with the possibility of infectious diseases, now largely conquered, that could wipe out a significant portion of the population in a few months. Nuclear weapons are new, but the threat of annihilation has been with mankind since the beginning. There is also no evidence of an increase in the incidence of serious emotional disorder since the advent of advanced industrialization. The best studies have failed to discover such a pattern of growth. To be sure, we talk more about our problems and seek help more often, but that is not the same as an increase in the number or severity of problems. The only sense in which it can be said that the number of problems has increased is that we now busily label as problems everything that limits and frustrates us.

I realize some will react with skepticism to these statements because they "know" that modern life exacts a horrendous toll. But we have to remember the apparently inherent human tendency to create good old days, mythical periods that were supposedly better than what we now have and when whatever is now bothering us presumably didn't exist. Good old days under closer examination invariably turn out to be not half as good as imagined. At Otto Bettmann says, after a lifetime studying the presumably better days of yore in America, *The Good Old Days — They Were Terrible!*

Alcoholism provides a fascinating case study of the good-old-days hypothesis because it is often attributed to the alienation, complexity, and strain of modern life, and statistics are presented demonstrating an increase in alcohol consumption in the last thirty to forty years. Presumably in earlier times life was easier and people weren't pushed to drink as much. But the truth is that Americans have always been heavy drinkers, more so two hundred years ago than today. John Adams asked, "Is it not mortifying . . . that we Americans should exceed all other people in the world in this degrading, beastly vice of intemperance?" and a Boston scholar in 1821 warned Thomas Jefferson that soon "we should hardly be better than a nation of sots." Heavy drinking and alcoholism have many causes, but it is difficult to conclude that modern living is one of them. Per capita consumption in 1975 was less than half of what it was in the years from 1750 to 1830.

Many of us believe that, as Erich Fromm wrote, "modern man is hardly capable of love." The idea has gone forth that we are a country of loveless, uncommunicative, hardly worthwhile relationships, all in need of therapeutic overhauls or at least tune-ups. Yet there is no evidence that we are less loving or less communicative than our ancestors. Up until the early nineteenth century, historian Edwin Shorter notes, "lovelessness was a common feature of the petty bourgeois and peasant marriage everywhere." We are today far more concerned with promoting relationships that are loving and also provide security and opportunities for sexual and emotional expression. That our efforts often fail does not signify that things were better in the past, but instead point to the great difficulty of what we are trying to achieve. With regard to communication, Shorter observes: "Whatever vexing dilemmas that Mom, Dad, and the Kids are wrestling with nowadays, they do not include some 'new' kind of uncommunicativeness." We probably communicate better than any people in history. Because we are better educated and more sophisticated, and more concerned with internal goings-on and relationship dynamics, we are better at recognizing, labeling, and expressing feelings, desires, and hurts than were our ancestors.

One thing many of us are certain of is that parent-child relationships and family life have deteriorated badly in modern times. In the good old days, the story goes, parents were much more loving toward their children, spent more time with them, and were more attentive to their needs. It's a nice story but it couldn't be farther from the truth. The supposedly close and warm families before the age of industrialization were hardly paragons of virtue. Infanticide and the abandonment of children were widespread until the early 1800s, and the beating of children by parents so common that it seemed the norm. There was little privacy for anyone and, by our standards, little understanding of children's needs. The now common idea that parental love was important for children was nonexistent until the modern era. Compared to our ancestors, we have much greater respect for children as individuals and are far more knowledgeable about their requirements. And America has always been the most child-oriented society in the world. To be sure, there are still problems, to which we devote more attention and concern than previous generations. But problems in this area are nothing new, having existed ever since family life began. In some cases, professional or nonprofessional assistance may be of benefit, but it cannot eliminate what the poet Rilke called "the drama that is always stretched taut between parents and children."

Evidence that family life has not declined over the past fifty years, and in fact has improved in many ways, comes from a recent follow-up to the classic Middletown studies. In the late 1970s, a team of sociologists did an exhaustive investigation of the families of Muncie, Indiana, to determine what changes had occurred since the work there in the 1920s and 1930s by Robert and Helen Lynd. Much to their surprise, they found "increased family solidarity, a smaller generation gap," and "closer marital communication." In addition, "contrary to the myth, suicide, mental breakdown, and domestic violence appear to be less frequent today than they were two generations ago. . . ." There is good reason to believe that these trends are similar for the whole country.

Work is yet another area that many think is worse than before. Visions of happy artisans and peasants float through our minds and we have the idea that their work was natural, holistic, and fulfilling, as compared to our own, which we feel is joyless, dronelike, and harmful, described by terms such as *alienation* and *dehumanization*. But, as George Will notes, "Almost all work has almost always been drudgery. What is new is that many people are surprised by the drudgery." Although much of our work is not interesting or fulfilling, we have far greater choice about what kind of work to do, we work fewer hours and under safer conditions, have longer breaks and vacations, and receive larger rewards. All of which means we have more time, energy, and money to pursue other activities to fulfill needs not met at work.

Of course not everyone locates the golden age in the past. Many look forward to the good new days, a future utopia where our lives will be more exciting, happier, and without the kinds of problems that now trouble us. All manner of panaceas are put forth that will presumably get us to this better place, but rarely is much said about their inherent limitations and about the tendency of people to feel bad, perhaps even worse than before, when they try the new ways and fail to achieve the advertised results.

Proper communication is supposed to be one of the main routes to a better life and there has been an unending supply of material telling us how better to communicate with our spouses, lovers, children, those we work with and for, and those we want to sell to or buy from. People have taken the message seriously and often feel themselves to be inadequate communicators when things don't turn out as they wish. But that doesn't necessarily mean they didn't communicate properly. It may simply mean that communication is not the answer or that no better outcome can be had in the situation regardless of what is done. Expressiveness, like all human activities, is limited in what it can do; and it can also be harmful. Too much communication, for instance, can be deadly. In organizations, it can hamper decision-making and reduce efficiency, as many businesses discovered to their horror after sending employees to therapeutic activities designed to help them get in touch with and express themselves. Having spent a fair amount of time in meetings with people who felt obliged to communicate openly and fully, I believe there are few things worse. Most of the time I left the meetings unable to determine what, if anything, had been decided. The only certain result I observed was that far less work got done on meeting days, not only because of the time spent in the meetings, but also because many of the participants devoted much of the rest of the day trying to figure out what had occurred during them.

Too much communication, or the wrong kind, can also cause harm in relationships. I have seen marriages destroyed or made worse by admissions of things that should have been kept secret, and I have seen couples suffer needlessly because of endless discussions (actually the same discussion repeatedly endlessly) about things that could not be changed or reconciled. There are both limits and prices to expressiveness, but all in all, I don't think most of us are deficient in this area. Rather than berating ourselves and others for not being sufficiently or properly communicative, we might be better off celebrating how much and how well most of us do express ourselves.

Something similar can be said about the issue of child-rearing. For a long time now, parents have been duped into believing that if only they did the right things, their children would develop in certain healthy ways. As already noted, when this doesn't happen, parents feel guilty and blame themselves. While I have no desire to let off the hook parents who have abused or in some other way mistreated their offspring, there are a lot of parents torturing themselves unnecessarily. Aside from a few points obvious to anyone — e.g., that children shouldn't be battered or made to feel totally incompetent — we really don't know how to raise the kind of children we have been told we should raise. The experts themselves disagree tremendously about what should be done. It is not easy to be either a parent or a child, but if we can give up some of our great expectations and our sense of great responsibility for how the children turn out, we might conclude that most of us are doing quite well and be able to enjoy our children more.

The number of things we now feel unnecessarily bad about is too long even to list. The making of evaluations or value judgments, as they are often called, is an informative example. Many of us feel that it is unhealthy, unwise, or just plain neurotic to make right/ wrong assessments. We should be empathic, understanding, accepting, and above all nonjudgmental. People strive to accept what is unacceptable to them and feel bad when they cannot do so. They apologize for their backwardness — "I don't want to seem to be passing judgment . . ." or "I guess I'm just old fashioned (or uptight)" — or else keep their mouths shut in order to avoid offending someone's sensibility and looking like judgmental fools. Many worry about their lack of acceptance or what some call their "closed-mindedness," and there are now courses and workshops where they can shed some of their rigidity.

Yet it is difficult to imagine an activity more common to all animals than the making of good/bad, right/wrong distinctions. Consider pets and children. Like and dislike are immediately manifest in their reaction to people, places, and things. What they don't like they respond to with aggressiveness, flight, or disgust. There is no problem discovering if your child likes a certain food or person: you'll get an immediate gut reaction.

That something comes easily to us does not necessarily make it right or useful, but neither does it necessarily make it wrong or destructive. Making evaluations does not seem particularly harmful most of the time and is often of value, for example by affirming for a person or a group what he or it believes in, or by indicating to others what is expected of them. Even if this were not the case, abolishing or even seriously decreasing judgmentalness is extremely difficult for most people. It is noteworthy that those in the vanguard of the struggle against making value judgments are themselves quite judgmental. If nothing else, they believe that value judgments and those who make them are bad or wrong. If *they* can't achieve the standards they preach to us about, why should we feel bad for thinking in terms of good and bad?

Of course it is sometimes nice to talk to someone who seems totally accepting and who doesn't judge what we say. But it is also good to be around people who are just the opposite: who know exactly what they like and dislike, what is right and wrong, and who mince no words about it. Such people are often admired and called men and women of principle. The standards of unconditional acceptance and nonjudgmentalness are unrealistic and probably not worthwhile even if they could be achieved.

We have succeeded in turning human limitations and natural differences between people into problems. Although it seems ridiculous once put on paper, we appear to believe that we all should be psychologically minded; in touch with our feelings; free of stress; open; expressive; spontaneous; creative; using all of our brain-power and other potential; assertive; free of biases, compulsions, addictions, depressions, and "irrational" fears; possessed of high self-esteem; independent yet capable of warm, loving relationships with others; and happy to accept the advice of those who set these standards and presumably know better than we do how we should live our lives. By meeting all these criteria, we are assured, we will feel good, be productive, avoid mental disorders and probably physical ones as well, and be as happy as possible. But this is a fantasy model of life, based not on the study of real people or on the study of anything at all, not much more than the opinions and fantasies of certain people who want to tell us how life ought to be.

This fantasy model ignores the obvious fact that people are different. I am certain that the response of some readers to the previous discussion is something like this: "Sure, we shouldn't aim for unattainable goals, but it has to be admitted that some people — my clients, my spouse, my friends, or I — are less expressive than others, feel less good about themselves, are less productive, or less happy. Since other people do better in these areas, why can't they?" It sounds like a reasonable question but it overlooks the fact that people are different. What is possible for one may not be possible for another. Just because Einstein had the intelligence and creativity to do what he did does not mean that others can do the same thing. Just because Martha is able to be a good wife and mother, do very well in her law practice, and still find time for swimming and reading does not mean that those of us who aren't doing as much or as well are guilty of not using all our potential. Maybe Martha had more potential to begin with. And just because, to use one of Joyce Brothers's success stories, Avery became a wealthy realtor by telling himself every day, "You must succeed. You're going to succeed," doesn't mean that you have the discipline to make a habit of this ritual or, even if you do, that you'll also become rich. Maybe you and Avery, and your susceptibility to positive thinking, are just different.

Our expectations have simply gotten out of hand. There are few, if any, real people who measure up to the standards of well-being now accepted by millions of Americans. Consider the following men and women, none of whom fit these standards. Assuredly not all were happy, but they were creative, productive, admirable in many ways, and among them are some that may be the best our race is capable of producing.

Charles Darwin was a recluse, a hypochondriac, and probably an agoraphobic. Other famous hypochondriacs include Lord Byron, Shelley, and Tennyson. Byron himself was a whole case study: he was a "nervous wreck" who bit his fingernails to the quick and kept two loaded pistols at his bedside, the better to fight off the enemies who appeared in his nightmares; though reputed to be a great lover, his bedroom was filled with pills and potions for his many imagined diseases and smelled more like a pharmacy than a love nest; he had an uncontrollable temper and apparently enjoyed torturing women; and, obsessed with retaining his slender figure, he ate only one meal a day, usually consisting of a small potato. Goethe was depressed much of his life, as was the great American psychologist William James. The latter also seems to have had something of a self-image problem; he described his classic work, *The Principles of Psychology*, as "a loathsome, distended, tumefied, bloated, dropsical mass." Founding Father Alexander Hamilton was a good example of self-hate ("I hate Congress — I hate the army — I hate the world — I hate myself," he wrote to a friend) and self-destructiveness (making a lurid public confession of adultery; attacking the character of President John Adams, the head of Hamilton's own party; and getting into a duel he couldn't hope to win with Aaron Burr). August Strindberg was probably schizophrenic and wrote a book about his own case. Virginia Woolf was manic-depressive and took her own life, as did a number of other luminaries including Sylvia Plath, Jack London, Ernest Hemingway, and inventor George Eastman. Thomas Edison was the complete workaholic, laboring day and night on his inventions, exactly the type of person now so often called unhealthy by therapists. Van Gogh did not fit anyone's model of a healthy personality — though he seems to have had more than his share of spontaneity — and was psychotic before he killed himself. Florence Nightingale suffered from what we might now call anxiety neurosis and was bedridden much of her life. She also talked to herself and carried around a pet bird in her pocket wherever she went. When the bird died, she had it stuffed and continued to carry it about. Mary Baker Eddy, the founder of Christian Science, was tortured by maladies of various sorts her whole life long, including panic attacks (for which she was treated with morphine), paranoia, colic, and probably hysteria. Nonetheless, the success of Christian Science, the only one of a host of mind-cure treatments to achieve the dignity of a popular and established religion, was due entirely to her efforts. Alcoholic writers are legion: in addition to Hemingway and London, we can add Edgar Allan

Poe (who was obsessed with death, depressed, and a consumer of every known drug), F. Scott Fitzgerald, John O'Hara, William Faulkner, Edwin Arlington Robinson (who was painfully shy and unable to make friends), Malcolm Lowry (another shy man), Jack Kerouac (who was also addicted to drugs), Raymond Chandler, Eugene O'Neill, James Joyce, Sinclair Lewis, and Thomas Wolfe. The great Victorian critic John Ruskin was manic-depressive, attracted to little girls, and, though married, celibate his whole life, a characteristic he shared with Isaac Newton. Sexologist Havelock Ellis barely escaped the same fate, overcoming his lifelong impotency at the age of sixty. I have indicated earlier that many famous therapists, including Freud, Harry Stack Sullivan, and Fritz Perls, suffered from various emotional difficulties and destructive habits.

Psychiatrist Anthony Storr writes that two of the greatest creative geniuses of all time, Newton and Einstein, were schizoid personalities. Einstein's teachers thought him to be "mentally slow, unsociable and adrift forever in his foolish fantasies." At the age of sixteen he had what was called a nervous breakdown. Had he gone to school in modern America, Einstein would undoubtedly have been sent to the school counselor or another therapist to get himself straightened out. Newton was even more solitary than Einstein and his lack of sexual interest and involvement would now be sufficient to earn him the label of misfit or neurotic. Like Einstein, Newton was often adrift in his foolish fantasies, many times forgetting to eat and sleep. He also had what we might call a publication phobia: he had a paralyzing fear of exposing his thoughts and discoveries, and published his work only under extreme pressure from friends. He also had what seems to have been a nervous breakdown.

Abraham Lincoln manifested many of the behaviors we are now so concerned about. He suffered deep bouts of depression his whole life and was preoccupied with death and fascinated by madness. He revealed almost nothing of his feelings to anyone, a characteristic that led his law partner to call him the most "shut-mouthed" man who ever lived. His marriage had a number of problems, many caused by his unwillingness to share more time and his feelings with his wife. She preferred a good fight to clear the air, but Lincoln "often withdrew at the first sign of a quarrel, for he hated fussing, avoided it whenever he could." Needless to say, Lincoln would not be given the stamp of approval by our current experts. But he carried on nonetheless — using humor to combat his depressions and more than making up for his deficiencies with compassion, political acumen, and sheer determination — to become one of the greatest and most admired of American politicians.

The point of this list, which could easily be expanded, is not to glorify emotional problems, to sling mud at greatness, or to suggest a link between neuroses and creativity. It is rather that neuroses, emotional difficulties, or whatever you call them, are quite common, close to universal. Even those people we call great, whom we admire and respect, who have in one way or another made it, have their share. Even those people who presume to tell the rest of us how to live also have their share, and perhaps more than their share. And consider these people I talked to, all of whom by most standards are living good lives:

A professional woman who has what she calls a "thing" about driving on freeways. She's scared to death of the highways and has to prepare carefully for each trip. She psyches herself up for about half an hour and loads up the front and back seats of her car with fruit, candies, and other snacks. The car looks like a mobile grocery store but she can go where she has to, though with great trepidation.

A writer with half-a-dozen books and scores of articles to his credit, lots of money in the bank, and one of the warmest and most supportive families I have seen. Yet he is a bundle of insecurities, always thinking that what he is working on is worthless and will be rejected or, if accepted, will receive humiliating reviews. He is also highly opinionated and critical, taking strong positions on every possible issue, including those he knows absolutely nothing about.

An educator who can't have a lasting intimate relationship. She has had several marriages and many romances. She says she wants a permanent union but is unsure she has what it takes, and finds this distressing. On the other hand, she does very well in her work and is sought out by colleagues and students for personal advice.

A therapist who is severely depressed and has been so most of his life. He is at least as depressed as most of his depressed patients, but at the same time he is witty, well read, and has a lot of interesting things to say.

A successful businessman who has a good family life, is active in community affairs, and is well liked by most who know him. He also smokes nonstop and drinks heavily. His family doesn't like these vices but has learned to live with them and has stopped making helpful suggestions on how to end them.

I suggest that all these people are normal, not much different than most other people except perhaps for being more successful. This statement will undoubtedly ruffle some feathers because we have come to believe that normal or healthy means the absence of problems and difficulties, and at least an approximation of the virtues held out by therapeutic experts. But this is an unrealistic notion. Whether physically or emotionally, there are always disorders, distresses, symptoms, and problems. Health or well-being does not consist of their absence but rather of being able to function *reasonably* effectively and to feel *relatively* content in their presence.

The ubiquity of physical disorder is well documented. Sociologist Renée Fox states:

> If we include into what is considered to be sickness or, at least, nonhealth in the United States, disorders manifested by subjective symptoms which are not brought to the medical profession for diagnosis and treatment, but which do not differ significantly from those that are, then almost everyone in the society can be regarded as in some way "sick."

Studies have found that up to 90 percent of apparently healthy samples had some physical aberration or clinical disorder. The more intensive the examination, the higher the rate of significant but previously undiagnosed and untreated problems. If we look closely enough, we find that most people have symptoms of illness. Defined as the presence of clinically serious symptoms, illness is the statistical norm. What is true physically is also true emotionally. If we look closely enough, all of us have signs and symptoms of emotional dis-ease.

If you want to conduct your own experiment on the ubiquity of behavioral problems, here is one. Pick some people you admire, respect, or think are doing well (e.g., have good marriages, are successful or happy), but they must be people about whom you can get detailed personal information through observation, questioning, or reading. For all of them, list the problems they have: addictions, anxieties, compulsions, depressions, phobias, trouble with the law or on the job, relationship and sexual difficulties, and so on. My guess is that you won't find many people, maybe any, who are free of these problems. If that is true, if almost everyone has them, why do we make such a big deal about them? Maybe they are just part of life, not abnormal but just the opposite. Does it make any sense to try to eliminate them?

Some will give a strong affirmative answer to this question and will take the discussion leading up to it as evidence of just how urgently we need more, new, and better ways of changing people. Many therapists will feel vindicated: there really are a tremendous number of complaints and difficulties requiring their attention; there are scores of millions of people who need their help. All the symptoms should be cured and all the problems resolved. But this position leads to a number of difficult problems and, in my opinion, is itself the greatest problem now confronting us. It assumes and affirms what many people already fear is true — that they are fundamentally flawed and in need of fixing — and we have earlier seen the effects of this assumption. This point of view also assumes that there really are ways of making life better and of substantially resolving problems, a proposition of doubtful validity. And adherence to such a position would mean even greater involvement in change efforts than what we currently have. The whole country would have to be turned into a hospital or clinic in which almost everyone would be undergoing some form of treatment or therapy much of the time. It is worth asking whether we want to have this kind of society and pay the kinds of prices it would entail.

It seems to me that we would be far better off to consider whether we really need to change everything, and I would hope that such consideration would include the thought that there are no perfect arrangements, personalities, traits, or relationships. There are only different characteristics, styles, and behaviors, each with its own strong and weak sides, each with something good and something missing. Every human characteristic, activity, relationship, and organization is double-edged. In short, everything has a price. When we think about change, we see only the positive in the way we hope we can become. It takes longer to see the prices and defects in the new way. If we thought about them ahead of time, and about the strengths as well as the shortcomings of our present situation, we might not be so quick to try to change; we might, in fact, conclude that what we now have isn't all that bad.

We have all heard much about the advantages to assertiveness. Without denying them, it seems fair to point out also that there are prices to be paid. For one thing, not everyone likes people who are always saying what they want and don't want, no matter how tactfully they say it. For another thing, being assertive can result in disagreements and quarrels with others; they too may be assertive and not agree with your desires. And last, the very act of making your desires public and having them rejected, which is inevitable some of the time, can lead to greater disappointment and frustration than if you had kept quiet. Unassertiveness also has its costs. You may be less able to get what you want and may feel that no one takes your wishes, unspoken though they may be, into account. On the other hand, you may find it easier to get along with others, with fewer hassles. It is extremely difficult to have the advantages of both assertiveness and nonassertiveness. Prices have to be paid either way.

One thing we all seem to desire is good health. Yet we have it on the authority of two of our greatest geniuses that even health exacts a toll and that there is something to be said for physical dis-ease. Albert Einstein suffered from sporadic attacks of stomach pain for over thirty years. Gall bladder trouble was suspected but it was never cured and Einstein often refused to take his doctor's advice. While it would be going too far to say he enjoyed his pain, he did welcome its appearance because it helped him work. He wrote to an old friend:

> When I suffer such an attack, I can often work very successfully. It does not seem to be very favorable for the imagination if one feels too well. At least the gods seem well intentioned toward me when they squeeze the gall bladder.

If that sounds strange, consider what another chronic sufferer of various pains had to say. Some of the writing in *The Interpretation of Dreams* was bad, stated Freud, because he was "feeling too well physically; I have to be somewhat miserable in order to write well." Elsewhere he noted that he needed a "moderate amount of discomfort" to do good work. His biographer Ernest Jones concludes that "happiness and well-being" were not conducive to Freud's best work and, indeed, that he made his most original contributions when his neurosis was at its height. Freud continued to smoke his daily quota of cigars long after he had contracted cancer of the jaw, a practice that did nothing to decrease his pain or improve his health, but he wrote that he owed "to the cigar a great intensification of my capacity to work and a facilitation of my self-control."

A lot of what we now call problems and want to get rid of are what make people interesting. That the great captain of industry is afraid of dogs or airplanes, that the strong man or woman is obsessed by fear of failure, that someone who appears to have it all together feels confused most of the time or can't get much of anything together in the bedroom, that the preacher of positive thinking is often depressed, that some great changers of others can't change themselves — these "flaws" are often what make them appealing, more human, and draw us to them. Many of these people would be far less interesting and attractive without their problems. As critic Anatole Broyard comments: "When I look at some of my friends who have 'outgrown,' or been psychoanalyzed away from, the peculiarities that originally drew me to them, I wish there were something like an Institute of Regression where they could go and have their psyches turned back like a clock or speedometer."

I am not arguing against change: people are free to try to alter themselves if they so desire. But it may not be necessary to do so and it may entail a larger price than they foresee. What they take to be problems can also be viewed as attractive or at least not terribly unattractive peculiarities or eccentricities. Newton and Einstein, I believe, would be far less interesting and appealing had they resolved their problems and conformed more to conventional social standards. Since their eccentric behavior is largely what allowed them to do their creative work, it is entirely possible that resolution of their problems would have seriously hampered that work. Something similar can be said for Darwin, whose many disorders and reclusiveness are what allowed, or perhaps forced, him to stay home and write the books by which we remember him. Achilles is unthinkable without his vulnerable heel, as is Lincoln without his anguish and depression, Van Gogh without his outbursts of passion and craziness, Patton without his impulsiveness, and Woody Allen without his neuroses. These lives each fit together and make sense. That there was discomfort and pain in each does not detract from them nor does it differentiate them from other lives.

Another way of putting much of the preceding discussion is, as Lewis Thomas says, "that most people are . . . abundantly healthy." Sure, they have problems, hassles, idiosyncrasies and even idiocies, bad habits, and all the rest, but that's the way people are. Change may be possible for some of them, but whether it is or not, they can have relatively productive and meaningful lives. People as they are are not paragons of virtue and they are often difficult to get along with, both for others and themselves; that's the way it is. Not only are most people reasonably healthy, so long as we use realistic standards, they are also tough, resilient, and resourceful, capable in one way or another of handling what life offers them. As already noted, many of them are pretty good therapists for themselves and those around them. They do not need more or less constant surveillance and guidance from experts. My guess is that the vast majority of people need no surveillance and guidance at all from professional therapists. The maintenance of physical and emotional well-being, and the amelioration of present distress, is far less dependent on what experts do than on what people, in their families and communities and on their own, do for themselves and each other. Of course, awareness and use of one's personal and social resources will not rid the world or even oneself of distress and disability, the suffering human flesh and psyche are heir to, but neither will an increasingly large and expensive mental health apparatus. There are limits to change and to what life can be.

We have entered a time when we have no choice but to face our limits in many areas: economics, international politics, and the military. Whatever else the future holds, it is clear that the period of American exceptionalism, as it is often called, is over. We will have to live as one nation among many, stronger and richer than most but no longer so powerful that we alone can decide our fate. This fact may make it possible for us to also face our social and personal limits, to acknowledge that we can't solve all the ills that have troubled mankind from the beginning and that we don't have the ability to make perfect people. The self-improvement endeavor has moved too fast and too far. Without realizing what was happening, we now find ourselves firmly enmeshed in it. Just as we used our great resources and industrial capabilities to fool ourselves about how much power we had, we have used therapeutic thinking to lie to ourselves and one another about what life is like, what we can do, and what therapy can accomplish. This may be a good time to reevaluate our thinking about personal change and to recognize our limits, and doing so may be less terrible than it at first appears.

It may help to recognize that the aimlessness, loneliness, confusion, dissatisfaction, and many other things that we feel and that lead many of us to try to change, are simply some of the prices we have to pay for liberating ourselves from traditional belief systems and the institutions that supported them. Not knowing what else to do, we try to change ourselves and eliminate or mitigate the feelings, but this is not necessarily the best course to follow. The simple fact is that freedom is not easy to live with. But neither is anything else. Living without the traditional supports may not be all fun and games, but neither was living with them. There may have been a stronger sense of belonging and identity, but there were also far more constraints, fewer options, and much less freedom. Neither the therapeutic ideology nor any other contemporary ideology is powerful enough to assuage our sorrows and guide our lives. The care provided by counselors may be comforting, at least for a while, but it has no answers to the riddles and hazards of our time. The kind of help we often seem to want simply does not exist, and maybe it never did.

One can search for answers in self-improvement and elsewhere, but there is another option, that of accepting ourselves as we are, because that seems to be good enough or, even if not good enough, that is what we are stuck with. Freud's statement — "I have examined myself thoroughly and come to the conclusion that I don't need to change much" — is a good illustration of this position, as is William Sloane Coffin's idea that it's okay that none of us is okay. Given the ridiculous standards we have accepted for ourselves, hardly any of us can be given a clean bill of health and feel that we finally are the way we ought to be. Perhaps to some extent we can accept that we will never achieve these standards and that we don't need to, that we really don't need to change much or at all. If this position was good enough for Freud, maybe it can be good enough for us.

The recognition and acceptance of limits can be liberating in its own way. To say we'll never be thin, assertive, cheerful, or overcome our fear of speaking in public, that we'll never write a book or win an election, that we'll never reach the top of our field or overcome our psychosis or straighten out our confusion and feel that we have our lives in order — to say any of these things or a myriad of others can be as relieving and freeing as it first appears to be depressing. It frees us from having to confront day after day the possibility of finally doing whatever it is we keep thinking we will do and from blaming ourselves and others for not doing it. If we can make some peace with ourselves for giving up in one or more areas — and keep in mind that professional assistance is probably not required for this — there is one less thing to be concerned about, one less thing to feel bad about, and more time and energy to devote to things we can do something about.

A woman I talked to had spent most of her adult life trying to lose weight; she had participated in more diets and weight-loss programs than she can remember. While she often lost weight, she just as often and just as quickly put it on again. Then, a few years ago, she gave up. "It's such a feeling of relief. No more diets, no more hating myself for thinking about food and eating more than I should, and for not being slim. I have come to terms with the fact that I'm fat and always will be. It's not as bad as I thought. I do everything I want and really haven't lost much except for the fantasy that someday I'll be svelte. The other things I lost, the constant worrying and self-criticism, I was glad to lose. I'm sure there are neurotic reasons why I eat so much, but it's also true that I love food: talking about it, shopping for it, preparing it, eating it, and then talking about how good it was. I can live with my fatness and feel that a weight has been lifted off of me since I accepted this is who I am."

A similar account comes from a man who spent about six years in seven different therapies. There were changes in each, but all changes were short-lived. He finally realized he wasn't going to change in any important way. "At first I felt terrible about this, but over a period of time I took careful stock of myself and decided that I didn't need to change. I'd been blowing things out of proportion, seeing my problems as totally bad. For example, I'm very critical and aggressive, and this turns some people off; it used to turn me off and was one of things I had tried to change. But I discovered there is also a positive side. People trust me, they know I won't bullshit them, and my aggressiveness gets me a lot of things; without it I wouldn't be half as successful a businessman as I am. Also, I don't get taken in as much as my less critical friends. I'm not saying criticalness and aggressiveness are all good. I hurt when someone is offended by my behavior or says that I rain on their parade. But all in all, I think the positive in my personality outweighs the negative. I have a good deal and I'm glad I stopped trying to remake myself. I've been more content since I made that decision."

And here is the experience of a much separated and much therapized couple, now married almost twenty years, as told by the wife: "I can't truly say our lives are wonderful, but they sure as hell are a lot better than before. We spent so many years in futile attempts to change our relationship, by ourselves and with more therapists than I care to remember. Finally, maybe just before we had exhausted ourselves with all these attempts and all our separations, we both gave up and decided that what we had wasn't so bad, actually was pretty good, if we would only stop trying to make it better. So we pretty much accepted our differences. They haven't gone away and we still sometimes wage war over them, but basically we accept them. We also accept the fact that some parts of our lives together are far from perfect. I suppose you could say it's a kind of resignation, which it is, but that's far from bad; we sure have lots more energy for other things and for enjoying each other. I feel we did the right thing."

I don't wish to make the acceptance of limits sound like a new peak experience, although it may be like this for some. Accepting our limitations can be frustrating, anxiety-provoking, depressing, and just plain unpleasant. It's not always easy to give up the fantasies of how great life will be once we change. But these possibilities need to be weighed against the consequences of not accepting ourselves and of trying to change. Needless to say at this point, there are costs either way.

I cannot say for certain that we will be happier if we let go of some of our fantasies and some of our preoccupation with altering ourselves, but there are benefits. Acceptance of ourselves as we are, and this would include acceptance of our desire to be different than we are, would mean less disappointment and less self-hatred for not being all the things we believe we should be. A fair amount of money now spent on attempts at modifying ourselves would be saved, money that might be better spent on other comforts and amusements. Acceptance can provide a clearer picture of reality, no longer seen through the spectacles of utopian possibilities, and I think this clearer view would be refreshing. If we stop trying to change everything about ourselves and others, we may develop a better understanding of what can be readily changed and do better jobs of dealing with those things, and also of what can't be changed and so stop trying to do the impossible. With a more realistic view of ourselves and of the possibilities and limits of change, therapy itself could be used more wisely, resulting in less frustration, less wasted effort, and fewer of the problems caused by inappropriate therapeutic thinking and indiscriminate therapy-going. We might even find that our unaltered bodies, psyches, relationships, communication patterns, and so forth, aren't as bad as anticipated and be able to enjoy them more. Last, we may be able to take pride in living more honest lives, bearing the limits, contradictions, vulnerabilities, and burdens of our humanity as best we can, taking our place in the long stream of men and women who have done the same since the beginning of time. And that, I think, is quite a lot.

Appendix

Some Uses of Professional
Therapy and Guidelines for Consumers

If we are willing to say that the goal of therapy is to make people feel better, whether or not symptoms remain or behavior changes, it is clear that counseling is very effective. As a result of therapy, clients don't feel as alone, as overwhelmed, or as hopeless, and they believe they can better cope with their lives. These feelings may not last long but they are highly valued in any case. In short, therapy is a great morale booster and comforter for many of its consumers and it is also helpful in changing the behavior of some of them. Therapy, however, is not without risk: some people are harmed by it. A last point is that professional counseling is not unique. It is similar in process and outcome to the informal counseling that goes on all around us and that we practice on ourselves and others.

As far as we know, your chances of feeling better, being comforted, resolving a problem — and probably also of suffering harm — seem approximately equal if you:

- try to work things out by yourself, with or without self-help material written by professionals;
- talk to a friend, spouse, religious adviser, nonpsychiatric physician, or anyone else you feel comfortable with;
- join a self-help group;
- see a professional therapist for many years or a few months.

Does this mean that professional counseling is useless and should be done away with? Not at all. While it is overpromoted, overused, and overvalued, it can be beneficial when used prudently, with clear understanding of its powers, limitations, and risks.

One of the major values of professional therapy is treatment with medication. Although this extends the definition of therapy that we started with, we have seen that problems such as schizophrenia, some depressive disorders, and agoraphobia respond best to drugs or a combination of drugs and psychotherapy. If you have one of these problems and are willing to try medication, you should consult a psychiatrist, the only mental health professional allowed to prescribe drugs.

Professional counseling may also be useful for people whose own efforts have failed. A number of people with sex problems have consulted me after failing to make changes by using my *Male Sexuality*. In some of these cases the problems were more complex than could be handled by any book. In others, however, this was not true and the clients got very little from me that they couldn't have gotten from the book, with one exception. The fact of seeing me regularly, and paying for it, gave them the incentive and discipline to carry out the necessary assignments, two things that were lacking before they came to therapy. Many people cannot, or at least do not, practice change-inducing tasks unless they have someone to report their progress to.

Some people fail in their attempts to get help from those around them. Your mother, for instance, may respond to your marital woes by reminding you that she warned you not to marry that good-for-nothing in the first place. Your employer may have little tolerance for listening to your emotional troubles. The people you turn to may not have the interest, knowledge, or skill to assist you. In some cases, they may be too involved in the problem to be of help. You and your spouse, for example, may be unable to resolve a family difficulty because you are both too close to it. An outsider such as a therapist might be able to bring a fresh perspective. There's also the matter of time. Dealing with some problems takes more time than nonprofessional helpers may be willing or able to give. Your physician, minister, or best friend may not be willing to hear for the fiftieth time how upset you are over your son's drug habits. If you feel the need to go over the story again, there may be no alternative other than to hire a professional listener. Although most therapists seem to have an infinite capacity for listening, there is no guarantee you'll accomplish more with them than you did on your own or with nonprofessional help. Nonetheless, the possibility exists and might be worth exploring.

Some people can't talk things over with a friend or someone else because they have no friends and are too shy to approach anyone. Therapy may be useful, especially if it helps them to develop the confidence and skills to make friends, and therefore informal therapists, of their own. Other people are neither shy nor unassertive and they do not lack willing listeners, but they don't want to talk with them. Having others in their lives know about their problems makes them feel too vulnerable or puts them under real or imagined obligations. Even though they have other resources, they prefer a professional, someone not involved in their daily lives. Some people who have friends to talk with prefer a professional because their experience is that friends are too protective, trying to make them feel better as quickly as possible and not aiding them in facing difficult issues, while a good professional therapist may allow them greater latitude to confront difficult problems and to feel bad, thereby producing a better long-term outcome.

Professional counseling also seems the best alternative for some people simply because they believe it is best. They have great faith in experts and don't believe that talking things over with a teacher or relative will accomplish as much as consulting a highly trained and high-priced specialist. This seems to be the main reason that millions of people with colds and influenza flock to physicians each year, even though the doctors have nothing to offer that their mothers and grandmothers couldn't have told them about. There's probably not much sense getting informal therapy or joining a self-help organization if you don't think you can get anything from it. Since there is undoubtedly a relationship between one's faith in the treatment and the results obtained, those who believe strongly in professionals will probably get more from them than from others.

Professional counselors have another value. Primarily through their popular books, but also to some extent through their media appearances, they provide information that enables some of us to help ourselves better and to help those around us. Counselors disseminate and popularize ideas and methods that are new to some people and put old information in new forms that make it more readily usable. Most people, for example, believe that talking things over is useful for dealing with misunderstandings and disagreements, but some people are not very successful at this until they follow specific suggestions they find in books on assertiveness or communication. A number of men and women I talked with vouched for the efficacy of self-help books in combating despair, providing solace, and, in some cases, changing behavior. As far as I know, there has not been any good research on the uses and limits of self-help materials, but my guess is they are similar to what we found for therapy proper. Although generally helpful, these materials promise more than they deliver and there is some risk to their use since some readers end up feeling worse rather than better. Nonetheless, if you are willing to accept the risk, you may find some of what you are looking for in a good self-help book.

On the basis of the preceding material, it is possible to offer some pointers about selecting resources for help with personal problems. It is clear that self-help efforts are worthwhile. You can do many things for yourself that a therapist does. For instance, thinking clearly about your current situation and how you would like it to be, and possible routes from the former to the latter, is something many counselors will get you to do, or do for you, yet most people can do the same without professional assistance. One thing all therapists do is listen, but you may be able to find someone else to listen to you. Pick a person you feel comfortable with and make sure to protect yourself. Don't tell intimate details to someone who may use them against you or who can't keep secrets. It's a good idea to make an agreement beforehand regarding what you want: e.g., "I'd like to talk to you about some problems I'm having at home, but only if you can agree not to tell anyone, including your wife." In thinking about whom to talk to, don't overlook professionals not in the mental health field — nonpsychiatric physicians, teachers, coaches, clerics, and so forth.

There's also something to be said for listening to yourself. Some people have derived considerable benefit from keeping a diary or speaking into a tape recorder. Such practices can be useful for defining problems and goals, as well as possible change procedures, and keeping track of feelings, behavior, and progress.

When problems involve more than one person — relationship and family disputes, for example — the main contribution of a therapist often consists in getting the parties to talk to and understand each other. This end can frequently be achieved without professional consultation. Presenting your case and listening to that of others is not always easy, but it will help if a safe and quiet place is used and everyone is allowed to have his say without interruption and without having to argue about and defend every point he makes. It also helps if the listeners, before presenting their sides, tell the speaker what they heard him say, so he knows that he has been properly understood.

As Eric Sevareid once noted, solutions are the main cause of problems, and many therapists will help you evaluate the solutions you are applying to determine whether they are more hindrance than help. But this is also something you can do on your own. For instance, a commonly used "solution" to some marital and sexual problems is withdrawal; the partners keep their distance in the hope of not making things worse or because of the fear of getting into a position where they can't deliver what is expected. Unfortunately, withdrawal often has the effect of making the situation worse or making a real solution impossible. If you or someone close to you is using withdrawal as a solution to a difficulty, you might want to consider whether tackling the problem head-on might not be a better alternative.

If you don't get anywhere on your own, think about using a self-help book. This is often the best way to get the advice of experts without having to pay the cost of a personal consultation. Remember, however, that just reading self-help books probably won't help. Most books of this kind contain exercises to be done, and doing them takes effort and discipline.

Don't overlook resources such as classes and self-help organizations. Many schools and community agencies offer courses on assertiveness, family relations, communication, sexuality, and so on, frequently at very reasonable prices. There are self-help groups for almost every imaginable situation and difficulty. Some of these organizations, such as Alcoholics Anonymous and Take Off Pounds Sensibly, have proven their effectiveness, and many are less expensive than professional treatment.

Whether you choose self-help, nonprofessional help, or professional treatment, you will serve yourself well by not burdening yourself and those you turn to with unrealistic expectations for change. You can have whatever fantasies you want, but counter them with the main message of this book: human beings and relationships are difficult to change and typically the alterations made are modest. I know of no better guide on this point than Allen Wheelis:

> The changes we achieve with ourselves, with or without therapy, are likely to be partial and provisional. The homosexual gets married, has children, but never feels entirely safe with women; . . . the depressive character can work, may occasionally feel glad to be alive, but is not likely ever to be described as of sunny disposition; the phobic woman becomes less anxious, no longer has to decline invitations, but always has sweaty palms at cocktail parties. Such changes must be counted success; for more frequent in outcome, even with considerable effort, is no change at all. He who undertakes to transform himself, therefore, should think not of all or none, sick or well, miserable or happy, but of more or less, better or worse. He should undertake only to do what he can, to handle something better, to suffer less. The kingdom of heaven need not concern him.

If you decide you want a professional therapist, you will do yourself a favor and save unnecessary frustration by accepting the fact that finding one who can help you may be difficult. Even therapists have trouble finding counselors for themselves. The advice usually given at this point — call your local medical or psychological society for a recommendation — is largely worthless. All you will get are the names of therapists who are licensed and belong to the organization. You could do as well by looking in the phone book, because belonging to professional organizations and being licensed are not indicators of competence or anything else of importance. Keep in mind the consensus that incompetence rather than competence is the rule and also that there are no sure guidelines. Type of therapy and therapist reputation, experience, and training do not necessarily mean much. Therapist reputation is often based on showmanship, charisma, and number of publications, none of which necessarily has anything to do with clinical skill. There is no evidence that psychologists and psychiatrists, who have the longest training and command the highest fees, are more effective than social workers, marriage counselors, and other therapists. Even those who regularly refer to a certain therapist frequently have no idea of what kinds of results are achieved.

Names suggested by satisfied customers you know — friends, relatives, colleagues — can provide a good starting place. It does not necessarily follow that someone who was able to help your neighbor will be able to help you, but a personal referral is the best place to begin. Regardless of who makes the referral, don't hesitate to ask what he knows of the therapist's abilities and how this information was obtained. A satisfied friend will probably be able to give you only his personal experience, but someone else, say your physician, may have referred a number of people to this particular therapist and have a lot of information about his work. Be wary when your referral source has no direct information and knows of the therapist only through his talks or writings.

If you simply want to talk to someone, it probably doesn't make a lot of difference whom you select, as long as you feel comfortable and that he or she is listening. If results are what count — keeping your marriage together, stopping drinking, and so forth — inquire about these. You have every right to ask the person who refers you and the therapist what kinds of results are obtained with a problem like yours. You might also want to compare these results with the outcomes of alternative treatments. Do not count on counselors to supply you with accurate information about other methods. They often are ignorant on this point and are also convinced that whatever they are doing is best, whether or not they have any empirical support for their conviction. General reference books, psychology and medical textbooks, and articles in professional journals are useful places to find out about the effectiveness of different approaches for your problem. Avoid popular and professional books written from only one point of view — whether pharmacological, behavioral, family systems, or whatever — because it is predictable they will tell you their way is best.

Obviously you will want to think about the time and money required. Since short-term methods usually accomplish as much as longer ones, find out how long the therapist you're thinking of seeing usually works with people like you. If the answer is three or four years, you can almost certainly find someone who doesn't take as long.

Since we know counseling can be harmful or just a waste of time, there are several things to be wary of. One of them is counselors who suggest strange activities like having sex with them. You can be sure they are more interested in taking care of *their* problem than in dealing with yours. Beware of therapists who demand you do anything you really don't want to do or that makes no sense to you. Although touchy-feely activities in groups are no longer unusual, you are not required to do any touching you don't want to do. Similarly, although masturbation is now viewed as a useful method for dealing with some sex problems, you need not masturbate if this is unacceptable to you. You needn't tell your spouse about past or present indiscretions and you needn't be in several different therapies at the same time. There is nothing wrong with counselors suggesting things they think may be helpful to you, but good therapists know there is more than one way to work on a problem and will respect your position if you are offended or made uncomfortable with their suggestions. You need be concerned only when pressure is applied to get you to do things you don't want to do. You should also be concerned about therapists who are unresponsive to your questions about the process and duration of their approach, and the results achieved by it. Refusal to discuss these issues is, in my opinion, indication that the counselor is not treating you as an intelligent and responsible adult. Similarly, a therapist who is not receptive to your negative comments about the counseling — your complaint, for example, that his interpretation or homework completely missed the point — is clearly not taking you seriously.

Therapists who make you feel bad much of the time, by blaming you for having problems and not resolving them, or by finding more and more things wrong with you that need work, should be avoided unless you are willing to spend the rest of your life in therapy. Do not stay with a counselor who mistreats you. Despite the mystique of professional therapy, we have seen that there is little mysterious about it. But many people think there is and put up with abuse and humiliation because they believe it is part of the program and therefore good for them. I know of no valid change technique that requires people to be treated disrespectfully and without due consideration for their rights as human beings. If your therapist belittles you, calls you names, reads a magazine while you are talking, refuses to take your fears and questions seriously, or in any other way does not treat you like an adult, responsible human being, you don't have to put up with such treatment, and I don't think you should.

One form of not taking you seriously is an unwillingness to work on the problems you consider important and in ways that make sense to you. If when you try to talk about your marriage, your therapist always responds by asking you to talk about your childhood, you should ask why. As far as is known, the best way to deal with a problem is to work on that problem. It is not necessary to spend a lot of time discussing your childhood in order to improve your marriage, help you become more decisive, or alleviate depression. In fact, it's not clear that long discussions of childhood are necessary or useful to achieve any therapeutic goal. The only certain result of such discussions is greatly to increase the duration of treatment. If your therapist believes it is necessary for you to discuss your childhood in depth, he should be able to explain the reasons why to your satisfaction. There are sometimes legitimate reasons for looking at areas other than the one that bothers you: high levels of tension, which you may not have thought about, may well interfere with your creativity, and problems at work may adversely effect how you deal with your family. But your goal should always be in view and there should be a clear, direct, and understandable connection between it and the areas the therapist wants you to work on. Some counselors are experts at distracting people from their goals and getting them to focus on largely irrelevant, though interesting, topics. Many fascinating conversations may result, and if you enjoy them that's your business. On the other hand, if your main desire is to achieve a certain goal, find someone who's willing to help you keep it in sight and to help you reach it in a direct way.

An excellent way of getting the kinds of information mentioned above, as well as answers to other questions that are important to you, is to interview counselors on the phone. Phone calls are useful for narrowing your choices and for getting a sense of what kinds of help are available to you. Call several therapists and tell each that you are thinking of coming to see him, but first you'd like some information about how he works. Start with a brief description of what you want therapy for and the results you hope to achieve. Then ask if he has worked with such problems, what the outcomes were, how long it usually takes, fees, and anything else you are concerned about. Whatever is important to you — e.g., the therapist's religious orientation; attitudes about divorce, social drinking, or open marriage; or the prescribing of medications (if he is a psychiatrist) — should be asked about. After all, if you want help in keeping a distressed marriage together, you don't want to end up with a therapist who believes that marriage is an outmoded institution unworthy of being preserved. Discussions revolving around these questions will give you a feel for the type of person you are talking to and your level of comfort in dealing with him or her. Since you want to find someone you feel comfortable enough with to tell intimate details of your life, trust your feelings on this point. Good signs are that you feel listened to, that the therapist seems to understand your problem and offers a general outline of how it could be dealt with that sounds reasonable to you, and that you have a sense it could be useful to work with him. Of course there are limits as to how much can be discussed on the phone and there is always the possibility that you'll feel differently about the therapist after meeting with him, but brief phone interviews are usually the best guide you'll have in deciding whom to see. Although I have no direct experience of this, several people have told me that some counselors refuse to be interviewed by prospective clients on the phone, insisting instead that callers come in for an appointment (which almost invariably must be paid for). I think this practice is unfortunate because it forces the client to pay for something that may be totally irrelevant or inappropriate. You can handle this any way you like, but I would not make an appointment with someone who would not give me a few minutes of information beforehand.

I firmly believe that the best results are achieved, regardless of the type of help employed, when the client plays an active role. Whether you are dealing with a friend, self-help group, or a professional healer, it is in your interests not to surrender your autonomy. Having someone else take over the running of your life can be relieving and comforting — it's an important reason why some people join religious cults or go to therapy — but it is your life that is at stake and you are going to have to live with the consequences. If you stay in therapy for ten years rather than one, using up all your savings in the process, take prescribed drugs to the point where you become addicted and are unable to function at work or home, or do assigned tasks you feel are wrong and that generate bad feelings about yourself, you and only you are stuck with the results. I suggest working with your counselor, which requires that you do not allow your behavior to be controlled by a fantasy of his curing you with some magical technique or pill. Bring up material that seems relevant, ask for information you want, criticize his interpretations and suggestions when they seem wrong, do not go along with ideas and tasks that offend you or seem inappropriate, and at fairly frequent intervals — alone and with your counselor — assess your progress. If you don't like how things are going, say so and see what can be done. If you are dissatisfied with the therapy and can't work something out with your therapist, you might do well to discuss the situation with someone close to you or seek an opinion from another professional. I hope you won't make the mistake of assuming that although nothing seems to be happening, something good will result if you just keep plodding along. Although this sometimes does happen, it is rare. I also hope you won't stay in counseling beyond the point where you feel progress is being made just because you don't want to offend your therapist or because he says you need to stay. If you want to end therapy or take a break, you have the right to do so. If your therapist disagrees with your decision, listen to his reasons and determine how much sense they make to you, but remember that the choice is, and has to be, yours.

Obviously what I have said about professional therapy also holds for other types of assistance. Getting help from others, be they professionals or nonprofessionals, can be of value, sometimes of very great value, but in the final analysis you have to be your own expert. You have to decide when to get help and what kind, how satisfied you are with the helping process, and when you should stop or find something else. To surrender your responsibility in these matters is to put yourself in peril.

References

Although space limitations preclude listing all of the sources that were of value in writing this book, I use this section to document quotations and citations, and also to list those works that are of particular interest for further reading. Unattributed quotations, whether from clients or therapists, are from personal interviews.

CHAPTER 1

Page
3: "the problem is not that so many . . ." Rosen, R. D. *Psychobabble*, 1977, 230.
4: Tocqueville, A. de. *Democracy in America*, Vol. 2, 1945, 35.
5: "Well, what do you say . . ." Skinner, B. F. *Walden Two*, 1948, 274.
"may be the elimination . . ." London, P. *Behavior Control*, 1977, 5.
"willing to be responsible . . ." From The Hunger Project, an offshoot of est, and quoted in Naipaul, S. *Journey to Nowhere*, 1981, 199.
8: "Critical works . . . are rare." Several exceptions to this statement are worth noting: a number of books by Thomas Szasz, especially *The Myth of Psychotherapy*, 1978 (though, surprisingly, Szasz says almost nothing about the limited powers of therapy); Martin Gross, *The Psychological Society*, 1978; Hans Strupp, The Limitations of Psychotherapy, in Strupp, H. H. *Psychotherapy: Clinical, Research, and Theoretical Issues*, 1973, 514–18; Paul Vitz, *Psychology as Religion*, 1977; and several works by Allen Wheelis, particularly *The Quest for Identity*, 1958, and *How People Change*, 1973. More than any other therapist I am aware of, Wheelis demonstrates an exquisite understanding of the limits of therapy and the limits of change.

CHAPTER 2

Page
11: Rieff, P. *The Triumph of the Therapeutic*, 1966.
12: "Schizophrenia Made Stockman Do It." *The New Republic*, 12/23/81.
"passivity is a disease." Toni Grant on *Donahue*, Donahue Transcript #02022, 1982.
"only dogs she can't train . . ." *Time*, 12/7/81, 80.
13: Menninger, K. *Whatever Became of Sin?*, 1973.
Leven, J. *Satan*, 1982, 466.
Schutz, W. *Profound Simplicity*, 1979, 4.
16: Rogers, C. *On Encounter Groups*, 1970, 29.
17: Rosenblatt, D. *Your Life is a Mess*, 1976, 2.
Midtown Manhattan study is the name given to the work of Srole, L., et al., *Mental Health in the Metropolis*, 1962.

Page
18: "other studies . . . have concluded . . ." See, for example, Leighton, D. C., et al. *The Character of Danger*, 1963.
Korchin, S. *Modern Clinical Psychology*, 1976, 561.
"In one of them . . ." Rosenhan, D. L. On Being Sane in Insane Place, *Science*, *179*, 250–58. For replications of this study, see interview with Rosenhan in *APA Monitor*, June/July 1981, 4.
19: "In another study . . ." Temerlin, M. K. Suggestion Effects in Psychiatric Diagnosis, *J Nervous & Mental Disease*, 1968, *147*, 349–53. Just how little therapists know about normal behavior is indicated by a study in which mental health professionals were asked to fill out self-image questionnaires the way they believed a mentally healthy adolescent would complete it. The therapists saw the teenagers as having far more problems than did the children themselves and as having more problems than were reported by psychiatrically impaired and delinquent teenagers.
Offer, D., et al. The Mental Health Professional's Concept of the Normal Adolescent, *Archives General Psychiatry*, 1981, *38*, 149–52.
Reusch, J., and Bateson, G. *Communication*, 1951, 71.
20: Rieff, P. *Freud: The Mind of the Moralist*, 1979, 330.
21: Freud's statement about Lourdes is in *New Introductory Lectures on Psychoanalysis*, in *The Standard Edition of the Complete Psychological Works of Sigmund Freud*, 1964, Vol. *22*, 152. Freud might not have made this comment had he had accurate information about the results at Lourdes. Though scores of millions of people have made the pilgrimage there, only about 5,000 "cures" have been recorded. There are limits to change even for those who believe in miracles. See Marnham, P. *Lourdes*, 1981.
Carl Rogers interview is in Bergin, A. E., and Strupp, H. H. *Changing Frontiers in the Science of Psychotherapy*, 1972, 318–19.
23: For the political and religious views of therapists, see Rogow, A. E. *The Psychiatrists*, 1970, and Henry, W. E., et al. *The Fifth Profession*, 1971.
Bergin, A. E. Psychotherapy and Religious Values, *J Consulting Clinical Psychology*, 1980, *48*, 98.
"anyone who gets involved in . . ." Hogan, R. Interview in *APA Monitor*, 4/79, 4.
Campbell, D. T. On the Conflicts between Biological and Social Evolution and between Psychology and Moral Tradition, *American Psychologist*, 1975, *30*, 1103, 1105.
24: Levenson, S. *You Don't Have to Be in Who's Who to Know What's What*, 1979, 111.
"expressed by a behavior therapist . . ." Weiss, R. L. Coupling Skills, BMA Audio Cassette, 1980.
25: "study of 4,000 professionals . . ." Henry, W. E., et al. *The Fifth Profession*, 1971, 170.
"therapy was recommended for all but four . . ." Frances, A., and Clarkin, J. F. No Treatment as the Prescription of Choice, *Archives General Psychiatry*, 1981, *38*, 542–45.
28: "therapists don't hold people in high regard." See Dan Wile's *Couples Therapy*, 1981, for a brilliant critique of the assumptions about people posited by the major models of therapy.
Rogers, C. R. *On Personal Power*, 1977, 6.

Page
31: "the proportion of Americans who had consulted . . ." Kulka, R. A., et al.
Social Class and the Use of Professional Help for Personal Problems:
1957 and 1976, *J Health & Social Behavior*, 1979, *20*, 10.
The statistics regarding participation in the new therapies have to be
regarded as estimates; in most cases I got them by calling the organizations in question. The figure for participation in encounter groups comes
from Yalom, I. D. *The Theory and Practice of Group Psychotherapy*,
1975, 457.
32: We are on somewhat safer group regarding the number of professional
therapists and the groups I use to compare them with. Among my sources
are: Brown, B. The Life of Psychiatry, *American J Psychiatry*, 1976, *133*,
489–95; Dorken, H., and Webb, J. T. Licensed Psychologists on the Increase: 1974–79, Paper presented at annual meeting of the American
Psychological Association, Montreal, 9/2/80; the chapters on psychiatric
nursing, social workers, and paraprofessionals in Kaplan, H. I., et al.
Comprehensive Textbook of Psychiatry, Vol. 3, 1980; Reisman, J. R. *A
History of Clinical Psychology*, 1976; U.S. Bureau of the Census, *Statistical Abstract of the United States: 1980*.

CHAPTER 3

Page
33: On the statistics, see the sources cited for page 31.
Storr, A. A Disciple's Chronicle, *N.Y. Times Book Review*, 8/5/79, 3.
34: Addington quoted in Wuthow, R. *The Consciousness Reformation*, 1976,
102.
35: Tocqueville, *Democracy in America*, Vol. 2, 106.
36: Potter, D. M. *Freedom and its Limitations in American Life*, 1976, 29.
37: Tocqueville, *Democracy in America*, Vol. 2, 105.
Heilbroner, R. *The Future as History*, 1960, 16, 54.
38: Lerner, M. *America as a Civilization*, 1957, 693.
Tocqueville, *Democracy in America*, Vol. 2, 144.
39: Boorstin, D. J. *The Republic of Technology*, 1978, 33.
40: "Somewhere there is a technique . . ." Bry, A. *Getting Better*, 1978, 11.
Davies, J. D. *Phrenology, Fad and Science*, 1955, 5.
41: Beard quoted in Meyer, D. *The Positive Thinkers*, 1965, 24.
44: For the quotes on mind cure, as well as further information, see, in addition to *The Positive Thinkers*, Hale, N. G. *Freud and the Americans*,
1971; James, W. *The Varieties of Religious Experience*, first published
in 1902; Parker, G. T. *Mind Cure in New England*, 1973; and Schneider,
L., and Dornbusch, S. M. *Popular Religion: Inspirational Books in America*, 1958.
46: "If you are in poor health . . ." Seth quoted in Schutz, W. *Profound
Simplicity*, 1979, 29.
"When we concentrate on a thought . . ." Silva, J., and Miele, P. *The
Silva Mind Control Method*, 1977, 58.
"Love, power, riches . . ." Brothers, J. *How to Get Whatever You Want
out of Life*, 1978, 1–2.
47: "Magazines eagerly printed . . ." Hale, *Freud and the Americans*, 235.

Page
48: On Coué and his methods, see his book, *How to Practice Suggestion and Autosuggestion*, 1923, and the brief account in Peter, L. J. *Peter's People*, 1979, 53–57.
49: "Every morning when I shave . . ." Brothers, *How to Get Whatever You Want out of Life*, 100–01.

CHAPTER 4

Page
51: "neighborhood villages . . ." Brown, R. D. *Modernization*, 1976, 54.
Laslett, P. *The World We Have Lost*, 1971, 22.
52: "a perception of one's environments . . ." Antonovsky, A. *Health, Stress, and Coping*, 1979, 125.
54: Wheelis, A. *The Quest for Identity*, 1958, 20.
55: Keniston, K. *Youth and Dissent*, 1971, 6.
57: Lifton, R. J. Protean Man, *Archives General Psychiatry*, 1971, *24*, 299.
Erikson, E. H. Identity and the Life Cycle, *Psychological Issues*, 1959, *1*.
58: "I have an extraordinary number of masks . . . ." In Lifton, Protean Man, 300.
Bach, R. *Jonathan Livingston Seagull*, 1970, 53.
60: Statistics on living arrangements are from two publications of U.S. Bureau of the Census: *Historical Statistics of the United States, Colonial Times to 1970*, Part 2, 1975, 42, and *Statistical Abstract of the United States*, 1980, 47.
61: "less than one-third of those eligible . . ." Brown, *Modernization*, 81.
"almost every state . . ." Lipset, S. M. *The First New Nation*, 1963, 34.
On Civil religion, see Robert Bellah, Civil Religion in America, in McLoughlin, W. G., and Bellah, R. N. *Religion in America*, 1968.
63: Heilbroner, *The Future as History*, 14.
64: Lapham, L. H. *Fortune's Child*, 1980, 166–67.
65: Kristol, I. *Two Cheers for Democracy*, 1978, 262–63.
66: Schutz, W. *Profound Simplicity*, 1979, 32, 34.
68: Larkin, R. W. *Suburban Youth in Cultural Crisis*, 1979, 153–54.

CHAPTER 5

Page
70: Wolfe, T. The "Me" Decade, *New York*, 8/23/76, 30.
72: Maslow, A. *Toward a Psychology of Being*, 1962.
Wolfe, T. The "Me" Decade, 32.
73: Hacker, A. *The End of the American Era*, 1972, 209.
77: Wheelis, A. *Quest for Identity*, 1958, 39.
78: Szasz, T. S. *The Myth of Mental Illness*, 1961, xvi.
80: Keniston, K. *Youth and Dissent*, 1971, 10.
82: For a thoughtful and disturbing essay on American individualism, psychology's acceptance of it, and the link between individualism and androgyny, see Sampson, E. E. Psychology and the American Ideal, *J Personality & Social Psychology*, 1977, *35*, 767–82.
84: Bach, R. *Jonathan Livingston Seagull*, 1970, 88.
85: "I deserve . . ." Ray, S. *I Deserve Love*, 1976, front cover.

CHAPTER 6

Page
87: "The key to a successful . . ." Spooner, J. D. *Smart People*, 1979, 5.
88: Frank, J. D. *Persuasion and Healing*, 1973, 8.
90: *Time*, 4/7/80, 62.
     "the profound mental benefits . . ." Lilliefors, J. *Total Running*, 1979, 1.
     "the idea that athletics . . ." *San Francisco Examiner*, California Living
     Magazine, 9/9/79, 50.
91: Rome, H. P. Psychiatry and Foreign Affairs, *American J Psychiatry*, 1968,
     125, 729, and The Psychiatrist, the APA, and Social Issues, *American J
     Psychiatry*, 1971, *128*, 686.
     Polster, E., and Polster, M. *Gestalt Therapy Integrated*, 1973, 23.
     Stachnik, T. J. Priorities for Psychology in Medical Education and
     Health Care Delivery, *American Psychologist*, 1980, *35*, 8.
92: Dorken, H., and associates. *The Professional Psychologist Today*, 1978,
     292.
     Thomas, L. *The Lives of a Cell*, 1974, 96.
     "we lack the kind of understanding . . ." *Task Panel Reports Submitted
     to the President's Commission on Mental Health*, 1978, Vol. 4, 1830.
     "These would include . . ." *Report to the President from the President's
     Commission on Mental Health*, 1978, Vol. 1, 51.
     Albee, G. W. A Competency Model Must Replace the Defect Model, in
     Bond, L. A., and Rosen, J. C. *Competence and Coping During Adulthood*,
     1980, 95. Albee is hardly the first mental health professional to believe that
     society rather than the individual should be the focus of treatment. He
     follows in the footsteps of psychiatrists and psychologists such as Harry
     Stack Sullivan, Henry Murray, C. B. Chisholm, and Lawrence Frank,
     whose 1948 book *Society as the Patient* says it succinctly: "our culture
     is sick, mentally disordered, and in need of treatment." For more on
     these therapists and ideas, see Lasch, C. *Haven in a Heartless World*,
     1977, 97–110.
93: "*reforming* the criminal justice system." Fenster, C. A., et al. Careers in
     Forensic Psychology, in Woods, P. J. *Career Opportunities for Psycholo-
     gists*, 1976, 124–25.
     Brayfield, A. H., and Lipsey, M. W. Public Affairs Psychology, in Woods,
     Career Opportunities, 259, 263.
94: Lasch, C. *Haven in a Heartless World*, 1977, 136.
95: Dyer, W. W. *Your Erroneous Zones*, 1976, 36.
     Brothers, J. *How to Get Whatever You Want*, 191.
     Lobsenz, N. M. Make Your Marriage Better, *Reader's Digest*, 7/80, 144.
96: "How much of yourself . . ." Bry, A. *Getting Better*, 1978, 117.
     "The vast majority . . ." Gross, L. *Good Sex*, 21.
     "Sex is life. . . ." Reuben, D. *How to Get More out of Sex*, 1974, xv.
     "The couple that satisfies . . ." Abelow, D. *Total Sex*, 1976, 21.
     Zimbardo, P. G., and Radl, S. *The Shy Child*, 1981, 26–27.
99: Benson, H. *The Relaxation Response*, 1975.
100: "transform the level . . ." quoted in Bry, A. *est*, 1976, 25.
     Bry, A. *Visualization*, 1978, 31–32.
     Janov, A. *The Primal Scream*, 1970, 162–63, 166, 168–69.
101: Corriere, R., and Hart, J. *Psychological Fitness*, 1979, jacket.
     Bird, J., with Bird, L. *Freedom to Live*, 1979, 6.

Page
101: Goulding quoted in Curing the Fear of Becoming a President, *San Francisco Examiner*, 5/31/81, D2.
      Ellis, A. *Reason and Emotion in Psychotherapy*, 1962, 375–76.
102: Kohut quoted in Crews, F. Analysis Terminable, *Commentary*, 7/80, 31.
      Breuer, J., and Freud, S. *Studies on Hysteria, Standard Edition*, 1955, Vol. 2, 6.
      Bry, *est*, 206.
103: "the initial enthusiasm . . ." Tourney, G. A History of Therapeutic Fashions in Psychiatry, 1800–1966, *American J Psychiatry*, 1967, *124*, 785. The example of counting as successes the repeated recoveries of the same patient is on 786.
104: Sobell, L. S., and Sobell, M. B. Individualized Behavior Therapy for Alcoholics, *Behavior Therapy*, 1973, *4*, 49–72. The first follow-up study is by the Sobells (Second Year Treatment Outcome of Alcoholics Treated by Individualized Behavior Therapy, *Behaviour Research & Therapy*, 1976, *14*, 195–214) and the second is by Caddy, G. R., et al., Individualized Behavior Therapy for Alcoholics: A Third Year Independent Double-blind Follow-up, *Behaviour Research & Therapy*, 1978, *16*, 345–62.
      "no evidence . . ." Pendery, M. L., et al. Controlled Drinking by Alcoholics? New Findings and a Reevaluation of a Major Affirmative Study, *Science*, 1982, *217*, 174.
105: Brown, B. B. *Stress and the Art of Biofeedback*, 1977, xiii, 3.
      "On the whole . . ." Ray, W. J., et al. *Evaluaton of Clinical Biofeedback*, 1979, 52. See also Orne, M. T. The Efficacy of Biofeedback Therapy, *Annual Review Medicine*, 1979, *30*, 489–503, and Shapiro, D. H. Overview: Clinical and Physiological Comparison of Meditation with Other Self-Control Strategies, *American J Psychiatry*, 1982, *139*, 267–73. Shapiro notes that a number of studies "suggest no physiological differences between meditation and other self-regulation strategies" such as hypnosis and biofeedback, and often no differences between these activities and "just sitting."
      "friends and supporters of psychotherapy." Kadushin, C. *Why People Go to Psychiatrists*, 1969.
106: The story of Curtiss Anderson and the *Ladies' Home Journal* is taken from Chase, C. *The Great American Waistline*, 1981, 199–200.
108: "Reading their own journals . . ." For an important discussion about defects in psychological thinking and literature, see Samelson, F. J. B. Watson's Little Albert, Cyril Burt's Twins, and the Need for a Critical Science, *American Psychologist*, 1980, *35*, 619–25.
110: Thomas, L. *The Medusa and the Snail*, 1979, 102.

CHAPTER 7

Page
115: "therapists tend to see more improvement . . ." Feifel, H., and Eels, J. Patients and Therapists Assess the Same Psychotherapy, *J Consulting Psychology*, 1963, *27*, 310–18; Gillian, P., and Rachman, S. An Experimental Investigation of Desensitization in Phobic Patients, *British J Psychiatry*, 1974, *124*, 392–401; Harty, M., and Horwitz, L. Therapeutic Outcome as Rated by Patients, Therapists, and Judges, *Archives General Psychiatry*, 1976, *33*, 957–61; Lieberman, H. A., et al. *Encounter*

Page
     Groups, 1973, 96–97 (groups' leaders exaggerated positive gains made by participants and underestimated negative results); Rogers, C., et al. *The Therapeutic Relationship and Its Impact*, 1967, 77–79.

116: "The tendency to accentuate the positive . . ." This tendency is apparently common in most areas of life. For a review of relevant studies, see Matlin, M., and Stang, D. *The Pollyanna Principle*, 1978. Although it is well known that people like to accentuate the positive and that casual questions, general questions, and questions asked in the absence of rapport or the time for more questions result in spuriously high levels of positive response, therapists and even many therapy researchers rely heavily on these kinds of questions (as, for example, when therapists call former clients and ask only "How are you getting along now?" or "How satisfied are you with the therapy you had with me?"). It is only when, as one writer puts it, "an interviewer establishes rapport and goes into detailed questioning" that "elements of discontent, concern, and difficulty" surface. Antonovsky, A. *Health, Stress, and Coping*, 1979, 35.

117: Wheelis, A. *The Quest for Identity*, 1958, 158.
     "these studies imply . . ." Wincze, J., et al. Multiple Measure Analysis of Women Experiencing Low Sexual Arousal, *Behaviour Research & Therapy*, 1978, *16*, 48.

121: Zilbergeld, B., and Evans, M. The Inadequacy of Masters and Johnson, *Psychology Today*, 8/81, 29–43.

123: "A follow-up study of a stop-smoking program . . ." Brockway, B. E., et al. Non-aversive Procedures and Their Effect on Cigarette Smoking, *Addictive Behaviors*, 2, 121–28.

125: "many problems . . . are self-limiting . . ." David Malan and colleagues write, "A review of the available evidence suggest strongly that *symptomatic* improvement is the rule rather than the exception in untreated neurotic patients." They also found that a significant number of the untreated patients they followed improved on presumably more stringent psychodynamic criteria. See their article, A Study of Psychodynamic Changes in Untreated Neurotic Patients, *British J Psychiatry*, 1968, *114*, 525–51.
     "A very well done study . . ." Sloane, R. B., et al. *Psychotherapy Versus Behavior Therapy*, 1975, 101.

131: Meehl, P. Psychotherapy, *Annual Review of Psychology*, 1955, *6*, 373.

132: The delinquency study is described in Powers, E., and Witmer, H. *An Experiment in the Prevention of Delinquency*, 1951.

133: McCord, J. A Thirty-Year Follow-up of Treatment Effects, *American Psychologist*, 1978, *33*, 288.

134: "one critic said . . ." Sobel, S. B. Throwing the Baby Out with the Bathwater, *American Psychologist*, 1978, *33*, 290, 291.

135: Kuhn, T. *The Structure of Scientific Revolutions*, 1970, 13.

136: "a large number of therapeutic approaches . . ." Herink, R. *The Psychotherapy Handbook*, 1980, gives 250 "different therapies in use today."

137: "Freud never offered any evidence . . ." Fisher, S., and Greenberg, R. P. *The Scientific Credibility of Freud's Theories and Therapy*, 1975, 285.
     "the material worked upon . . ." Freud S. *New Introductory Lectures on Psychoanalysis, Standard Edition*, 1964, Vol. 22, 152.
     "In a later publication . . ." Freud, S. *An Outline of Psycho-Analysis, Standard Edition*, 1964, Vol. 23, 144.

Page
137: "The heart has reasons . . ." Nemiah, J. Classical Psychoanalysis, in
      Freedman, D. X., and Dyrud, J. E. *American Handbook of Psychiatry*,
      1975, 181.
139: Eysenck, H. J. The Effects of Psychotherapy, *J Consulting Psychology*,
      1952, *16*, 322.
140: Those desiring further information about the evaluation of therapies might
      want to start with the best short treatment of the subject I know, Alan
      Kazdin and Terence Wilson's Criteria for Evaluating Psychotherapy,
      Archives General Psychiatry, 1978, *35*, 407–16.

CHAPTER 8

Although I do not give direct quotations from all of them, the following
works are invaluable in providing information about and understanding
of the issues in this and the following chapter: Franks, C. M., and Wilson, G. T. *Annual Review of Behavior Therapy*, Vols. 2–7, 1974–79; Garfield, S. L. *Psychotherapy*, 1980; Garfield, S. L., and Bergin, A. E. *Handbook of Psychotherapy and Behavior Change*, 1978; Gruman, A. S., and
Razin, A. M. *Effective Psychotherapy*, 1977; Parloff, M. B., et al. Assessment of Psychosocial Treatment of Mental Disorders, 1978 (unpublished
report by Advisory Committee on Mental Health, National Academy of
Sciences); Rachman, S., and Wilson, G. T. *The Effects of Psychological
Therapy*, 1980; Smith, M. E., et al. *The Benefits of Psychotherapy*, 1980.
Page
142: The conclusions that most of the well-known therapy methods achieve
      about the same results and that behavior therapies do better with some
      circumscribed problems is supported by most of the references cited above.
      For example, after a comprehensive review, Allen Bergin and Michael
      Lambert write that insight therapies, humanistic therapies, and behavior
      therapies "have been found to be about equally effective with the broad
      spectrum of outpatients to whom they are typically applied. . . . [But] it
      seems clear that with circumscribed disorders, such as certain phobias,
      some sexual dysfunctions, and compulsions, certain technical operations
      [behavioral methods] can reliably bring about success." In Garfield and
      Bergin, 170.
143: Lazarus, A. A. Where Do Behavior Therapists Take Their Troubles, *Psy-
      chological Reports*, 1971, *28*, 350.
      "couples therapy is superior . . ." Gurman, A. S., and Kniskern, D. P.
      Research on Marital and Family Therapy, in Garfield and Bergin, 883.
      "analysts have claimed . . ." For example, in Anna Freud's words, "In
      competition with the psychotherapies [analysts] are justified to main-
      tain that what they have to offer is unique, i.e., thoroughgoing person-
      ality changes as compared with more superficial symptomatic cures."
      Difficulties in the Path of Psychoanalysis, 1969, 17.
144: "The cases he wrote about . . ." Fisher, S., and Greenberg, R. P. *The
      Scientific Credibility of Freud's Theories and Therapy*, 285.
      One ought not to be . . ." Freud, S. *Analysis Terminable and Interminable*,
      Standard Edition, Vol. *23*, 1964, 228, 230.
      Fisher, S., and Greenberg, R. P., 341. Bergin and Lambert write that
      because of its great length and cost, and because of "its failure to show
      success exceeding other briefer forms of psychotherapy, psychoanalysis

Page
    can hardly be considered the treatment of choice for particuluar clients
    or types of psychological disturbance." In Garfield and Bergin, 169.
    "A report published by . . ." Hamburg, D. A., et al. Report of the Ad
    Hoc Committee on Central Fact-Gathering of the American Psycho-
    analytic Association, *J American Psychoanalytic Association*, 1967, *15*,
    841–61.

146:    On phobias, including the effects of antidepressant medication on agora-
    phobia, see Mavissakalian, M., and Barlow, D. H. *Phobia*, 1981.

147:    For a comprehensive review of the outcomes of sex therapy, see Kilmann,
    P. R., and Mills, K. *All About Sex Therapy*, 1983.
    On the results of therapy with marital and family problems, there is noth-
    ing more comprehensive than Gurman, A. S., and Kniskern, D. P. *Hand-
    book of Family Therapy*, 1981.
    On the effects of shock treatment on depression, see Scovern, A. W., and
    Kilmann, P. R. Status of Electroconvulsive Therapy, *Psychology Bul-
    letin*, 1980, *87*, 260–303. On antidepressive medication, including lithium,
    there are the chapters on antidepressants and lithium in the *American
    Handbook of Psychiatry*, 1975, 476–513, and Wender, P. H., and Klein,
    D. F. *Mind, Mood, and Medicine*, 1981.

148:    "An encouraging note . . ." Rush, A. J., et al. Comparative Efficacy of
    Cognitive Therapy and Pharmacotherapy in the Treatment of Depressed
    Outpatients, *Cognitive Therapy & Research*, 1977, *1*, 17–38. McLean,
    P. D., and Hakstian, A. R. Clinical Depression, *J Consulting Clinical Psy-
    chology*, 1979, *47*, 818–36.
    Stunkard, A. J. The Management of Obesity, *New York State J Medicine*,
    1958, *58*, 79.
    For AA and professional therapies for alcoholism, see Emrick, C. D., et
    al. Nonprofessional Peers as Therapeutic Agents, in Gurman and Razin,
    1977, 120–61. For overview of various addictions and their treatments, see
    Dole, V. P. Addictive Behavior, *Scientific American*, 12/80, 138–54. On
    smoking, see Levenberg, S. B., and Wagner, M. K. Smoking Cessation:
    Long-Term Irrelevance of Mode of Treatment, *J Behavior Therapy &
    Experimental Psychiatry*, 1976, 7, 93–95.

149:    Regarding the effectiveness of psychotherapy and drugs on schizophrenia,
    see Parloff et al., 1978, 136–57, and Snyder, S. H. *Biological Aspects of
    Mental Disorder*, 1980, 58–68.

150:    For a review of the treatment of sexually deviant behavior, albeit one
    that gives too much weight to the results of case reports, see Kilmann,
    P. R. The Treatment of Sexual Paraphilias, *J Sex Research*, 1982, *18*,
    193–252.
    Masters, W. H., and Johnson, V. E. *Homosexuality in Perspective*, 1979.
    For criticisms of this work, see reviews by D. Barlow and C. Silverstein in
    Contemporary Psychology, 1980, *25*, 355–58, and by L. M. Lothstein,
    J Sex & Marital Therapy, 1980, *6*, 145–46.
    Martinson, R. What Works? — Questions and Answers About Prison Re-
    form, *The Public Interest*, Spring, 1974. As for the effects of behavior
    modification programs on adult offenders, "the results following release
    have not been encouraging. At best, these programs have resulted in only
    a slight or temporary decrease in recidivism." Agras, W. S., et al. *Be-
    havior Therapy*, 1979, 43.
    Storr, A. *The Art of Psychotherapy*, 1980, 161

292   *References*

Page
152: "Perhaps the import of encounter groups . . ." Lieberman, M. A., et al. *Encounter Groups*, 1973, 452.
153: Cox, H. *Turning East*, 1977, 96.
"People come to the psychiatrist . . ." Quoted in Lipp, M. R. *The Bitter Pill*, 1980, 116.
154: "a wonderful sense of camaraderie . . ." Bry, A. *est*, 131.
155: "For a weekend . . ." Quoted in Gordon, S. *Lonely in America*, 1976, 263.
156: "I have experienced a feeling of self-confidence . . ." Quoted in Strupp, H. H., et al. *Patients View Their Psychotherapy*, 1969, 71.
157: "In some ways therapy is similar to prayer." The results of therapy can also be compared with the results of pilgrimages to Lourdes. The number of cures at Lourdes is very small, far less than what many people seem to believe, but nonetheless something positive happens for many who go there. As Patrick Marnham says in his book *Lourdes*, "The sick pilgrims feel better, not in the sense of receiving a cure — that occurs in only a tiny fraction of cases — but in the sense of feeling stronger and happier and more reconciled to their lives." (1981, vii)

CHAPTER 9

Page
159: Panov, *Primal Scream*, 168.
160: Storr, A. *The Art of Psychotherapy*, 151.
"One psychiatry textbook . . ." Redlich, F. C., and Freedman, D. X. *The Theory & Practice of Psychiatry*, 1966, 270.
Rogers, C. R. The Process Equation of Psychotherapy, in Stollack, G. E., et al. *Psychotherapy Research*, 1966, 416.
161: "average weight loss is . . ." Agras, W. S., et al. *Behavior Therapy*, 1979, 118. Actual average weight loss is about eleven pounds.
Malcolm, J. *Psychoanalysis: The Impossible Profession*, 1981, 55–62, 108.
163: On Freud's smoking and medical problems, see Schur, M. *Freud: Living and Dying*, 1972.
"Perls was incapable of . . ." Dolliver, R. H., et al. The Art of Gestalt Therapy, *Psychotherapy: Theory, Research & Practice*, 1980, *17*, 136–42; Dolliver, R. H. Some Limitations in Perls' Gestalt Therapy, *Psychotherapy*, 1981, *18*, 38–45.
"Freud was, by his own admission . . ." Jones, E. *The Life and Work of Sigmund Freud*, Vol. 1, 1953, 304–11.
164: Regarding Freud's disciples and their relationship to the master, see Jones, Vols. 1 *and* 2; Roazen, P. *Freud and His Followers*, 1974; and Weisz, G. Scientists and Sectarians: The Case of Psychoanalysis, *J History Behavioral Sciences*, 1975, *11*, 350–64.
Sullivan's story is told in H. S. Perry, *Psychiatrist of America*, 1982.
Regarding suicides among therapists, see Cartwright, L. K. Sources and Effects of Stress in Health Careers, in Stone, G. C., et al. *Health Psychology*, 1979, 419–45, which also deals with drug abuse and marital problems; Freeman, W. Psychiatrists Who Kill Themselves, *American J Psychiatry*, 1967, 846–47; and Torrey, E. F. *The Mind Game*, 1972, 40.
Kirchner, M. What Makes Other Marriages Lousy, *Medical Economics*, 10/1/79, 43.

Page
165: Luborsky, L., et al. Comparative Studies of Psychotherapies, *Archives General Psychiatry*, 1975, *32*, 1001. The efficacy of brief therapy is also indicated by the fact that behavior therapy and sex therapy, usually relatively brief, have not been shown to accomplish less than other methods lasting far longer.

166: "A study done at MRI in Palo Alto . . ." Weakland, J. H., et al. Brief Therapy: Focused Problem Resolution, *Family Process*, 1974, *13*, 141–68.
"A number of analysts . . ." A good sampling of psychoanalytic brief therapies can be found in two edited works: Davenloo, H. *Basic Principles and Techniques*, in *Short-Term Dynamic Psychotherapy*, 1978, and Budman, S. H. *Forms of Brief Therapy*, 1981.
"But even the analytic literature . . ." In the major research production of psychoanalysis in recent years, analytically oriented therapy averaging 289 sessions per patient was compared with full-scale psychoanalysis averaging 835 hours per patient. Despite the fact that psychoanalysis involved almost three times as many therapy hours, there were no differences attributable to duration in the results between patients in the two treatments. While 289 hours does not exactly equal brief therapy, the idea that longer is better was hardly supported by this research, usually called the Menninger Study. See Kernberg, O. F., et al. Psychotherapy and psychoanalysis. *Bulletin of the Menninger Clinic*, 1972, *36*, 1–276.

168: Rubin, J. *Growing (Up) at 37*, 1976, 42.

169: Lazarus, A. A. *Behavior Therapy and Beyond*, 1971.
Masters, W. H., and Johnson, V. E. *Human Sexual Inadequacy*, 1970. The two studies of sex therapy with far higher relapse rates are Levay, A. N., and Kagle, A. A Study of Treatment Needs Following Sex Therapy, *American J Psychiatry*, 1977, *134*, 970–73, and Zussman, L., and Zussman, S. Continuous Time-limited Treatment of Standard Sexual Disorders, in Meyer, J. K. *Clinical Management of Sexual Disorders*, 1976, 107.

169: "the backsliding after treatment for addictions . . ." See the Dole and Levenberg and Wagner references for page 148, and Stunkard, A. J., and Penick, S. B. Behavior Modification in the Treatment of Obesity, *Archives General Psychiatry*, 1979, *36*, 801–06.
"In the large majority of psychotherapeutic endeavors . . ." Goldstein, A. P., et al. introduction, in Goldstein, A. P., and Kanfer, F. H. *Maximizing Treatment Gains*, 1979, 2–3.
Farson, R. The Technology of Humanism, *J Humanistic Psychology*, 1978, *18*, 17.

170: Cummings, N. A., and Vandenbos, G. A. The General Practice of Psychology, *Professional Psychology*, 1979, *6*, 433.
An excellent source for the issue of negative effects, which includes reviews of the clinical and research literature, is Strupp, H. H., et al. *Psychotherapy for Better or Worse*, 1977. Another important source is Bergin, A. E., and Lambert, M. J. The Evaluation of Therapeutic Outcomes, in Garfield, S. L., and Bergin, A. E., 1978, 152–62.
"On the whole . . ." Gurman, A. S., and Kniskern, D. P., in Garfield and Bergin, 1978, 832.
"A large study of encounter groups . . ." Lieberman, M. A., et al. *Encounter Groups*, 1973, 108.

173: "81 percent of growth center users . . ." Lieberman, M. A., and Gardner,

Page

J. A. Institutional Alternatives to Psychotherapy, *Archives General Psychiatry*, 1976, *33*, 157–62.

"one hundred phobic patients . . ." Zitrin, C. M., et al. Behavior Therapy, Supportive Therapy, Imipramine and Phobia, *Archives General Psychiatry*, 1978, *35*, 307–16.

"In another sample of therapy clients . . ." Sloane, R. B., et al. *Psychotherapy versus Behavior Therapy*, 1975.

Wheelis, A. *Quest For Identity*, 42.

"salted peanut effect." Howard, K. I., and Orlinsky, D. E. Psychotherapeutic Processes, *Annual Review of Psychology*, 1972, *23*, 651.

"By the time he was referred to me . . ." Lazarus, A. A. *The Practice of Multimodal Therapy*, 1981, 20.

174: "only 18 percent said they had no need . . ." Strupp, H. H., et al. *Patients View Their Psychotherapy*, 75.

Rubin, J. *Growing (Up) at 37.*

CHAPTER 10

Page

178: Aronson, E. *The Social Animal*, 1980, 291.

179: "One study found that laypersons . . ." Carkhuff, R. R., and Truax, C. B. Lay Mental Health Counseling, *J Consulting Psychology*, 1965, *29*, 426–32. The study dealing with simulated therapy interviews is Pope, B., et al. The Experienced Professional Interviewer versus the Complete Novice, *J Consulting Clinical Psychology*, 1974, *42*, 680–90.

"professional training decreases the level of relationship skills." Carkhuff, R. R., et al. Effects of Professional Training. *J Counseling Psychology*, 1968, *15*, 68–74.

181: The book that launched modern behavior therapy in America is Wolpe, J. *Psychotherapy by Reciprocal Inhibition*, 1958; it contains numerous examples of desensitization, as well as theories about behavior and behavior change that have since been discarded by most behaviorists. Briefer descriptions of desensitization can be found in almost any behavior therapy textbook; e.g, Goldfried, M. R., and Davison, G. C. *Clinical Behavior Therapy*, 1976.

182: Wolpe, J. *Our Useless Fears*, 1981. The example of the mother desensitizing her baby to the water is on page 68.

184: Barbach, L., and Levine, L. *Shared Intimacies*, 1980, 173.

185: "The expression of anger . . ." Lieberman, M. A., et al. *Encounter Groups*, 1973, 375.

186: "Patients undergoing psychotherapy with professors . . ." Strupp, H. H., and Hadley, S. W. Specific vs. Nonspecific Factors in Psychotherapy, *Archives General Psychiatry*, 1979, *36*, 1134. The other quotations in the text are from page 1136 of this article.

"Professional therapists, by virtue of their training . . ." One might think that professional counselors, because of their training, would do better than lay therapists with difficult clients. But this was not what Strupp found. As he puts it, "Professional therapists are no more effective in dealing with patients' resistances and negativism than untrained counselors (in fact, there was a slight trend in the opposite direction). . . ." Strupp, H. H. Success and Failure in Time-limited Psychotherapy,

Page

Archives General Psychiatry, 1980, 37, 716. The value of professional training is very difficult to explain and defend in light of this finding.

187: Durlak, J. A. Comparative Effectiveness of Paraprofessional and Professional Helpers, *Psychological Bulletin*, 1979, 86, 89. Two other important sources regarding the effectiveness of laypersons and paraprofessionals are Anthony, W. A., and Carkhuff, R. R. The Functional Professional Therapeutic Agent, and Emrick, C. D., et al. Nonprofessional Peers as Therapeutic Agents, both in Gurman, A. S., and Razin, A. M. *Effective Psychotherapy*, 1977.

188: The tape-led encounter groups formed part of the study reported in Lieberman, M. A., et al. *Encounter Groups*, 1973. In a comprehensive review of the encounter group literature, Gibb found a number of examples of tape groups producing better results than professionally led groups; he also found that the leaderless groups generally produced fewer negative effects (Gibb, J. R. A Research Perspective on the Laboratory Method, in Benne, K. D., et al. *The Laboratory Method of Changing and Learning*, 1975, 66).

The comparison between negative effects in the Stanford and Berkeley encounter group studies is in Hogan, D. B. *The Regulation of Psychotherapists*, Vol. 1, 1979, 135.

189: Stunkard, A. J., quoted in Gartner, A., and Riessman, F. *Self-Help in the Human Services*, 1977, 85.

An illuminating discussion of Synanon's claims and what appears to be its much lower success rate is in Mitchell D., et al. *The Light on Synanon*, 1980, 143–46.

For more on self-help groups, see Emrick, C. D., et al. Nonprofessional Peers as Therapeutic Agents, in Gurman, A. S., and Razin, A. M., 1977, 120–61, and Gartner, A., and Riessman, F. *Self-Help in the Human Services*, 1977.

"Most people who have given up smoking . . ." We know from several surveys that literally millions of men and women have given up smoking, most without any formal therapy, and we know from Lee Robins's study of drug addicts among American soldiers in Vietnam that most of them, without outside assistance, overcame their addictions (with low relapse rates) once back in the U.S. After reviewing these studies, plus research of his own, Stanley Schachter concludes: "People can and do cure themselves of smoking, obesity, and heroin addiction. They do so in large numbers and for long periods of time, and in many cases apparently permanently." Recidivism and Self-Cure of Smoking and Obesity, *American Psychologist*, 1982, 37, 442.

190: The estimates of professional competence by Strupp, Meehl, and Bergin are all in Bergin, A. E., and Strupp, H. H. *Changing Frontiers in the Science of Psychotherapy*, 1972, 199, 226.

"are ineffective or harmful." Truax, C. B., and Mitchell, K. M. Research on Certain Therapist Interpersonal Skills in Relation to Process and Outcome, in Bergin, A. E., and Garfield, S. L. *Handbook of Psychotherapy and Behavior Change*, 1971, 340.

Rogers, C. R. *A Way of Being*, 1980, 244.

Kovel, J. *A Complete Guide to Therapy*, 1976, 227. Another example of how many leading therapists assess the competence of their colleagues is found in a recent article by Albert Ellis, Must Most Psychotherapists

Page
Remain as Incompetent as They Now Are?, *J Contemporary Psychotherapy*, 1982, *13*, 17–28.

191. "For too long we have viewed . . ." Truax, C. B., and Mitchell, K. M., in Bergin and Garfield, 1971, 340–41.

CHAPTER 11

Page
195: Farson, R. The Technology of Humanism, *J Humanistic Psychology*, 1978, 8.

"When it comes down to it, therapy isn't more accepting . . ." A leading proponent of "unconditional positive regard," Carl Rogers, provides some good examples of therapy's lack of acceptance of people as they are in his book *On Encounter Groups*. He notes that the group "finds it unbearable that any member should live behind a mask or front." What constitutes a mask or front? Among other things, "polite words," "intellectual understanding of each other and of relationships," and "the smooth coin of tact," all of which "are just not good enough." Members displaying such characteristics are criticized and attacked until they conform to group standards, and Rogers acknowledges that "the group is quite violent at times in tearing down a facade or defense . . ." (quotes are on pages 29–30 of Rogers's book). So much for unconditional positive regard.

197: Tocqueville, A. de. *Democracy in America*, Vol. 2, 145.

198: "Mental health experts have helped create . . ." Writer Leo Rosten claims that the main message in the land now is "that discontent is unnecessary, unnatural, and unAmerican," and he feels it necessary to assert that we "have a right to be unhappy." *Passions and Prejudices*, 1978, 90–93.

Burns, D. D. *Feeling Good*, 1980, 24.

Janov, A. *The Primal Scream*, 1970, 168.

May, R. *The Meaning of Anxiety*, 1977, xix.

Dyer, W. W. *Your Erroneous Zones*, 1976, 97.

199: Cummings, N. A. Turning Bread into Stones, *American Psychologist*, 1979, *34*, 1119–20.

Farson, The Technology of Humanism, 1978, 11.

201: "My orgasms have always come from intercourse." Quoted in Ellison, C. R. Harmful Effects of Sex Therapy, paper presented at the convention of the American Psychological Association, Washington, D.C., 8/25/82.

Masters, W. H., and Johnson, V. E. *Human Sexual Inadequacy*, 1970, 240.

203: "Did you spurt?" This and the following quote are from Ladas, A. K., et al., *The G Spot*, 1982, 167, which means that the authors of this book have advance warning of the harm that could be done by dissemination of their ideas. My review of *The G Spot* is in *Psychology Today*, 10/82, 82–84.

Comfort, A. *More Joy of Sex*, 1974, 153, 154.

204: Talese, G. *Thy Neighbor's Wife*, 1980, 343, 541.

205: Chisholm, C. B., quoted in Lasch, C. *Haven in a Heartless World*, 1977, 99.

"every action and every word of theirs . . ." Skolnick, A., and Skolnick, J. H. *Intimacy, Family, and Society*, 1974, 377.

Page

Storr, C. Freud and the Concept of Parental Guilt, in Skolnick and Skolnick, 387.

206: Freud, A. *Normality and Pathology in Childhood,* 1965, 8.
Pogrebin, L. C. Growing Up Free, 1980, 6–7.

207: "ban pink and blue . . ." Pogrebin, 112.
"It took just two pages to tell me how wrong I was . . ." Brown, L. Review of *Growing Up Free* in *SIECUS Report,* 9/81, 16–17.

208: "When a member of my family . . ." Freud S. *Psychopathology of Everyday Life, Standard Edition,* 1960, Vol. 6, 180.

209: Freud's comment about Dora is in *A Case of Hysteria, Standard Edition,* 1953, Vol. 7, 45.
Schutz, W. *Profound Simplicity,* 1979, 38.
"it is oneself who determines . . ." Fritz Perls, cited in Schutz, 1979, 31.
Greenwald, H., cited in Schutz, 1979, 31.

210: Schutz, 1979, 32.
Farson, R. Technology of Humanism, 1978.

212: Scarf, M. Images That Heal: A Doubtful Idea Whose Time Has Come,
Psychology Today, 9/80, 45. Simonton's methods, as well as anecdotal
illustrations of their success, is presented in his *Getting Well Again,* 1978.
The medical community, however, has not been persuaded. Jimmie Hol-
land, chief of psychiatry at the Sloan-Kettering Institute for Cancer
Research, has called Simonton's treatment a "cruel hoax" and "unethical"
(quoted in Scarf, 45).
Most of my discussion of obesity follows from information contained in
perhaps the most important book ever written about the subject, William Bennett and Joel Gurin's *The Dieter's Dilemma,* 1982. The depressing results of various therapies for obesity are reviewed in Wing,
R., and Jeffery, R. Outpatient Treatments of Obesity, *International J
of Obesity,* 1979, *3,* 261–79. On the American preoccupation with bodyweight, see Kim Chernin's *The Obsession: Reflections on the Tyranny of
Slenderness,* 1981.

214: The Dan White case and the dimished capacity defense are briefly discussed in Noble, J., and Noble, W. *The Psychiatric Fix,* 1981, chapter 9.
A thoughtful consideration of what therapists in the courtrooms are doing
to all of us is psychiatrist Willard Gaylin's *The Killing of Bonnie Garland,*
1982.

216: Bach, G., and Torbet, L. *A Time for Caring,* 1982, 283.

217: "There were times when I actually believed . . ." Quoted in Westin, J.
The Coming Parent Revolution, 1981, 55.
Thomas, L. On the Science and Technology of Medicine, in Knowles,
J. H. *Doing Better and Feeling Worse,* 1977, 43–44.

219: Farson, R. The Technology of Humanism, 12.

CHAPTER 12

Page
222: Marshall, S. L. A. *Men Against Fire,* 1947, 54, 60–61, 78.

223: Regarding the general effectiveness of brainwashing and its results on
American POWs in Korea, see Scheflin, A. W., and Opton, E. M. *The
Mind Manipulators,* 1978, 22–105.
Frank, J. D. *Persuasion and Healing,* 1972, 102.

Page
224: Bromley, D. G., and Shupe, A. D. *Strange Gods: The Great American Cult Scare*, 1981. Information about the last day in Jonestown is on pages 65 and 113–14.

225: Statistics on agricultural production in the Soviet Union are from Brand, D. Back to the Soil, *Wall Street Journal*, 3/4/81, 1.

226: On adherence to the doctor's orders, see Scakett, D. L. and Haynes, R. B. *Compliance with Therapeutic Regimens*, 1976.
Zablocki, B. *Alienation and Charisma*, 1980, 320.

227: Freud, S. *The Dynamics of Transference*, in *Standard Edition*, 1955, Vol. 12, 103.
Perls, F., quoted in Leonard, G. B. *The Transformation*, 1972, 76.
Ellis, A. *Reason and Emotion in Psychotherapy*, 1962, 377.

228: A number of thoughtful discussions of the obstacles encountered in trying to help people change are in Wachtel, P. L. *Resistance*, 1982.

229: For the response of scientists to new findings and ideas, see Barber, B. Resistance by Scientists to Scientific Discovery, *Science*, *134*, 596–602, and Kuhn, T. S. *The Structure of Scientific Revolutions*, 1970, 150–59.

230: My discussion of limits to change owes much to Albert Ellis's chapter on the limitations of psychotherapy in his *Reason and Emotion in Psychotherapy*, 1962.

231: Passmore, J. *The Perfectibility of Man*, 1970, 269n.
Freud's comment about Jones is in McGuire, W. *The Freud/Jung Letters*, 1974, 145.
"I should not even claim that every case of hysteria . . ." *Freud/Jung Letters*, 12.
Sulloway, F. J. *Freud, Biologist of the Mind*, 1979, 443.

232: Regarding biological aspects of emotional problems, see Snyder, S. H. *Biological Aspects of Mental Disorder*, 1980, and Wender, P. H., and Klein, D. F. *Mind, Mood, and Medicine*, 1981.

235: "The relationship between childhood and adult behavior . . ." Brim, O. G., Jr., and Kagan, J. *Constancy and Change in Human Development*, 1980, reviews current research and thinking.

236: Regarding high ego-strength, psychoanalysts have always stressed this variable as essential for successful treatment, and many analysts reject patients deficient in it. The importance of "the patient's character makeup, the nature and depth of his disturbance, and his ability to become productively involved in psychotherapy" were supported by the results of the Vanderbilt Study (Strupp, H. H. Success and Failure in Time-limited Psychotherapy, *Archives General Psychiatry*, 1980, *37*, 953) and many other research projects. Although some have argued that such characteristics may be more important for success in psychoanalytic therapies than in behavioral ones, it is of interest that Kilmann finds them to be influential in the outcome of sex therapy (*All About Sex Therapy*, 1983).

243: Appelbaum, S. A. *Out in Inner Space*, 1979, 296.

247: Lazarus, A. A. *Behavior Therapy & Beyond*, 1971, 18.

248: "An important implication . . ." The message that follows, both in this and the last chapter, is similar in many respects to that in Leo Rosten's lovely essay, You Have a Right to Be Unhappy, in his *Passions and Prejudices*, 1978.

249: The belief that suicide prevention centers lower the suicide rate was based on the tentative conclusions of a 1968 study in Great Britain. Those con-

References 299

Page

clusions have not been supported in England or the U.S. Suicide expert
Herbert Hendin states: "The evidence . . . is fairly conclusive that suicide
prevention programs have no demonstrable effect on the suicide rate of
their communities" *Suicide in America*, 1982, 183. Suicide rates for various countries are from U.S. Bureau of the Census, *Statistical Abstract of
the United States: 1980*, 187.

CHAPTER 13

Page

251: "the belief that we are worse off . . ." One of the chief proponents of this
doctrine was Erich Fromm, who wrote that in modern society, which he
often called insane, people are overwhelmed by a sense of "individual
nothingness and helplessness. Paradise is lost for good. . . . The new
freedom is bound to create a deep feeling of insecurity, powerlessness, doubt,
aloneness and anxiety." All of which is due to the breakup of medieval
life and the development of capitalism (*Escape From Freedom*, 1965,
81). Presumably people were happier and healthier in the good old days
of the eleventh century.

252: "no evidence of an increase in the incidence of mental disorder . . ."
See Goldhammer, H., and Marshall, A. W. *Psychosis and Civilization*,
1949, and Srole, L., and Fischer, A. K. The Midtown Manhattan Longi-
tudinal Study vs. 'The Mental Paradise Lost' Doctrine, *Archives General
Psychiatry*, 1980, *37*, 209–21.
Bettmann's *The Good Old Days — They Were Terrible!* 1974, is the best
antidote I know for those suffering from the delusion that life was better
a century ago.
Quotes and statistics about alcohol consumption are from Rorabaugh,
W. J. *The Alcoholic Republic*, 1979.

253: Fromm, E., quoted in Coles, R. *The Mind's Fate*, 1975, 6.
Shorter, E. *The Making of the Modern Family*, 1975, 61.
"Whatever vexing dilemmas that Mom . . ." Shorter, 6.
On parent-child relationships in the good old day, see Shorter, 168–204.
As he notes, "Good mothering is an invention of modernization."

254: Rilke, R. M. *Letters to a Young Poet*, 1954, 39–40.
Caplow, T., et al. *Middletown Families: Fifty Years of Change and Con-
tinuity*, 1982, 332.
Will, G. F. *The Pursuit of Virtue & Other Tory Notions*, 1982, 366.

255: "In organizations, it can hamper. . . ." See Calane, B. E. The Truth Hurts:
Some Companies See More Harm than Good in Sensitivity Training, *Wall
Street Journal*, 7/14/69, 1.

257: "abolishing or even seriously decreasing judgmentalness . . ." Perhaps no
one has emphasized the nonjudgmentalness of the therapist as much as
Carl Rogers, so it is of interest that two independent studies done ten
years apart found that Rogers was not nonjudgmental with his clients:
he systematically rewarded verbal behavior that he liked and punished
expressions he didn't like. (Murray, E. J. A Content-Analysis Method
for Studying Psychotherapy, *Psychological Monographs*, 1965, *70*, Whole
No. 420, and Truax, C. B. Reinforcement and Nonreinforcement in
Rogerian Psychotherapy, *J Abnormal Psychology*, 1966, *71*, 1–9. Allen
Bergin puts the issue clearly: Rogers's "values significantly regulated the

Page

structure and content of therapeutic sessions. . . . If a person who intends to be nondirective cannot be, then it is likely that the rest of us cannot either." Bergin, A. E. Psychotherapy and Religious Values, *J Consulting Clinical Psychology*, 1980, *48*, 97.)

258: Among the sources I used regarding the emotional problems of famous men and women are: Goertzel, V., and Goertzel, M. G. *Cradles of Eminence*, 1962; Newlove, D. *Those Drinking Days*, 1981; Oates, S. B. *With Malice toward None: The Life of Abraham Lincoln*, 1977; Pickering, G. *Creative Malady*, 1974; Storr, A. *The Dynamics of Creation*, 1972.

262: Fox, R. C. The Medicalization and Demedicalization of American Society, in Knowles, J. H. *Doing Better and Feeling Worse*, 1977, 11.

264: Einstein quote from Browne, M. W. The Case in Favor of Suffering, *San Francisco Examiner*, This World, 3/22/81, 27.

265: "feeling too well physically . . ." Quoted in Jones, E. *The Life and Work of Sigmund Freud*, Vol. 1, 346. Jones's comment about Freud doing his most original work when he was most neurotic is on page 305.
"to the cigar a great intensification . . ." Quoted in Schur, M. *Freud: Living and Dying*, 1972, 62.

266: Thomas, L. On the Science and Technology of Medicine, in Knowles, J. H. *Doing Better and Feeling Worse*, 1977, 43.

268: Freud's comment about not needing to change was made in 1889 in a letter to colleague Joseph Breuer. Freud, E., ed. *Letters of Sigmund Freud*, 1960, 226.

APPENDIX

Page

274: Some self-help books people have said were especially helpful to them are: Barbach, L. *For Yourself: The Fulfillment of Female Sexuality*, 1975 (but I think her newer work, *For Each Other: Sharing Sexual Intimacy*, 1982, is far better); Burns, D. D. *Feeling Good: The New Mood Therapy*, 1980; Ellis, A., and Harper, R. A. *A Guide to Rational Living*, 1961; Fensterheim, H., and Baer, J. *Don't Say Yes When You Want to Say No*, 1975; Lazarus, A., and Fay, A. *I Can If I Want To*, 1975; Rush, A. K. *Getting Clear*, 1973; Zimbardo, P. G. *Shyness: What It Is, What to Do about* It, 1977.

275: "solutions are the main cause of problems . . ." The school of therapy most closely allied to this idea was developed at the Mental Research Institute in Palo Alto, and its principles and methods are given in Watzlawick, P., et al., *Change*, 1974.

276: Wheelis, A. *How People Change*, 1973, 106–07.

Index